Canadian Multiculturalism and the Far Right

Canadian Multiculturalism and the Far Right examines a neglected aspect of the history of 20th century Canadian multiculturalism and the far right to illuminate the ideological foundations of the concept of 'third force'.

Focusing on the particular thought of ultra-conservative Ukrainian Canadian Walter J. Bossy during his time in Montreal (1931–1970s), this book demonstrates that the idea that Canada was composed of three equally important groups emerged from a context defined by reactionary ideas on ethnic diversity and integration. Two broad questions shape this research: first, what the meaning originally attached to the idea of a 'third force' was, and what the intentions behind the conceptualization of a trichotomic Canada were; and second, whether Bossy's understanding of the 'third force' precedes, or is related in any way to, postwar debates on liberal multiculturalism at the core of which was the existence of a 'third force'.

This book will be of interest to students and researchers of multiculturalism, radical-right ideology and the far right, and Canadian history and politics.

Bàrbara Molas (PhD, York University) is a historian of, and expert consultant on, far-right ideology and radicalisation. Having published more than 20 articles and book chapters on the subject, her consulting experience is international and includes intergovernmental organisations, national prosecution services, and Big Tech companies.

Routledge Studies in Fascism and the Far Right
Series editors
Nigel Copsey, Teesside University, UK and Graham Macklin, Center for Research on Extremism (C-REX), University of Oslo, Norway.

This book series focuses upon national, transnational and global manifestations of fascist, far right and right-wing politics primarily within a historical context but also drawing on insights and approaches from other disciplinary perspectives. Its scope also includes anti-fascism, radical-right populism, extreme-right violence and terrorism, cultural manifestations of the far right, and points of convergence and exchange with the mainstream and traditional right.

Titles include:

The Dynamics of Right-Wing Extremism within German Society
Escape into Authoritarianism
Edited by Oliver Decker, Elmar Brähler and Johannes Kiess

Canadian Multiculturalism and the Far Right
Walter J. Bossy and the Origins of the 'Third Force', 1930s–1970s
Bàrbara Molas

The Fascist Faith Of Romania's Legion "Archangel Michael" in Romania, 1927–41
Martyrdom To National Purification
Constantin Iordachi

Nazi Occultism
Between the SS and Esotericism
Stéphane François

The Nature of Identitarianism
Göran Dahl

For more information about this series, please visit: www.routledge.com/Routledge-Studies-in-Fascism-and-the-Far-Right/book-series/FFR

Canadian Multiculturalism and the Far Right

Walter J. Bossy and the Origins of the 'Third Force', 1930s–1970s

Bàrbara Molas

LONDON AND NEW YORK

First published 2023
by Routledge
4 Park Square, Milton Park, Abingdon, Oxon OX14 4RN

and by Routledge
605 Third Avenue, New York, NY 10158

Routledge is an imprint of the Taylor & Francis Group, an informa business

© 2023 Bàrbara Molas

The right of Bàrbara Molas to be identified as author of this work has been asserted in accordance with sections 77 and 78 of the Copyright, Designs and Patents Act 1988.

All rights reserved. No part of this book may be reprinted or reproduced or utilised in any form or by any electronic, mechanical, or other means, now known or hereafter invented, including photocopying and recording, or in any information storage or retrieval system, without permission in writing from the publishers.

Trademark notice: Product or corporate names may be trademarks or registered trademarks, and are used only for identification and explanation without intent to infringe.

British Library Cataloguing-in-Publication Data
A catalogue record for this book is available from the British Library

Library of Congress Cataloging-in-Publication Data
A catalog record has been requested for this book

ISBN: 978-1-032-25089-2 (hbk)
ISBN: 978-1-032-25469-2 (pbk)
ISBN: 978-1-003-28334-8 (ebk)

DOI: 10.4324/9781003283348

Typeset in Times New Roman
by KnowledgeWorks Global Ltd.

Contents

Acknowledgements vii
Acronyms viii

1 Introduction 1

A history of Canadian multiculturalism 2
A history of far-right multiculturalism 5
A note on methodology 9
Book structure 12

2 Christian Revolutions 18

Walter J. Bossy 18
   A Call to Socially Minded Christian Canadians 21
The Christian left 26
The 'foreign problem' 29
Conclusion 36

3 Allegiances 51

New Canadians Friendship House 51
Fundraising 56
Allegiance day 62
The Ukrainian question 68
Conclusion 73

4 Networks 90

L'Action corporative 90
The Liberal Party 95
Fellow crusaders 102
A white 'third force' 108
Conclusion 113

5 The 'Third Force' 128

The Ethnic Canadian Mosaic Institute 128
Biculturalism and bilingualism 131
Partial stories 135
The 'third force' 137
Self-preservation 141
Conclusion 144

6 Conclusion 151

References 158
Index 173

Acknowledgements

When I first met Professor Adrian Shubert in 2016 at the Universitat Pompeu Fabra de Barcelona to ask him about Canada, I would have never imagined that I would end up pursuing my PhD there. I also didn't expect to write a dissertation, and later a monograph, in Canadian history – a country of which unfortunately I did not know much until 2017. Today, not only has Canada become my scholarly interest, but also my home. This wouldn't have been possible without the unconditional support, invaluable mentorship, and advice of Professors Marcel Martel, Roberto Perin, and Adrian Shubert at York University. I would be a different scholar, but also a different person, if it weren't for each and one of them. This book is the result of their constant care and guidance, for which I will always be grateful. *A vosaltres, gràcies de tot cor.*

I would like to thank the History Department at York University at large, and especially the HIST6030 2017/2018 cohort, whose feedback, encouragement, and friendship made a difference in my early years as a doctoral student.

I thank my wonderful husband, Justin Mott. Thank you for reminding me that the sun will come out soon, like it always does in the Mediterranean.

I would like to dedicate this book to my family in Catalunya, Spain: Eva Gregorio (Mami), Xavier Molas (Papi), and Alba Molas (Tati). I especially thank my mom, Eva, who began studying English in her mid-fifties to be able to read my work and attend my talks – including my dissertation defence. I have never seen anyone strive so much to show unconditional love. I hope this book is worthy of her efforts.

Acronyms

AC	L'Action Corporative
AFL	American Federation of Labour
ALN	Action Libérale Nationale
B&B	Biculturalism and Bilingualism
BUKMH	Brotherhood of Ukrainian Classocrats-Monarchist Hetmanites
CCES	Catholic Church Extension Society
CCF	Cooperative Commonwealth Federation
CIL	City Improvement League
CIO	American Committee for Industrial Organization
CLC	Classocracy League of Canada
COTC	Canadian Officers Training Corps
CPC	Communist Party of Canada
ECMI	Ethnic Canadian Mosaic Institute
ESP	L'École Sociale Populaire
LSR	League for Social Reconstruction
MCSC	Montreal Catholic School Commission
MRA	Moral Re-Armament
NCB	New Canadians Bureau
NCF	New Canadian Citizens Federation
NCFH	New Canadian Friendship House
NUP	National Unity Party
RCMP	Royal Canadian Mounted Police
UCC	Ukrainian Canadian Committee
UHO	United Hetman Organization
ULFTA	Ukrainian Labour-Farmer Temple Association
UNF	Ukrainian National Federation of Canada
UWVA	Ukrainian War Veterans' Association
WAAJA	World Alliance Against Jewish Aggressiveness

1 Introduction

I have been asked many times why I decided to look at 30 years of the life of someone who was ultra-conservative, a white supremacist, quite unstable, and seemingly a rather irrelevant individual. Canadian historiography already says that Walter J. Bossy was a far-right Ukrainian immigrant who didn't do much besides stirring some Nazi sympathy among fellow expats in the Prairies. This supposed insignificance could explain why none of the local newspapers in Montreal, the core of his years of activism, mentioned his passing on January 3, 1979. But Bossy contributed to the history of Canada in a way that determined how we think of this nation up to this day. He was the first to imagine a trichotomic Canada; a united nation composed of three elements: the French-speaking group; the English-speaking group; and *the third force*. This study follows the life and thought of Ukrainian Canadian Walter J. Bossy from his arrival in Montreal in 1931, when he was 32 years old and had lived in Canada for seven years, to his retirement from public activities in 1972. It begins in 1931 and not in 1924 or at an earlier time because it was in 1931 that Bossy began developing an interest in Canadian nationhood and governance. It is in Montreal that he began conceptualizing Canada as a trichotomic nation, and it is that specific thought that constitutes the focus and interest of this book.

Bossy's idea of a trichotomic Canada emerged in a context characterized by accelerated change. Indeed, the crash of the New York stock market in October 1929 signalled the start of economic turmoil that would deeply define Canada's 1930s. At the outset, the Conservatives under Prime Minister Richard Bedford Bennett (R. B. Bennett) attempted to deal with this unprecedented economic disaster by increasing trade within the British Empire and imposing tariffs for imports from outside the Empire. But his policies had only limited success. By 1933, tens of thousands had lost their jobs, and over 20% of the entire Canadian labour force remained unemployed. In Montreal, by 1933, there were 60,000 unemployed; counting their dependents, an estimated 250,000 people, or 30% of the city's population, were receiving relief from the city.[1]

In this climate, extreme left- and right-wing political movements grew. Although the latter proved less numerous than the former, during the

DOI: 10.4324/9781003283348-1

Depression many Canadians turned to religion for hope and direction. As a consequence, conservative and reactionary Christian groups flourished during the decade.[2] In Quebec, Adrien Arcand founded his Nazi-inspired Parti National Social Chrétien claiming to represent the last stand of Roman Catholicism against communists and other atheists.[3] While Arcand remained marginal, his fervent antisemitism was supported by French-Canadian nationalist organizations such as Jeune-Canada, the Ligue d'Action Nationale, and the provincial branch of the Social Credit Party of Canada.[4] On the other hand, large sectors of the Catholic church interpreted the Depression as evidence of divine punishment for modernity, epitomized by revolutionary communism and unrestrained capitalism. Based on the encyclical *Quadragesimo Anno* authored by Pope Pius XI in 1931, which rejected the competitive nature of capitalism as well as the class struggle, they suggested a return to a more cooperative and Christian system inspired by the European medieval guilds.[5] This was called corporatism.

In an era of extremes, many Canadians either created or looked for alternative ways of addressing the flaws of the existing economic and political systems. It is in this climate that Walter J. Bossy proposed a new model for the socio-economic organization and governance of Canada. The model consisted in having a small elite oversee a society structured in guilds. Inspired by contemporary elitist socio-political theories and corporatism, Bossy proposed the establishment of a Canadian state in which peoples of European descent would organize in guilds or professional units and integrate under a common Christian framework. Like many others, he was trying to achieve a third way out of the crisis, that is, a way that was defined neither by capitalism nor by communism, and that was built upon Christian principles. Thus, his early theories for the reorganization of Canada are not especially original. Yet, what was new about his approach was that he believed that the integration of Canadians through a guild system would not be possible without first ensuring the cooperation between three Canadian components: the English-speaking group, the French-speaking group, and what in 1937 Bossy called the 'third group'. In other words, he envisioned the socio-economic reform of Canada as resulting from the integration of three national groups. Bossy understood Canada to be trichotomic almost 30 years before the idea of 'third force' was even employed in debates around multiculturalism.

A history of Canadian multiculturalism

Above all, this study constitutes a contribution to the study of Canadian multiculturalism. A mechanism which seems to offer a means to combine both the recognition of ethnic differences and the continuation of unified nationhood, Canadian multiculturalism has been widely praised in Canada and abroad.[6] Part of the reason for this is that, in principle, multiculturalism offers minorities the possibility to claim rights and recognition. It's a compromise by which unequal group relations are meant to be bridged, rather than reproduced, with a view to create a more unified nationhood. However, Canadian multiculturalism was shaped after Pierre Elliott Trudeau's own understanding of pluralism, which was based on the idea that individual rights must prevail over group rights. Indeed, what Ian McKay calls 'the liberal framework'[7] was an essential force in leading to the proclamation in 1971 of Canada as a multicultural nation within a bilingual framework.

For Canadian Francophones as for First Nations, multiculturalism 'remains ambiguous since it undermines their claim for more autonomy'.[8] Both these groups have been fighting for that since they became British subjects in the eighteenth century. At first, the British expected *Canadiens* (French Canadians) and Indigenous peoples to either assimilate or perish. Later in the eighteenth century, the idea of a plural nation emerged in part from the concessions given to Indigenous peoples and French Canadians through the Royal Proclamation of 1763 and the 1774 Quebec Act. Those concessions were used to ensure unity against the expansion of Americans into Canadian territory;[9] to contain the French-Canadian fact to a specific territory;[10] and to protect the Anglophone minorities in Quebec.[11] Seventeen years later, British authorities divided the province of Quebec into Lower Canada and Upper Canada, giving both colonies representative parliamentary institutions.[12]

Following the 1837–1838 rebellions, however, Britain attempted to assimilate French Canada by decreeing the union of Lower Canada and Upper Canada, the use of French in the colonial parliament being initially disallowed. But the presence of two national communities created tensions that made colonial governance in the United Canadas difficult, and by mid-1800s Confederation was proposed as an alternative form of political and geographical organization. Established in 1867, the new federal government would have 'limited control over issues at the heart of French-Canadian concerns', like education, language, and religion.[13] Ultimately, Confederation 'served to solidify the power and autonomy of the largest number of French Canadians within Canada: Quebecers ... protecting French-Canadian culture and society in his home province.'[14]

Critical of French-Canadian claims to a special status within Confederation, postcolonial scholars like Eve Haque, Richard Day, or Himani Bannerji argue that the federal state remains a mechanism of subordination of minorities of descent other than British and French that facilitates the perpetuation of colonial structures to the benefit the 'two founding nations' only.[15] Questioning postcolonial assessments on Canadian multiculturalism, Marcel Martel and Martin Pâquet, as well as Kenneth McRoberts or Guy Laforest, stress that the idea of multiculturalism within a bilingual framework in fact leads to cultural relativism, as it divorces language from culture, and language alone can't protect the structures that ensure the development of a society.[16] As a consequence, they argue, Canadian multiculturalism undermines French-Canadian claims to rights and recognition as a national entity within the federation.

French Canadians had relied on the Royal Commission on Bilingualism and Biculturalism (and especially on co-chair of the Commission André Laurendeau), established in 1963, to amend the relationship between the so-called 'two founding nations' and ensure that Quebec's hopes for equal demographic and economic development would be addressed. When Trudeau's Liberal Party ignored Laurendeau's recommendations on bilingualism and biculturalism and declared Canada a multicultural nation in 1971, those hopes disappeared. McRoberts insists that, before Trudeau, neither the Pearson Government nor the Royal Commission had seriously questioned the bicultural character of the country.[17] The establishment of official bilingualism and biculturalism was thus the attempt by French Canadians to reject the effects (economical and cultural) of a colonial power rather than to impose new unequal power relations over other minorities as postcolonial scholars suggest it does.[18] In fact, many francophone Canadians argue that Trudeau's multiculturalism was deliberately designed to obscure Quebec's constitutional agenda and bury its demands under an ever-growing pool of ethnic minorities.[19] Indeed, it is widely accepted that '*in practice* multiculturalism helped ... to undermine [Quebec's] distinctiveness in terms of its history and place in the Confederation'.[20]

Since 1971, many have tried to suggest alternative frameworks to multiculturalism that would allow to approach the Quebec question in a better (and less conflicting) way. In 1995, Guy Laforest suggested multi-*nationalism*. Building upon Henri Bourassa's compact theory, he argued that asymmetry would work more effectively than multiculturalism because it would be able to protect group identities attached to specific territories like Quebec. This theory, however, is difficult to apply to Indigenous peoples, as the dispossession of their lands has led to geographical dispersion, as Will Kymlicka argues.[21] Despite supporting the idea that what he calls 'national minorities' (which Kymlicka identifies as Quebec, and Indigenous groups) deserve unique rights by nature of their historical role in Canada, Kymlicka states that asymmetry could lead to secession, as it is based on the idea of separation or two distinct nations rather than on the idea of union and plurality.[22] Trying to re-conceive the place of Quebec within a plural Canada, Jocelyn Maclure suggests the establishment of a political framework in which Quebecers can freely express the 'polyphony' of their identities and their processes of (historical) memory.[23] He is, however, not too specific about what this framework should look like besides saying that it would reflect neither the sum of different ethnic enclaves nor the sole object of national identification for all its members.[24] Neither does he fully explain what the place of ethnic minorities of descent other than French who do not identify with what Maclure calls Quebec's 'common denominator' would be.[25]

A history of far-right multiculturalism

This book focuses on the historical efforts of one ethnic minority spokesperson to redefine Canadian identity, and the place of ethnic groups in it, decades before Trudeau's liberal multiculturalism was conceived. Specifically, it traces the ideological roots of the 'third force', a concept whose inception is believed to signal the origins of Canadian liberal and contemporary multiculturalism. I argue that this belief is a misconception caused by the absence of studies that interrogate the changing nature of the concept and, as a result, the changing nature of the socio-political perceptions that the concept has allowed for to this day.[26] This study represents a first attempt to change that. It also constitutes a first attempt to understand the meaning of the 'third force' from the perception of individuals belonging to ethnic groups other than English- or French-speaking. In doing so, I am actively responding to Marcel Martel's call to switch our focus from politicians to ethnic groups in our study of Canadian politics and political thought,[27] bringing new voices into the study of interwar and early postwar debates on Canadian multiculturalism.[28]

The existing literature on Canadian multiculturalism argues that concerns over the integration of minorities emerged from the experience of the Second World War among the political left. I demonstrate that these were first expressed in the 1930s by Canadian of Ukrainian descent Walter J. Bossy, a reactionary fellow who promoted the establishment of a Canadian totalitarian state defined by white and Christian supremacism. Indeed, it is among Bossy's papers that we find the earliest use of 'third element' (later 'third force') as a concept in 1937, including efforts to define and mobilize it. This discovery also challenges previous understandings of multiculturalism in Canadian scholarship which relate its ideological or conceptual origins to the establishment of policies and programs of the Canadian Citizenship branch in the 1940s; to the 'multicultural movement of the 1960s'; or to the Royal Commission on Bilingualism and Biculturalism between 1963 and 1969.[29] In particular, it shows that the conceptual origins of the 'third force' are intimately related to the interwar 'corporative wave', or the transnational impact of Pius XI's encyclical *Quadragesimo Anno*.[30] Thus, this book questions that the idea that the Canadian nation is composed of three groups or national forces as opposed to two founding nations resides in liberal secularism, while also rebalancing overly Eurocentric approaches to the study of corporatism.

In learning that the conceptual origins of the 'third force' lie in Bossy's particular ideas on Canadian nationhood, this study supports previous literature affirming that Ukrainian Canadians were a crucial driving force behind the multicultural movement.[31] And while this book focuses on Bossy's unexplored activism and life among English- and French-speaking milieus exclusively, I finish now what is merely one side of a surely more complex story in the hope that future research will look at Bossy's

6 *Introduction*

Ukrainian writings to further illuminate this early conceptualization of the 'third force'.

My research demonstrates that Bossy's efforts for the integration of Christian Canadians of European descent were unprecedented in two main ways. Firstly, his proposal differed from earlier attempts to 'keep Canada white and Christian'[32] through restricted immigration rules which aimed to *maintain* the ethnic status quo and ensure cultural and religious *assimilation* into one of the 'two founding nations'. Bossy's project was also different from the efforts of other ethnic groups who advocated the establishment of extreme forms of corporatism in Canada during the interwar period. For example, Italian Canadians who promoted the establishment of an authoritarian form of corporatism in Canada in the 1930s did so based on Mussolini's imperial aspirations, or international fascism.[33] Unlike them, Bossy's goal was to ensure the loyalty of the 'third group' towards the Canadian government, and as a consequence he never questioned the authority of the British monarchy. In addition, he believed that Canada must remain under the tutelage of the British empire, as Canada's diversity seemed to reflect the extent and nature of the empire, a characteristic that Bossy believed would eventually lead Canada to a position of world leadership.

It should be noted that the idea of ethnic diversity constituting precisely the essence of Canadian nationhood as well as Canada's potential source of world power was not new. The League for Social Reconstruction (LSR), for example, talked about the need to 'evoke a common loyalty amongst all races in Canada'. It also argued that 'National unity comes [from] the realization that whether we be ... English or French, Protestant or Catholic, we are Canadians with many common interests, despite our geographical, racial, economic and religious differences'.[34] But Bossy's thought was closer to that of Imperial Loyalists, as reflected in Carl Berger's *The Sense of Power* (1970). According to Berger, Loyalists in eighteenth-century Canada praised diversity and used it to claim a central and even dominant role for Canada within the British Empire. That diversity, however, was narrowly defined – the Loyalists saw Canada as solely composed by 'the northern peoples [of] Europe' or 'Nordic races'.[35]

Bossy's equally narrow view of pluralism, that is, one defined by racial and religious homogeneity, along with his authoritarian and theocratic aspirations for government, situates his thinking further to the right than mainstream conservatism in the 1930s. I understand the idea of *radical right* according to how it is used by the sociologist Jens Rydgren, who describes it as being a non-violent form of right-wing radicalism or far-right politics which is critical of liberalism institutions and values as well as democracy as a system of government.[36] Often, the radical right suggests reform along the lines of reactionary politics, that is, returning to an earlier form of socio-economic organization and government – such as the medieval guild system under absolutism.[37] Reactionary politics are often influenced by monarchism, traditionalism, and Christian supremacy, all of which emphasize a desire for strong authority, illiberal politics, religious devotion, and Eurocentrism. This is in opposition to what we would call the mainstream right or conservative right, which is situated at the centre-right of the political spectrum and is often shaped by values related to liberal conservatism or Christian democracy. It is also in opposition to the extreme right, which is a far-right form of politics that is violent in nature and actively hostile to democracy. Because Bossy's proposals for socio-economic and political reform were characterized by a return to the pre-Enlightenment guild system; a strict hierarchy on the basis of origin and group association (status); the defence of shared Christian principles as the basis for intergroup cooperation; Christian nationalism or the idea that divine guidance should define our laws and our political and social life; the rejection of liberal democracy; and the close cooperation of Church and State; his ideas fall under the reactionary type, and therefore their analysis constitutes a contribution to the study of radical-right thought and, more broadly, the far right.

Most studies of the radical right associate its discourse on nation-building with ethno-nationalism and its variant racial (white) nationalism; anti-immigrant nationalism; nativism; and even ultra-regionalism.[38] Even though the sort of 'white nationalism' we will look at here is characterized by an explicit distancing from groups like Blacks and East Asians as a means to uplift other (white) minorities, it was not characterized by such communities 'abandoning their European ethnic identities' and merging into the Anglo-Protestant mould, as has been considered typical of this type of nationalism – like the idea of the American 'melting pot'.[39] To Bossy, European cultural specificities were a contribution rather than a burden to the identity and progress of the Canadian nation. His theory of pluralism, then, didn't represent 'an affirmation of the dominant group's ability to capture and define the identity of the country', as explained by Ashley Jardina.[40] Rather, Bossy thought that different ethnic groups should preserve their distinct cultures as much as possible – away from the idea of biculturalism.

Unlike other radical-right movements characterized as representing a backlash against cultural change, Bossy's ideas on pluralism triggered it. Even though Bossy hoped for traditional Christian values to shape a newly defined 'strong national identity', there was no Canadian 'golden age' to go back to.[41] Moreover, he did not 'reject multiculturalism and the integration of foreigners' or claim protectionist policies on behalf of the dominant ethnic group, as is common in radical-right movements.[42] This sets Bossy's thought as one defined by a sort of multi-cultural[43] ideal shaped by reactionary ideology. For, even if in a restrictive way, it ultimately rejected assimilation (or the idea that ethnic groups must choose to join one of the 'two founding nations') to suggest instead the expansion of national belonging through a process of ethnic and spiritual integration, while promoting the exclusion of those deemed unfit. Thus, in spite of the seemingly opposing use of terminology, it is safe to argue that Bossy's ideas on diversity can be defined as a unique form of radical-right multiculturalism in which *whiteness* is not 'defined as the loss of identity',[44] but as the multiplicity of identities.

Bossy's 'multiculturalism of the right' was different from what political scientist Alberto Spektorowski has described as 'a rhetorical trope designed to include one's own ethnic communities and exclude Others from the body politic'.[45] According to Spektorowski, 'multiculturalism of the right' supports cultural diversity as long as this is defined by a plurality of separate states. That is, by a political system characterized by restrictions on the basis of ethno-cultural and geographical boundaries – this is called 'ethnopluralism'. While Bossy's idea of multiculturalism would oppose this form of inter-ethnic organization, ethnopluralism originated from a philosophy that closely resembles Bossy's own understanding of diversity: Herderian multiculturalism. An eighteenth-century and anti-Enlightenment German philosopher, Johann Gottfried Herder promoted the cultural independence of different German groups combined with their harmonious intercultural relations under the state. Whereas he rejected internal assimilation, Herder stated that 'foreign cultures' were a threat, 'a cancer', to what he considered to be the 'spiritual' German community.[46] Based on Herder's philosophy, some scholars argue that modern multiculturalism and right-wing populism share common roots: they maintain that the Herderian idea of group or cultural difference 'gave rise to both racial and pluralist views and these remain ... common bonds between racial and multicultural notions of human difference.'[47]

Herder influenced emerging theories on group survival based on social Darwinism and biological determinism, including the 'integral' or 'tribal nationalism' proposed by French author and politician Charles Maurras.[48] Maurras proposed the restoration of the *ancien régime* or old rule (prior to the French Revolution of 1789) by using the monarchy and the Catholic Church as unifying cultural elements, sources of social hierarchy and order, national solidarity, and centralisation. In addition, he sought to forge a national community out of the disparate linguistic and regional identities of the French state, and he defined that larger community based on what he considered to be 'common' criteria, namely Catholicism, agrarianism, and historical rule under the French monarchy.[49] In Canada, Maurras' ideas against the heritage of the Enlightenment and the French Revolution influenced a relevant number of French-Canadian nationalist intellectuals, particularly during the 1920s (or before Pius XI condemned his ideas), including Henri Bourassa, Lionel Groulx, and Esdras Minville.[50] While there is extensive literature on these and other individuals and groups influenced by right-wing forms of corporatism, none of the existing scholarship mentions Bossy's corporatist organization Classocracy League of Canada (CLC), which was active (albeit with minor support) between 1934 and 1938. It is precisely by studying the short-lived CLC that Bossy's subsequent projects for ethnic integration can be interpreted as a continuation of his early reactionary thoughts on Canadian diversity rather than as a precedent to liberal multiculturalism.

Walter J. Bossy was a Christian nationalist. Different from white nationalism, Christian nationalism is related to but not exclusively defined by racialist sentiments, mainly equating cultural purity with ethnic exclusion. Ultimately, it seeks the preservation of a 'unique Christian identity', unable to distinguish between religious and national identities.[51] It is essentially a 'cultural schema advocating the synthesis of [national] life with a particularist (almost ethnic) form of Christianity'.[52] Because Christian nationalism is about culture as much as about race, religion, and politics, it conveniently elucidates how Bossy was able to suggest multi-culturalism under a Christian framework while sustaining a white supremacist view of the nation. 'Christian nationalists are one example of a convergent social identity arising out of the perception of a high degree of overlap between three identities', namely the religious (Christian), the national (Canadian), and the racial (white, European).[53] Christian nationalism will help explain the incoherence inherent in Bossy's attempt to use Christian notions of universalism while insisting that groups of descent other than European and Jewish communities were unfit for his idea of nationhood. It will thus also explain the racist nature of his rhetoric, of which I warn the reader.

A note on methodology

The focus of this book is not a person as much as an idea: the 'third force'. Thus, this study will address the *conceptual origins* rather than simply the *origins* of the 'third force'.[54] As a consequence, I use a methodological approach characteristic of the study of the history of ideas or conceptual history, which deals with the evolution of ideas and value systems over time.

Firstly, this study builds upon Mark Bevir's understanding of hermeneutic meaning. On the one hand, I disagree with Bevir's interpretation of ideas as existing only *once* due to (he argues) an idea being utterly dependent on a specific subject situated within a specific context. As I see it, this approach leaves the historian without the possibility of comparing two ideas expressed at two different points in time or by different individuals, which denies any two thoughts having anything in common – and therefore any form of communication. On the other hand, Bevir's stress on subjectivity and context is important. His insistence upon the fact that 'historians should concern themselves with ... meaning as it exists for particular individuals' in particular reveals that signification is a process that results from both perception and intention.[55] Accordingly, in this study, I do not try to find the truth about the 'third force' or an objective and stable definition of it. Rather, I seek to reveal how a very particular individual understood it in order to comprehend the subjective intentionality behind the first trichotomic interpretation of the Canadian nation.

Bevir maintains that historians 'should generally presume that [the subject's] beliefs are sincere, conscious and rational'.[56] However, because Bossy's life was characterized by a firm desire to either attain or highly influence

10 *Introduction*

power, I believe that Bossy's discourse was often shaped by the wish to manipulate meaning. A clear example of this is when he began using the term 'New Canadians' (which had been historically understood as generally defining any Canadian of descent other than British or French) and linked it to individuals of European descent (except for Jewish communities) and Christian faith only. This is why this study will combine Bevir's approach to language with semiotics. Above all, semiotics distinguishes between *signifier* and *signified*, that is signs (words on a page, facial expressions, an image...) and the concept they communicate in order to find meaning. [57] I am especially interested in the poststructuralist interpretation of semiotics, which rejects the idea that words relate directly to anything specific, true, unchangeable, or objective. This leads to the conclusion that, while text (signifier) might remain through time, the ideas these texts express (signified) are subject to change.

This also happens the other way around. Considering a poststructuralist interpretation of semiotics allows us to identify the persistence of an idea through time despite alterations in the vocabulary used to express it. For example, I see 'third force' as a sign or a signifier, which means that the two words together are only the means by which the *idea* or signified of a trichotomic Canada is transmitted. This is why, throughout this book, I will show how different words like 'New Canadians', 'foreign group', or 'third element', were used to express the same idea. Using such words or signifiers to trace the persistence of a concept through time as expressed by a specific subject has been my main interest. It is important to highlight that I reject the poststructuralist idea that, ultimately, meaning does not exist. While poststructuralism helps demonstrate that there is no 'one-to-one correspondence between language and an external reality',[58] as well as locate historical shifts in meaning, it can also impede historical research altogether if used to fuel a nihilist perception of the world. Indeed, I believe truth is subjective. Yet that doesn't mean that truth does not exist, it simply means that truth may result from perception rather than fact.

It is through poststructuralism that I am able to find the ideological biases that, in turn, determine the vocabulary I use when framing the beliefs of the historical actors I study. That vocabulary is mine alone and it is subject to my own context and perception of reality, as is the narrative that I created from fragments of the past left by people whose experiences were also dependent upon their own context and perception of reality. It is part of the historian's craft to try our best to make sense of those fragments through an objective lens. Unfortunately, this is complicated, to say the least. This is why my goal throughout this study hasn't been to be as objective as possible, but rather to be reflective as often as possible. That is, at times I didn't simply let the sources talk but incorporated my own understanding of the events as they unfolded. I did this exclusively when I thought it necessary to justify my approach, as it is this which determines the order of events and encounters, the inclusion and exclusion of historical actors, the analysis of this and not that idea, etc. In this process, my main goal always remained to uncover meaning to the best of my ability.

Poststructuralists like Michel Foucault argue that meaning can't be found because it is permanently changing. As I see it, the changes in meaning are precisely our doors to subjectivity. So, to go back to the previous example, it is only when I realized that Bossy's use of 'New Canadians' was different from any previous definitions of the concept that I realized that he was intentionally altering meaning for his own purposes. In this case, a clear shift in the signification of a concept revealed intention. On the other hand, Foucault explains that such shifts reveal patterns of power. They show how individuals try to protect or modify power relations – or the unequal way in which they relate to others. To Foucault, the circulation of power is ensured by constantly constructing meaning through differentiation, ultimately producing epistemes or systems of truth.[59] This indicates that Bossy's aiming to change or create meaning implies a wish to alter power relations. This understanding of language helps illuminate Bossy's uplifting of Canadians of European descent and the creation of a new 'other' through discourse. In showing the capacity for individuals on the right side of the political spectrum to change or create meaning, this study questions Ian McKay's Gramscian assessment of Canadian history as defined by a liberal mechanism of 'coercion and consent'.[60]

It is my understanding that ideas or concepts are context sensitive, and that we need to see their histories as dynamic processes of transformation. In other words, I reject that ideas are either incomparable (Bevir) or untraceable (poststructuralism). For if ideas can't be found because they change (Foucault), and only transformation allows for change to be noticeable, then transformation implies that something has remained.[61] After philosopher Jouni-Matti Kuukkanen, I think that 'a concept in history should be seen to be composed of two components: the *core* of a concept and the *margin* of a concept.'[62] If the core concept (the central defining element of an idea) remains unchanged through time, there is conceptual continuity. However, conceptual continuity might still experience significant changes in the margin of a concept (less central ideas characterizing the concept at a certain point in time) if new meanings are attached to the core idea. In this book, I consider the trichotomic conceptualization of Canada to be the core idea characterizing the concept 'third force', while I situate Bossy's illiberal definition of the 'third force' at the margin of it.

Based on the above, my study demonstrates that while alterations occurred at the margin of the idea of 'third force' between the 1930s and the 1970s, the conceptual core remained the same. In other words, there was *conceptual continuity*. This is not to say that Bossy's conceptualization of the 'third force' was the same, or anticipated in any way, liberal postwar understanding of ethnic minorities and their cultural contribution to the Canadian fact. Indeed, between 1934 and the 1970s, the ideas at the *margin* of the concept 'third force' developed by Bossy were altered by him as well as by other historical actors

12 *Introduction*

(with the latter being the only one to promote those new meanings effectively), and by the different contexts in which the concept became employed. On the other hand, the *core* idea of the concept 'third force', namely that Canada is a nation composed of three elements rather than two, didn't change. In uncovering the reactionary nature of the marginal ideas that originally surrounded the 'third force', I demonstrate that this concept became part of a progressive discourse on pluralism only when the marginal ideas which first defined it were altered by liberal elements in the postwar era.

In showing that the idea of 'third force' was transformed from being an expression of radical-right thoughts on cultural integration to symbolizing modern Canadian multiculturalism, this contribution brings attention to the problematic histories of concepts we now deem progressive and urges the study of their changing meanings through historical inquiry. It is the questioning of terms and the ideas behind them that can bring us closer to the intention behind language, and that is the starting point to bring clarity to rhetoric, and truth to historical narrative.

Book structure

This book is structured into six chapters, including an introduction (Chapter 1) and a conclusion (Chapter 6). Chapter 2 focuses on the ideological currents and individuals that shaped Walter J. Bossy's thought before and shortly after his arrival to Montreal in the early 1930s, determining his early projects for Canadian nation-building. Chapter 3 illuminates the origins of Bossy's trichotomic understanding of Canada, while reflecting upon Bossy's complex identity in order to shed light upon the sincerity of, and actual commitment towards, his Canadian ideal. Chapter 4 focuses on the question of whether Bossy's idea of the 'third force' in the 1940s and the early postwar can be related to other visions of a plural Canadian nationhood (and the role of 'New Canadians' in it) developed before and during that period. Chapter 5 analyses Bossy's attempts to alter his own ideas at the margin of the concept 'third force' to present a more inclusive discourse. The book ends with a discussion on whether Bossy's idea of the 'third force' was ever related to an actual concern towards Canada; whether he was concerned solely on the fate of the Ukrainian community in the diaspora; or whether he was strictly preoccupied with a personal quest for power.

Notes

1. Paul-André Linteau, René Durocher, Jean-Claude Robert, François Ricard, eds., *Quebec Since 1930* (Toronto: James Lorimer&Company, 1991), 50–1; Jean Hamelin, Nicole Gagnon, *Histoire du catholicisme québécois*, Tome 1, 1898–1940 (Montreal: Boréal Express, 1984), 365–70.
2. For an overview of the interwar far right in Canada, see: Martin Robin, *Shades of Right: Nativist and Fascist Politics in Canada, 1920–1940* (Toronto: University of Toronto Press, 1992).

3. Hugues Théoret, *The Blue Shirts: Adrien Arcand and Fascist Anti-Semitism in Canada* (Ottawa: University of Ottawa Press, 2017).
4. Théoret, *The Blue Shirts*; Ninette Kelley, M. J. Trebikcock, eds., *The Making of the Mosaic: A History of Canadian Immigration Policy* (Toronto: University of Toronto Press, 2010), 220; Janine Stingel, *Social Discredit: Anti-Semitism, Social Credit, and the Jewish Response* (Montreal: McGill-Queen's University Press, 2000).
5. Hamelin, Gagnon, *Histoire du catholicisme québécois*, 396–401.
6. See, for example: Will Kymlicka, *Multicultural Citizenship: A Liberal Theory of Minority Rights* (Oxford: Oxford Clarendon Press, 1995); Ian Angus, *A Border Within: National Identity, Cultural Plurality, and Wilderness* (Montreal: McGill-Queen's University Press, 1997).
7. Ian McKay, "The Liberal Framework", in Jean-François Constant, Michel Ducharme, eds., *Liberalism and Hegemony. Debating the Canadian Liberal Revolution* (Toronto: University of Toronto Press, 2009).
8. Elke Winter, "Bridging Unequal Relations, Ethnic Diversity, and the Dream of Unified Nationhood: Multiculturalism in Canada", *Zeitschrift für Kanada-Studien*, vol. 1, no. 52 (2007): 52, 38–57.
9. Eva Mackey, *The House of Difference. Cultural Politics and National Identity in Canada* (London: Routledge, 1999), 27.
10. Denys Delâge, "Quebec and Aboriginal Peoples", in M. Venne, ed., *Vive Quebec! New Thinking and New Approaches to the Quebec Nation* (Toronto: James Lorimer & Co., 2001), 127–36.
11. Kenneth McRoberts, *Misconceiving Canada: The Struggle for National Unity* (Toronto: Oxford University Press, 1997).
12. Daniel Heidt, ed., *Reconsidering Confederation: Canada's Founding Debates, 1864–1999* (Calgary: University of Calgary Press, 2018), 76.
13. Heidt, *Reconsidering Confederation*, 85.
14. Ibid., 97.
15. Eve Haque, *Multiculturalism within a Bilingual Framework: Language, Race, and Belonging in Canada* (Toronto: University of Toronto, 2012); Richard Day, *Multiculturalism and the History of Canadian Diversity* (Toronto: University of Toronto, 2000); Himani Bannerji, *The Dark Side of the Nation: Essays on Multiculturalism, Nationalism and Gender* (Toronto: Canadian Scholars' Press, 2000).
16. Marcel Marcel and Martin Pâquet, *Speaking Up: A History of Language and Politics in Canada and Quebec* (Toronto: Between the Lines, 2012); McRoberts, *Misconceiving Canada*; Guy Laforest, *Trudeau and the End of a Canadian Dream* (Montreal: McGill, Queen's University Press, 1995).
17. McRoberts, *Misconceiving Canada*, 44.
18. Martel and Pâquet, *Speaking Up*, 72–3.
19. Vince Seymour Wilson, "The Tapestry Vision of Canadian Multiculturalism", *Canadian Journal of Political Science*, vol. 26, no. 4: 645–69.
20. Winter, "Bridging Unequal Relations": 45.
21. Will Kymlicka, "Federalism, Nationalism, and Multiculturalism", in Dimitrios Karmis, Wayne Norman, eds., *Theories of Federalism: A Reader* (New York: Palgrave Macmillan, 2005).
22. Ibid., 283.
23. Jocelyn Maclure, *Quebec Identity: The Challenge of Pluralism* (London: McGill-Queen's University Press, 2003), 75.
24. Maclure, *Quebec Identity*, 84.
25. Ibid., 109.
26. See, for example: Roberto Perin, *The Immigrant's Church: The Third Force in Canadian Catholicism, 1880–1920* (Toronto: Canadian Historical Association, 1998); Evelyn Kallen, *Ethnicity and Human Rights in Canada* (Oxford: Oxford

14 *Introduction*

University Press, 2010); Julia Lalande, "The Roots of Multiculturalism – Ukrainian-Canadian Involvement in the Multiculturalism Discussion of the 1960s as an Example of the Position of the 'Third Force'", *Canadian Ethnic Studies Journal*, vol. 38, no. 1 (2006): 47–64; Miriam Smith, ed., *Group Politics and Social Movements in Canada* (Toronto: University of Toronto Press, 2014); Valerie Knowles, *Strangers at Our Gates: Canadian Immigration and Immigration Policy, 1540–2006* (Toronto: Dundurn Press, 2007); Hugh Donald Forbes, *Multiculturalism in Canada: Constructing a Model Multiculture with Mulicultural Values* (Toronto: Palgrave Macmillan, 2019).

27. Marcel Martel, "Managing Ethnic Pluralism: The Canadian Experience, 1860–1971", in T. Greven and H. Ickstadt, eds., *Meeting Global and Domestic Challenges: Canadian Federalism in Perspective* (Berlin: John F. Kennedy-Institut für Nordamerikastudien/Freie Universität, 2004), 110.

28. Examples of multiculturalism studied from the perspective or as a project of the political left and/or English- and French-speaking groups include: Charles Taylor, *Multiculturalism and the Politics of Recognition* (US: Princeton University Press, 1992); Kay Anderson, "Thinking 'Postnationally': Dialogue across Multicultural, Indigenous, and Settler Spaces", *Annals of the Association of American Geographers*, vol. 90, no. 2: 381–91; Ghassan Hage, *White Nation: Fantasies of White Supremacy in a Multicultural Society* (New York: Routledge, 2000); Forbes, *Multiculturalism in Canada*; Day, *Multiculturalism and the History of Canadian Diversity*. Ian McKay framed all nation-building processes in Canada as liberal in *The Liberal Framework*. In general, Canadian scholarly work in the social sciences has tended to mostly focus on the left, the liberal, or the progressive side of the political spectrum, see: R. Francis, Richard Jones, Donald Smith, *Canadian History Since Confederation: Destinies* (Nelson Education Limited, October 11, 2011), 311–2 (bibliographical account). For an analysis of how certain elements of the Ukrainian immigrant community in postwar Canada tried to combine the policies of Canadian multiculturalism with anti-communist and antisemitic rhetoric, see: Grzegorz Rossolinski-Liebe, "Celebrating Fascism and War Criminality in Edmonton. The Political Myth and Cult of Stepan Bandera in Multicultural Canada", *Pamięć i Sprawiedliwość* no. 2 (2012): 453–78. For Ukrainian-Canadian processes of 'selective memory' regarding a fascist past (including antisemitism and Nazi collaboration) in the wake of Canadian multiculturalism, see: Per A. Rudling, "Multiculturalism, memory, and ritualization: Ukrainian nationalist monuments in Edmonton, Alberta", *The Journal of Nationalism and Ethnicity*, vol. 39, no. 5 (2011): 733–68.

29. Nador F. Dreisziger, "The Rise of a Bureaucracy for Multiculturalism: The Origins of the Nationalities Branch, 1939–1941", in Norman Hillmer, Bohdan S Kordan, Lubomyr Luciuk, eds., *On Guard for Thee: War, Ethnicity, and the Canadian State, 1939–1945* (Ottawa: Ministry of Supply and Services, 1988). Dreisziger's article explains that the Nationalities Branch (Department of National War Services) aimed at controlling and regulating ethnic minorities within the country's borders to ultimately gain their support for the war effort. See also: Ivana Caccia, *Managing the Canadian Mosaic in Wartime* (Montreal: McGill-Queen's University Press, 2010); Leslie A. Pal, *Interests of state: the policies of language, multiculturalism, and feminism in Canada* (Montreal: McGill-Queen's University Press, 1993); Franca Iacovetta, *Gatekeepers: Reshaping Immigrant Lives in Cold War Canada* (Toronto: Between the Lines, 2006); Reva Joshee, "An Historical Approach to Understanding Canadian Multicultural Policy", in T. Wotherspoon and P. Jungbluth, eds., *Multicultural Education in a Changing Glocal Economy: Canada and the Netherlands* (New York: Waxmann Munster, 1995); José Igartua, *The Strange Demise of*

British Canada: The Liberals and Canadian Nationalism, 1964–1968 (Montreal: McGill-Queen's University Press, 2010); Haque, *Multiculturalism Within a Bilingual Framework*; David Seljak, "Protecting religious freedom in multicultural Canada", *Diversity Magazine*, vol. 9, no. 3 (2012); Lalande, "The Roots of Multiculturalism", 47–62, among other works by the same author dealing with this issue; Lee Blanding, "Re-branding Canada: The Origins of Canadian Multiculturalism Policy, 1945–1974", dissertation (University of Victoria, 2013); Shibao Guo and Lloyd Wong, eds., *Revisiting Multiculturalism in Canada: Theories, Policies and Debates* (Rotterdam: Sense Publishers, 2015).

30. António Costa Pinto, *Corporatism and Fascism: The Corporatist Wave in Europe* (London: Routledge, 2017), 124.
31. See particularly the works by Julia Lalande on Ukrainian Canadians and the issue of bilingualism in the 1960s.
32. On earlier efforts to keep Canada British and Christian specifically, see: Phillip Buckner, R. Douglas Francis, eds., *Canada and the British World: Culture, Migration, and Identity* (Vancouver: UBC Press, 2006), 222. On more radical or violent attempts do so do, see: Allan Bartley, *The Ku Klux Klan in Canada: A Century of Promoting Racism and Hate in the Peaceable Kingdom* (Toronto: James Lorimer & Company, 2020); James M. Pitsula, *Keeping Canada British: The Ku Klux Klan in 1920s Saskatchewan* (Vancouver: UBC Press, 2013). On postwar endeavours to define or characterize the country as exclusively white and Christian, see: Gary Richard Miedema, *For Canada's Sake: Public Religion, Centennial Celebrations, and the Re-making of Canada in the 1960s* (Montreal: McGill-Queen's University Press, 2005), 16.
33. Roberto Perin, "Good Fascists and Good Canadians" in Gerald L. Gold, ed., *Minorities and Mother Country Imaginary* (St. John's: ISER, Memorial University of Newfoundland, 1984), 138–56; Angelo Principe, *The Darkest Side of the Fascist Years. The Italian-Canadian Press: 1920–1942* (Toronto: Guernica, 1999), 26–8, 60.
34. Sean Mills, "When Democratic Socialists Discovered Democracy: The League for Social Reconstruction Confronts the Quebec Problem", *The Canadian Historical Review*, vol. 86, no.1 (March 2005): 56, 53–82.
35. Carl Berger, *The Sense of Power* (Toronto: University of Toronto Press, 1970), 53.
36. Jens Rydgren, ed., *The Oxford Handbook of the Radical Right* (Oxford: Oxford University Press, 2018), 2.
37. "Mark Lilla on reactionary nostalgia and identity politics", *SRF Kultur*, Interview, July 2, 2018. Accessed in November 2020.
38. Damon T. Berry, *Blood and Faith: Christianity in American White Nationalism* (New York: Syracuse University Press, 2017), 194; Terri E. Givens, *Voting Radical Right in Western Europe* (Cambridge: Cambridge University Press, 2005), 20; Cas Mudde, *Populist Radical Right Parties in Europe* (Cambridge: Cambridge University Press, 2007), 22; Tamir Bar-On, "Fascism to the Nouvelle Droite: The Dream of Pan-European Empire", *Journal of Contemporary European Studies*, vol. 16, no. 3 (2008): 339.
39. Karen Brodkin, *How Jews Became White Folks & What That Says About Race in America* (London: Rutgers University Press, 1998); Noel Ignatiev, *How the Irish Became White* (New York: Routledge Classics, 1995); Matthew Frye Jacobson, *Whiteness of a Different Color* (Cambridge: Harvard University Press, 1999); David Roediger, *Working Toward Whiteness: How America's Immigrants Became White* (New York: Basic Books, 2006).
40. Ashley Jardina, *White Identity Politics* (Cambridge: Cambridge University Press, 2019), 152.
41. Yotam Margalit, "Economic Insecurity and the Causes of Populism, Reconsidered", *The Journal of Economic Perspectives* vol. 33, no. 4 (2019): 165.

16 *Introduction*

42. Uwe Backes and Patrick Moreau, eds., *The Extreme Right in Europe: Current Trends and Perspectives* (Göttingen: Vandenhoeck and Ruprecht, 2012), 75–6; Tamir Bar-On, "The Radical Right and Nationalism", in Rydgren, ed., *The Oxford Handbook of the Radical Right*, 31; Ja-Wener Muller, *What Is Populism?* (Philadelphia: University of Pennsylvania Press, 2016), which concludes that at the core of populism there is a rejection of pluralism.
43. I will use the word *multi-culturalism* to encapsulate Bossy's specific ideas on ethnic pluralism because these challenged a bicultural understanding of Canada. I will limit the use of *multiculturalism* (no hyphen) to refer to the liberal understanding of ethnic and cultural pluralism, to address the term in a generic manner, or when citing it.
44. Jardina, *White Identity Politics*, 118–9.
45. Alberto Spektorowski, "The French New Right: multiculturalism of the right and the recognition/exclusionism syndrome", *Journal of Global Ethics*, vol. 8, no. 1 (2012): 41–61.
46. G. Adamson, A. Carlbom, P. Ouis, "Johann Herder: Early Nineteenth-Century Counter-Enlightenment, and the Common Roots of Multiculturalism and Right-Wing Populism", *Télos* 169 (2014): 30.
47. Ibid., 29.
48. Zeev Sternhell, *The birth of fascist ideology* (Princeton: Princeton University Press, 1995), 9.
49. On Charles Maurras and Catholic integralism, see: Tamir Bar-On, *Where have all the Fascists Gone?* (London: Routledge, 2016), 120, 138, 167, 192.
50. On the influence of Maurrassisme upon French Canada, see: Maurice Torrelli, "Le nationalisme intégral, c'est selon Maurras, la monarchie", *L'Action nationale*, vol. 65, no. 1 (September 1975): 16–27; and Pierre Trépanier, "Le maurrassisme au Canada français", *Les Cahiers des dix*, vol. 53 (1999): 167–233. Trépanier argues that, although Maurras influenced to a certain extent the traditionalist currents occurring in French Canada – especially throughout the 1920s – his influence did not create nor determine the duration of it, which he argues was genuinely French Canadian.
51. Andrew Whitehead, Samuel L. Perry, Joseph O. Baker, "Make America Christian Again: Christian Nationalism and Voting for Donald Trump in the 2016 Presidential Election", *Sociology of Religion*; Washington, vol. 79, no. 2 (summer 2018): 147–71.
52. Philip Gorski, *American Covenant: A History of Civil Religion from the Puritans to the Present* (Princeton: Princeton University Press, 2017).
53. Samuel L. Perry and Andrew Whitehead, "Christian Nationalism and White Racial Boundaries: Examining White's Opposition to Interracial Marriage", *Ethnic and Racial Studies*, vol. 38, no. 10 (August 9, 2015): 1675–6.
54. In this monograph, concepts (roughly, group perceptions), just like ideas (individual perceptions), are interpreted as mental representations of reality that are abstract or have no accurate reflection in the physical world necessarily. To stress such nature in notions like 'New Canadians' or 'third force', for example, I will use single quotes. This is to indicate that any meanings attached to these words are considered subjective and may only be revealed through desconstructive analysis.
55. Mark Bevir, *The Logic of the History of Ideas* (Cambridge: Cambridge University Press, 1999), 31–52, 54.
56. Ibid., 128, 142–71.
57. The person who first distinguished signifier from signified was Ferdinand de Saussure. He argued that the sign arises from the association between the signifier and the signified. Saussure's theories were used by post-structuralists to criticize the organisation of social conceptualisation. See: David Holdcroft,

Saussure: Signs, System, and Arbitrariness (Cambridge: Cambridge University Press, 1991), 64–7; "Saussure's Theory of Language" in Jonathan D. Culler, *Ferdinand de Saussure* (New York: Cornell University Press, 1986).
58. Daniel I. O'Neill, "*Symposium:* The Logic of the History of Ideas", *The Journal of the History of Ideas*, vol. 73, no. 4 (October 2012): 589.
59. Michel Foucault, *Power/Knowledge: Selected Interviews and Other Writings, 1972–1977* (New York: Pantheon Books, 1980), 200–1. See the use of Foucault to analyse shifts in meaning and the subsequent establishment of new power relations in: David R. Roediger, *The Wages of Whiteness: Race and the Making of the American Working Class* (London: Verso, 1999); Ann Stoler, *Race and the Education of Desire. Foucault's History of Sexuality and the Colonial Order of Things* (London: Duke University Press, 1995).
60. Ian McKay, "The Liberal Framework", in Constant, Ducharme, eds., *Liberalism and Hegemony,* 628.
61. Christopher Peacocke, *A Study of Concepts* (Cambridge: MIT Press, 1992), 3.
62. Jouni-Matti Kuukkanen, "Making Sense of Conceptual Change", *History and Theory*, vol. 47, no. 3 (October 2008): 351.

2 Christian Revolutions

> CANADIANS! Without ... a spiritual revolution there has never been developed in any part of the world a new life or a better future for a nation.
> Walter J. Bossy, *The Montreal Beacon*, June 29, 1934[1]

Walter J. Bossy

Walter J. Bossy[2] was born on May 21, 1899, in the Carpathian town of Yaslo[3], although he always liked to stress his Ukrainian origins.[4] Raised a Catholic, Bossy grew up to become an ardent anti-communist, fighting against the Bolsheviks with Ukrainian military formations between 1916 and 1920, and fleeing to Canada in April 1924, less than two years after the Soviet Union was established.[5] Already able to speak and write in several Slavic languages, including Polish, Ukrainian, Russian, Czech, and Serbian, in Canada he quickly learned to communicate in both English and French (Canada's two official languages).[6] He first lived in Saskatchewan and Manitoba, where he spied for the Royal Canadian Mounted Police (RCMP) reporting on 'suspicious' elements among the Ukrainian-Canadian community while also leading the Ukrainian Hetmanate movement.[7] The Hetmanites supported Hetman (Commander) Pavlo Skoropadsky, a descendant of the 18th century Ukrainian Cossak Hetmans.[8] Skoropadsky had ruled Ukraine with the backing of the German army between April and November of 1918.[9] After November 1918, most of Ukraine was conquered by the Red Army, resulting in the creation of the Ukrainian Soviet Socialist Republic in 1922, while an independent Poland seized most of the territory of present-day western Ukraine. As the Hetmanate was overthrown by the socialist Directorate, Skoropadsky left Kiev along with the Germans.[10] Even though the Hetmanate existed for less than eight months – during which real power lay in the hands of the Germans – 'ideologist of modern Ukrainian conservatism' Viacheslav Lypynsky noted that the Hetmanate had a broader significance. He argued that the Hetmanate allowed for the expansion of and broader attraction to the idea of a Ukrainian statehood.[11]

DOI: 10.4324/9781003283348-2

Precisely, after the fall of the Hetmanate in 1918, Bossy believed that only obedience ('submission') to the exiled Hetman Pavlo Skoropadsky 'would provide the order, discipline, and stability required to achieve [a Ukrainian] independent statehood in Europe and harmony among Ukrainian immigrants in North America.'[12] Just like Bossy, during the 1920s, Ukrainian Canadians who 'were tired of political and denominational bickering' and 'yearned for a strong authority figure to provide a sense of direction' jumped on the Hetmanate bandwagon.[13] However, by the early 1930s, the 'Polish government's assimilatory and repressive measures against its Ukrainian minority, and Stalin's genocidal policies in soviet Ukraine, drove many Ukrainian Canadians ... to despair', and began steering towards more reactionary and Canada-focused movements.[14]

Looking for socio-political alternatives that suited Ukrainian Canadians unable to return home, Bossy delved into the works of Viacheslav Lypynsky, who in 1930 had created the Brotherhood of Ukrainian Classocrats-Monarchist Hetmanites (BUKMH) with a small group of followers in Prague.[15] A short-lived organization, the BUKMH promoted a universal theory that defended the existence of three main kinds of state: democracy, ochlocracy (mob rule), and classocracy. As Lypynsky saw it, while democracy 'promoted personal freedom', ochlocracy fomented 'the absolutist rule of warriors-non producers', and suppressed liberty and civic initiative. Classocracy, he explained, offered the 'balance between power and liberty, and between conservative and progressive forces.' Under classocracy, church and state would cooperate as two autonomous and equal institutions. The religious theme was omnipresent in Lypynsky's works: '[H]e professed that "the ultimate purpose of human activity is to realize, as far as possible, the eternal truth in the life of nations".'[16]

Lypynsky's idea of classocracy was influenced by a number of contemporary European thinkers, such as Georges Sorel and Gustave Lebon, but especially by the Italian School of Elitist Theory and the works of Italians Gaetano Mosca and Vilfredo Pareto and the values of traditional European conservatism they represented. These fundamentally aimed at solving the problems caused by 'narrow nationalism and Marxism'.[17] Mosca and Pareto believed that elite rule is inevitable, and that rule by a small minority consisting of members of the economic elite and policy-planning networks should hold power.[18] In other words, class is the decisive factor in the organizing of society, as it alone determines the capacity for every individual to contribute to the nation.[19] The elitist theory developed in part as a reaction to Marxism, arguing that egalitarian society was an illusion, and thus simultaneously attacking liberal democracy. This critical approach to equality encouraged interwar European fascist ideologues to widely support the elitist theory.[20] Inspired by this theory, Lypynsky argued that societies should be organized hierarchically based on class, and united politically through solidarity among the different social strata for the sake of national unity.[21] As he saw it, classocracy allowed for such 'political integration', as it overcame class conflict while also surpassing quarrels based on ethnicity.[22]

20 Christian Revolutions

In general, the ideas of Lypynsky did not find broad support, either in Europe or in North America.[23] However, they sparked a profound interest in Bossy, who in 1931 toured Canada promoting Lypynksy's thought and the classocratic state as a remedy to what he saw as the bolshevization of Canada. At that point in time, Bossy argued that communism was penetrating the Canadian press, associations, and the schools, and that the only way to stop them was through the establishment of a state rooted in the principles of Christianity that promoted class cooperation.[24] Highlighting the relationship between intergroup cooperation and religious fulfilment was a very timely choice, or rather an opportunistic one, as it followed the publication of *Quadragesimo Anno*, issued only days before Bossy began his tour. Published on May 15, 1931, *Quadragesimo Anno* commemorated the 40th anniversary of Pope Leo XIII's encyclical *Rerum Novarum*. This earlier encyclical addressed the problems encountered by an increasingly industrialised world, especially the condition of the working classes, and discussed the relationship and mutual duties between labour and capital, as well as government and citizens. It supported the rights of labour to form unions, rejected socialism and unrestricted capitalism, and proposed guidelines for limited state intervention to improve conditions and wages.[25] In particular, *Rerum Novarum* advocated retrieving some sort of medieval guild system as a means to return to the organic constitution of societies against the accelerating social disintegration triggered by industrialization and modernization. His encyclical was thus 'built around a neo-Thomistic idealization of the medieval guild system', and presented corporatism as a 'third way' between atheistic communism and rampant capitalism. As Leo XIII saw it, corporatism offered a cooperation-based system that transcended both class conflict and extreme individualism.[26]

To those who accused Christian corporatism of sustaining the emerging Italian Fascist experiment, self-defined as a corporatist state,[27] Catholic proponents responded rejecting fascism due to its statism, which according to them differed from Leo XIII's Christian ideal. Certainly, the Catholic praise of the structural elements of corporatism came from comparing it to a 'romanticized medieval guild system' rather than to Fascist Italy, which unlike Christian corporatism subdued the envisaged voluntary corporative bodies under a 'state-controlled labour system'.[28] Yet, few could argue against the fact that corporatism was an organizational framework that could adapt itself well to different political systems and beliefs – including the non-democratic ones.[29]

Building upon Leo XIII's 1891 encyclical, in 1931 Pius XI's *Quadragesimo Anno* proposed combating the failures of the modern forms of government through the reconstruction of the social order based on the Christian principles of justice and social charity. Fearing the class conflict promoted by communism, the selfish individualism encouraged by capitalism, and the unrestrained rise of the masses initiated by democracy, Pius XI advocated a system based on hierarchy, class solidarity and the common good.[30]

A corporatist view of society seemed a valid alternative inspired by the 'principle of subsidiarity', which encouraged grass-roots socio-political engagement and collaboration against social 'atomization' and the centralization of power. Pius XI was calling for a Christian a revolution; a return to the 'right and sound order'.[31]

In Canada, there were many attempts to institute a new social order inspired by the Christian principles promoted by *Rerum Novarum* and *Quadragessimo Anno*. For example, in 1911, Jesuit Joseph-Papin Archambault co-founded L'École Sociale Populaire (The Popular Social School, or ESP) in Montreal, which brought together lay people and clerics who saw 'in professional organization, to civil personality and to the denominational base, the best means of preserving and restoring social peace and improving the lot of workers'.[32] In 1931–1932, historian Frank Underhill and law professor F.R. Scott led the constitution of the League for Social Reconstruction which, influenced by Christian socialist and reformist liberal ideals, pursued social and economic reforms and political education on the basis of Christianity.[33] In 1934, Paul Gouin founded l'*Action libérale nationale* (National Liberal Action, or ALN), which presented corporatism as an alternative path to capitalism and communism and as an effective response to the Great Depression.[34] In 1935, Baptist evangelist William Aberhart founded the Social Credit Party of Canada, which combined C.H. Douglas' social credit theories with radical Christian corporatism.[35] The city in Canada that was influenced the most by Christian corporatism was Montreal, where Bossy settled in late 1931.[36]

A Call to Socially Minded Christian Canadians

Thanks to the help of Toronto's Archbishop Neil McNeil, in 1931 Bossy received an offer to work with the Montreal Catholic School Commission (MCSC) as an instructor.[37] Although Bossy was living in Winnipeg at that time, he 'sold everything ... and with 3 dollars' in his pocket (as he would recall in 1972) he moved to Montreal.[38] While working for the MCSC, Bossy kept studying the works of Lypynsky, spreading his thought on classocratic state-building among 'Slavic groups'.[39] He also kept spying for the RCMP, something he had done since the late 1920s.[40] The nature of this particular activity was by no means unique. The RCMP had relied on Hetmanate leaders to obtain information on other Ukrainian organizations and communist infiltration all through the interwar period. Although the Hetmanites had shown sympathy for Nazi Germany and other fascistic emergent states, the RCMP considered the Hetmanites 'small and unpopular' and so it did not see them as a threat. Instead, the Hetmanite movement was used as a source to obtain information on other, 'more dangerous and subversive' groups, such as the Ukrainian War Veterans' Association (UWVA) and the Ukrainian National Federation of Canada (UNF).[41] Bossy's main contact at the RCMP was English-born Frederick John (Jack) Mead. Over the years,

Colonel Mead and Bossy had become friends, and Mead was well aware of Bossy's thoughts on government and his special admiration for Lypynsky's classocratic thought. This is why, in 1934, Mead suggested that Bossy meet John J. Fitzgerald.[42]

Fitzgerald was the editor of the English-speaking Catholic newspaper *The Montreal Beacon*. Mead thought that the Catholic English-speaking community of Montreal could benefit from Bossy's thoughts on class cooperation and national unity under a Christian framework – and Fitzgerald could certainly help spread the word.[43] Following Mead's advice, Bossy met with the editor of the *The Montreal Beacon*, a newspaper self-described as 'advocate of Social Justice and the Christian Reconstruction of the Social Order'.[44] Son of well-known Irish philanthropists established in Montreal, Fitzgerald was born in Sherbrooke (Quebec) in 1892 and educated at a high school in Denver, Colorado, and at the English Catholic Loyola College in Montreal.[45] In the 1920s, Fitzgerald became a member of the Self-Determination for Ireland League, a pro-republican organization formed in Montreal in 1920 by Prince Edward Island native Katherine Hughes following instructions from Irish nationalist leader Éamon de Valera.[46] By the early 1930s, Fitzgerald had become Grand Knight of the global Catholic fraternal organization the Knights of Columbus, and editor of the only English-speaking Catholic newspaper in Montreal.[47] At that time, *The Montreal Beacon* was a relatively modest diocesan newspaper with a weekly circulation of 5000.[48]

In a rather broken English, Bossy shared with Fitzgerald his interpretation of Lypynsky's classocracy, and its potential to facilitate the Christian unity of Canada. Fitzgerald made detailed notes.[49] A fervent Catholic, Fitzgerald gave Bossy's idea of a Canadian classocratic state his 'unqualified endorsement'. This was 'indeed a new social order for Canada ... [for] it is for *every* citizen of Canada', he claimed.[50] And so, on June 29, 1934, the *Beacon* introduced Bossy's call for the implementation of a Canadian classocratic Christian state. It presented Bossy's proposal as 'the most vital message submitted to the Canadian people by the medium of script ... [since] Jacques Cartier raised the cross on Canadian soil'. According to *The Montreal Beacon*, which not surprisingly highly recommended 'this essentially Christian movement', Bossy's project met with both 'the appeals of *Rerum Novarum* and *Quadragesimo Anno*', for it suggested 'a channel for the realization of all constructive plans offered by sincere and earnest men groping in the maze of a confused and chaotic actuality'.[51]

Bossy's idea of classocracy was received with enthusiasm by some. Having read his proposal in *The Montreal Beacon*, Jesuit teacher at Loyola College and fervent anti-communist William X. Bryan urged the 'many social-minded Christian Canadians' who were losing faith in the old forms of administration and government to 'get in touch with the Classocracy League' (the group Bossy was claiming to lead), for it had the key to the 'Christian revolution'. '[Their] task is tremendous,' said the Catholic weekly

Prairie Messenger (Saskatchewan), 'but that is not a reason for not undertaking it'. The time for revolution had come, argued the Saskatchewanian newspaper, and 'Classocracy [would] emerge as a leader, saviour and victor'.[52] The *Western Catholic* (Alberta) concluded that classocracy was a 'healthy, logical and Christian' solution to modern social evils.[53] In a society corrupted by materialism, classocracy could save Christian civilization, and 'isn't for this', asked the *Prairie Messenger*, 'that we have been praying for a long time?'[54] Even the liberal newspaper *Winnipeg Free Press* (Manitoba) affirmed that classocracy constituted a 'constructive ideology for Canadians'.[55]

Others argued that Bossy's arguments for a classocratic Canadian state were often confusing due to the constant use of philosophical terms that 'would cause even the minds of the most erudite to stagger', inevitably resulting in a 'terrible headache'. The 'Classocrats', said the associate editor of the Catholic newspaper *The Prairie Messenger* Cosmas W. Krumpelmann, need to present their theses in a way that 'an ordinary civilized man with some horse sense can understand'.[56]

The Montreal Beacon published a total of three articles on classocracy by Walter J. Bossy in the summer of 1934,[57] and the three of them were published shortly thereafter as a small book entitled *A Call To Socially Minded Christian Canadians* (henceforth *A Call*). *A Call* depicted a western world in decadence, and modern democracy as a social structure that no longer suited the material or the spiritual needs of the people.[58] It stated that only a new social order based on 'idealistic Christianity' could save civilization[59] from the moral chaos and poverty brought about by capitalism, secularism, rationalism, and democracy.[60] It advocated the spiritual unity of all Canadians or, rather, the unity of all Christian Canadians. For Bossy believed that, 'with the exception of an insignificant percentage ... Canadians are Christians', albeit from different denominations. According to Bossy, classocracy would allow for the harmonious integration of all Christian denominations into one nation.[61] In doing so, it would 'respect the traditions of Canadians' and their 'two main channels: French and English' while also allowing the 'variety of people' of Canada to cooperate.[62] Based on *Rerum Novarum* and *Quadragessimo Anno*, Bossy explained that the only divisions that would exist under such a state for the purposes of social organization would be those determined by professional units or 'guilds'.[63]

While in *A Call* Bossy called for the 'spiritual unification of all nations' in Canada, his 'universal' views were quite limited. On the one hand, Bossy claimed that he rejected the 'deification of race' exemplified by Nazi Germany, which led to 'bellicose imperialism'.[64] Instead, he explained, 'Christian universalism' allowed for the overcoming of the nation and, thus, for interethnic cooperation.[65] At the same time, some groups, in particular 'the yellow and black vandals' (as Bossy put it), were to be excluded from that nation-building project.[66] The specific word that Bossy was choosing to describe Canadians of East Asian and African descent is noteworthy.

Vandal is a word that refers to someone who deliberately destroys or damages public or private property and, in its origin from Latin, it refers to the Germanic peoples who ravaged Gaul, Spain, and North Africa in the fourth and fifth centuries.[67] It is thus a noun that ultimately signifies violence, paganism, and barbarism. The view that peoples of non-European descent are uncivilized had to that point been widely used by cultural, political, and economic colonizers, who justified their violent endeavours by arguing that the peoples they aimed to control were savages in need of (Christian and European) guidance. On the one hand, based on such an argument 'civilization' and 'civilized' became signifiers for *Christianity*, as reflected in *A Call*: 'Christianity reared for us during nineteen centuries the culture and the civilization out of which it has produced acceptable social arrangements'.[68] On the other hand, *civilization* also came to signify *European*, and according to Bossy it was precisely the Europeans who 'by real sacrifice and toil made Canada what it is (their heritage to us now seized by the greedy few)'.[69]

Bossy had a very clear idea of who those 'greedy few' were. In *A Call*, he explained that 'present-day democracy with its entire system – parliamentarism and capitalism' was the rule of 'plutocracy (those who control the whole economic machinery) ... Those who control democracy (plutocrats) speculate with this capital and thereby enrich themselves at the cost of the pauperization of the masses'.[70] The single enemy of the plutocrats was, he said, 'the Church of Christ', which they allegedly attacked with 'rationalistic liberalism'.[71] It was from 'plutocracy' that communism or 'internationalism' stemmed, explained Bossy; as did 'cosmopolitanism' and 'capitalism-democracy'. Against 'internationalism' or class-based commitment to international solidarity epitomized by socialism and communism, Bossy promulgated 'universalism', which aimed at a global spiritual union and class cooperation at the national level.[72]

During the interwar period, the association between democracy and so-called plutocracy had been widely utilized by fascist regimes, namely by Fascist Italy and Nazi Germany. In their conspiratorial narratives, *plutocracy* referred to 'democracy perverted by financial domination by the Jews'.[73] Fascist leaders argued that totalitarianism was 'democracy's fulfillment' while what they called 'plutocratic democracy' was the rule of the bourgeoisie or the Jewish capitalist.[74] Along with bolshevism, 'plutocracy or finance capitalism', which was allegedly dominated by an international Jewish conspiracy, were 'fascism's national enemies'.[75] *A Call* was an attempt to explain, or justify, this narrative. Democracy, argued Bossy, had 'rationalized' Europe and, as a consequence, it had exposed it to 'threatening Bolshevism'. Thus, to him, fascism was simply a response to the chaos caused between 'collectivist Communism ... and rationalist-democratic capitalism'.[76] Ultimately, he said, fascism had allowed for a Christian renaissance; created a Christian elite 'from among the most deserving, public-spirited and honest professionalists [sic]'; and reformed 'the failings of capitalism' and jeopardized 'the control of the anonymous capitalism-democracy'.[77]

Given that Lypynsky's classocratic theory was based on the elitist theories of Mosca and Pareto, which promoted the rule of the comfortable few, Bossy's rejection of a ruling class whose power derives from their wealth (i.e., plutocracy) can only be sustained if based on antisemitic prejudice.

Besides condemning plutocracy, *A Call* also rejected *cosmopolitanism*. Cosmopolitanism, explained Bossy, diminished the nations and promoted a false belief in the sameness of all people.[78] This, as he saw it, led to the 'atomization rather than to the construction of a unity'.[79] During the first half of the twentieth century, 'cosmopolitanism' was employed by antisemites when wanting to highlight that, lacking a nation state of their own, the Jewish community constituted a parasitic element, and an overall a 'destructive stranger' that infected self-described nations with intellectual and moral decadence.[80] In Canada, this type of antisemitism was not uncommon among the Ukrainian-Canadian community.[81] The Toronto's Hetmanate weekly *Ukrainskyi robintnyk* (Ukrainian Worker), for example, described Jews as 'a people without a Fatherland who felt no attachment to the countries in which they lived and who were averse to productive labour'. Bossy himself wrote for this paper stating that 'Jews were indifferent to their neighbours and only interested in securing material advantages for themselves'. The Jews, he argued, controlled the production and sale of armaments and influenced politics in the liberal democracies. They were doing 'all they could to promote international chaos and turmoil'.[82] References to the Judeo-Bolshevik conspiracy or to the disproportionately high percentage of Jews in the Communist Party and in the Soviet bureaucracy, for example, appeared in a number of Ukrainian-Canadian weeklies during this period. Ukrainian Catholic workers were implored to create an anti-Bolshevik front because 'what happened in Russia, in Mexico and in Spain can happen in Canada'.[83]

The idea that Jews, liberal democracy and communism were intrinsically related determined some of the social networks that Bossy connected with throughout the 1930s.[84] French-Canadian Adrien Arcand is a notorious example.[85] According to the *Ukrainskyi robitnyk*, during the 1930s Bossy and Arcand lived in the same neighbourhood in Montreal, Ahuntsic, and they established a relationship that led to subsequent discussions around an alleged global Jewish conspiracy and to book exchanges.[86] For example, Bossy kept a copy of Arcand's antisemitic *La Clé du Mystère* (The Key to the Mystery), published in 1938.[87] This booklet compiled several journal clippings containing Jewish 'testimonies' that were supposed to confirm the existence of a worldwide Jewish plot to cause communist revolutions and to control all nations. *La Clé du Mystère* argued that communism and free-masonry were the means by which the Jews conquer;[88] that communism in Russia and elsewhere was financed by the Jewish bankers in New York;[89] that rather than a persecuted minority, Jews have historically been the most ferocious persecutors;[90] and that the League of Nations was a Jewish organization.[91] Another central argument in *La Clé du Mystère*, and one that would shape Bossy's understanding of Canadian diversity for the rest of his life, is the idea that Jews could never become Canadian.[92] According to Arcand, the Jewish people would never be able (or willing) to contribute to the national common good, for they worked for the benefits of Jews only: 'They cannot be, they never will be Canadians, but always exclusively and fanatically Jews [...] They are, as everywhere else, a danger to the country'.[93]

Arcand made sure that Bossy became acquainted with the literature published by American Nazi sympathizer E. Sanctuary, author of *Are these things so? A study in modern termites of the Homo Sapiens Type,* which Bossy enthusiastically studied.[94] The book, edited by the World Alliance Against Jewish Aggressiveness (WAAJA), compared Jewish communities to termite infestations: '... [they] travel in colonies ... they are now in the lower part of the building and are making inroads on the supporting beams and joists, threatening demolition of the structure'.[95] The simile intended to express that Jews were inherently alien and conspired to destroy civilization. One of the main arguments of the book was that socialism and communism were Jewish both in inception and in direction. Sanctuary explained that Marx, Lassalles, and Engels, all described as Jewish (although Engels was not), seized Utopian socialism and turned it into a subversive, revolutionary movement, overshadowing socialism's sympathy for the poor by the Marxist hatred of the rich. As a consequence, the idea of cooperation was replaced by conflict. Jewish thought, Sanctuary concluded, naturally and logically introduced the idea of 'class war'.[96]

Throughout the 1930s, Bossy's acquaintance with Arcand continued, with the former repeatedly inviting the latter to events organized by the Ukrainian-Canadian community to speak about Bolshevism and the achievements of Nazi Germany. On November 29, 1937, for instance, Bossy invited Arcand to a banquet organized by a Ukrainian Catholic parish in Montreal to discuss the communist threat. At the time, Arcand had become a fervent admirer of German Nazi leader Adolf Hitler; an outspoken antisemite; the editor of the fascist newspaper *Le Fasciste canadien* (The Canadian Fascist); and the leader of the far-right Christian National Socialist Party. Influenced by Arcand's speeches, Bossy became certain that 'Hitler would save the Christian world from the Jewish menace' and that, with Germany's help, Jewish bolshevism would disappear to give way to a new world order.[97]

The Christian left

Besides urging to start a Christian revolution, *A Call to Socially Minded Christian Canadians* was also a public response to *The Regina Manifesto*, the political program of the Cooperative Commonwealth Federation (CCF) published in 1933. The CCF was a political party created in Calgary (Alberta) in 1932. In Quebec, the CCF was first regarded as a program for the establishment of 'the social and political ideals of English Protestant

Canadians'. On the other hand, its socialist-oriented program alarmed many who accused it of being communist – like l'École Sociale Populaire (ESP) did in its *Program of social restoration* issued in 1934.[98] Although, not unlike ESP, in *A Call* Bossy argued that the philosophy of the CCF 'remains essentially materialistic and it is bound ... to be found one day as a full-fledged member in the ranks of materialistic socialism', he also stated that the 'CCF represents the only serious attempt to diagnose Canada's ills and to present to the Canadian public a definite program of social reform'.[99] This is why, Bossy concluded, a new movement should be established to incorporate social justice in the material sphere of the CCF so that eventually both movements might merge.[100] The CCF must turn to 'those socially minded enthusiastic Catholics', wrote Bossy, for the world was dividing itself into militant Christianity and militant Bolshevism, and 'Canadians must choose'.[101]

Bossy considered 'CCFers' to be among the 'few social-minded citizens' that could 'serve the common good'. However, if the newly formed party did not modify its program by undermining its socialist dimensions, it would constitute 'a real danger', as Bossy saw it.[102] Thus, he resolved to approach the CCF as the leader of the Classocracy League of Canada (so far, a paper organization) and invite CCFers to Bossy's first symposium against 'the plutocratic regime ... so-called democracy' and 'the menace of the Communist movement'. According to Bossy, two CCFers answered the call: 'Prof. Scott' and 'Miss Sheridan'.[103] The records do not reveal whether 'Prof. Scott' was Francis Reginald (Frank) Scott, McGill Law Professor and founder of the League for Social Reconstruction (LSR) and active collaborator of the CCF; whether it was R. B. Y. Scott, Professor at the United Theological College in Montreal, and also member of the LSR and CCF sympathizer; or whether it was someone else.[104] On the other hand, 'Miss Sheridan' was for certain Madeleine Sheridan, a well-known Catholic of Irish descent and social worker from Montreal.

An upper-class unmarried socialist and a suffragist, Madeleine Sheridan had been active in women's organizations in Montreal for years, dedicating most of her life to social work.[105] As many others, her interest in politics arose with the Depression. She first became a member of the LSR in the early 1930s, and soon joined the National Council of the CCF, eventually becoming Vice-President of its Quebec section.[106] Given her political activism on the left of the political spectrum, Sheridan's interest in classocracy must have emerged from her thinking that Bossy's proposal might bring about progressive change. One possibility is that she believed that the reorganization of the social order based on professional units represented a means for women to achieve greater inclusion in modern society. Given that classocracy acknowledged all Canadians so long as they earned (as your capacity to contribute to the nation was measured by your capacity to join a guild)[107], and that Sheridan was economically independent, this assumption is not unfounded. Any other woman would have had to liberate herself from her (unpaid) duties[108] before even considering classocracy a step forward in equality, for classocracy was as much of a racialized socio-political and economic theory as a gendered one.[109]

In the fall of 1935, Sheridan wrote to Bossy inviting him over for tea to discuss the question of social reconstruction with New York Catholic leftist Dorothy Day and 'plenty of CCFers'.[110] Mainly known as the co-founder of the 1930s' newspaper *Catholic Worker* and the radical but theologically orthodox Catholic Worker Movement, Dorothy Day was a former member of the American Communist Party who converted to Catholicism and, influenced by Jacques Maritain, dedicated her life to 'revolutionary ... lay activism' through social work, greatly shaping twentieth-century 'Catholic Left'.[111] Acquainted at least since March 1934, throughout their lives Day and Sheridan exchanged their views on the relationship between the Gospel and political action, between Christianity and Socialism.[112] Day very much admired Sheridan's work in Montreal, and although she did not think that politics was the best way to support a 'Gospel view of life', she trusted Sheridan's engagement in Canadian politics and lamented that some 'oppose the CCF on the grounds of its "Moscow" flavor'.[113] In November 1935, Dorothy Day visited Canada to spread the word on the dangers of communism and the need to establish a new social order.[114] During her trip, Day stayed for a week at Madeleine Sheridan's house in Montreal, where Sheridan organized the 'tea party' she referred to when writing to Bossy.

Dorothy Day was acquainted with another Canadian social worker that highly influenced Bossy's plans for social reconstruction: Catherine de Hueck Doherty. A Russian baroness who had fled the Russian Civil War and established herself in North America, 'she became a dynamic lecturer against the 'reds' and a spokeswoman for the need for Christian love'.[115] De Hueck had gotten in touch with Day after learning about the latter's *Catholic Worker* 'and they became lifelong friends'.[116] Catherine de Hueck and Dorothy Day shared the idea that socialism 'could not be trusted', for it was 'based on large organizations'. Influenced by social corporatism, they believed that the creation of 'small self-help groups' would enhance collaboration and lead to another level of spirituality, paving the way for the establishment of a more cooperative society. Their Christian philosophy was more of what Gregory Baum calls 'Catholic anarchism', a philosophy which 'despised the major economic and political institutions and sought the reconstruction of humanity through small groups, whose operation embodied a new logic of love and simplicity'.[117]

In a letter de Hueck wrote to Day in April of 1934, the baroness shared her plans to open a social centre or Friendship House in Toronto, probably inspired by Day's own House of Hospitality, which had been providing temporary refuge and support services for the unemployed in New York.[118] In Toronto, the Catholic Church was very concerned about unemployed and low-paid Catholics, particularly the 'newly arriving [Catholic] immigrants', who were actively targeted by the Communist Party of Canada (CPC).

These immigrants were perceived as being vulnerable, innocent and ignorant, which allegedly explained why 'communists were preying [sic]' on them.[119] This situation motivated the establishment of St. Francis Catholic Friendship House at 122 Portland Street in September 1934. The House was located in a working-class area inhabited mostly by Czechoslovakians, Poles, Russians, Ukrainians, and Jews, and it was strategically positioned near the Protestant Church of All Nations (a United Church group trying to evangelize immigrants by providing services to them much like St. Francis House) and across from a Communist Hall. The Archdiocese of Toronto hired Catherine de Hueck to run it.[120]

When editor of *The Montreal Beacon* John J. Fitzgerald heard about the opening of Toronto's St. Francis Catholic Friendship House in 1934, he decided to pay a visit:

> It was the day after the federal elections in Ontario. I was looking for No. 122 Portland Street. I walked up from Wellington Street, crossed King Street, approaching my number when I noticed on the side wall of a large building housing a leather goods company the words: "VOTE COMMUNIST". The white chalk against the red brick stood out prominently [...] About ten feet farther on I again read: "VOTE COMMUNIST". But what was that written [sic] on the same wall in between these two; timid letters, also made with chalk, measuring about one brick high It was not easy to read but the message was clear and definite: "vote for Christianity". [...] There, a few feet away, on the opposite side of the street, was my number. "Friendship House" ran the sign over the door.[121]

That day, John J. Fitzgerald met Catherine de Hueck. Fitzgerald was extremely impressed by the work done by St. Francis Catholic Friendship House, a service that contributed in leading 'Canada and Canadians to safety'.[122] Back in Montreal, Fitzgerald told Bossy about the Friendship House projects and their success protecting Catholic immigrant groups. Impressed by the achievements of Dorothy Day's and Catherine de Hueck's Friendship Houses in New York and Toronto, Bossy decided that he too would establish a Friendship House in Montreal: a 'New Canadian Friendship House'.[123]

The 'foreign problem'

In July 1935, the Classocracy League of Canada (CLC) was constituted as a Catholic 'political and [social] organisation' composed of 'Canadians of different nationalities ... devoted to the reconstruction of the political, social and economic life of Canada'.[124] Following the inauguration of the CLC, its extended reform program entitled *Déclaration, theses, statuts* or Declaration, theses, and statutes (the *Déclaration*) was released in French in *l'École Sociale Populaire* magazine, reaching a readership of over 8000–9000.[125] The formation of the CLC, together with the release of its reform program, was announced in the social Catholic newspapers *L'Action Catholique* (Catholic Action) and *Le Progrès du Saguenay* (The Progress of Saguenay), the liberals *Le Soleil* (The Sun) and *Le Nouvelliste* (The Story-Writter), and the French-Canadian nationalists *Le Devoir* (The Duty) and *Le Bien Public* (The Public Good) – all of which were papers published in Quebec.[126] *L'Action Catholique* approved of the endeavour, citing the CLC's claims of it being based on 'Catholic philosophy and the teachings of the Supreme Pontiffs', which was also quoted by *Le Soleil* and *Le Nouvelliste*. *Le Devoir* gave details on the CLC's program, a 62-page-long proposal, and described it as offering 'a real State' based on professions. The *Déclaration* was introduced as the extended program of the Classocracy League of Canada (CLC) – the brief one being *A Call to Socially Minded Christian Canadians*, published a year earlier.[127] It presented the CLC as a movement dedicated to 'the establishment of a completely Christian system-State, of universal applicability: the Classocracy.'[128] Classocracy, it explained, was the re-organization of society by occupation or 'guilds', overseen by a minority. Since classocracy was based on social Catholicism, the *Déclaration* insisted that it alone would allow Canada to re-Christianize the country against liberal democracy, which according to the CLC promoted secularism, unrestrained capitalism, utilitarianism, neo-paganism, and the occult.[129]

The program of the CLC made no mention of Bossy, neither as founder nor as leader of the CLC.[130] This was deliberate. A few months earlier, Bossy had learned that the Irish Catholic community of Montreal was suspicious of the classocratic theory developed in *A Call* because 'a foreigner Ukrainian … Walter Bossy was behind [it]'.[131] Apparently, even Madeleine Sheridan had joined those critiques.[132] Because of this, Bossy came to believe that his identity was 'a tremendous obstacle' to the movement he wanted to lead.[133] That is why, in late 1934, he approached Edward LaPierre. A man of French and Irish descent and a devout Catholic born in 1899 in Quebec, by 1935 Edward LaPierre was an English Literature teacher at the Catholic Thomas D'Arcy McGee High School in Montreal, and a member of the Cercle Saint-Stanislas de L'Action Catholique de la Jeunesse canadienne-française or French-Canadian youth (whose ultimate goal was to develop Catholic and French-Canadian national feelings among youth).[134] At that time, LaPierre also worked for Fitzgerald at *The Montreal Beacon*, where he had met Bossy in 1934.[135] Bossy thought that LaPierre's ethnic origins and linguistic skills (i.e., the absence of an accent) would be enough to ensure the attention of the two major Catholic groups of the city – the Irish and the French Canadian. By the time the *Déclaration* was released, LaPierre had agreed to become the new leader of the CLC, and Bossy transitioned to a mere supportive role.[136]

Between 1935 and 1937, Edward LaPierre was the public representative of the CLC and, together with John J. Fitzgerald and William X.

Bryan (the Jesuit teacher at Loyola who had eagerly supported *A Call*), he organized bilingual public symposiums on corporatism and classocracy in Montreal.[137] In these symposiums, LaPierre promoted the aims of the CLC, inspired – he explained – by Pius XI's *Quadragesimo Anno* and exemplified by Benito Mussolini's policies in Fascist Italy. At the same time, he insisted on the 'democratic character' of the CLC and its wish to protect Canada's existing political institutions.[138] Only corporatism, however, could bring about true freedom – he explained.[139] Besides organizing symposiums, LaPierre also published on classocracy and its potential application to Canada. For instance, in *The Social Forum*, which was founded in Ottawa in 1935 by Catherine de Hueck after Dorothy Day's *Catholic Worker*, he defined classocracy as a 'Christian revolution'[140].[141] A classocratic Canada, he said, would truly embody a 'Christian, corporative, monarchical state-system'; a 'fourth' state: an alternative to democracy, socialism, and fascism. Classocracy, he argued, sustained the 'traditional teaching of Christianity concerning God, man, [...] and the state', their nature and function. Understanding society as an organism, classocracy organized it. Contrastingly, democracy atomized society, socialism distorted it, and statist fascism bullied it.[142]

While LaPierre was promoting classocracy, Bossy was practising English by writing regularly to Fitzgerald, and by reading aloud to LaPierre. Fitzgerald insisted that this was 'the most important thing [Bossy could] do for Classocracy' at the moment – losing his accent.[143] In addition to this, in October 1935 Bossy submitted a petition to president of the MCSC Victor Doré concerning the possibility of him being employed as a 'Special Representative' charged with studying and preventing the communist radicalization of 'foreign pupils' attending Catholic schools – in addition to his duties as an instructor.[144] Together with the petition, Bossy attached statistical information about schooled foreign children (including their faith, family members' occupation, and ethnic origin), and the religious, social and civic instruction they were receiving. From such statistics, he had concluded 'that a certain number [of] former foreign Catholics have definitely renounced their faith', emphasizing that some Catholic children were now attending Protestant schools.[145]

Doré and the MCSC were pleased to have Bossy investigate what they called the 'foreign problem', and for roughly a year Bossy kept supplying lists of Catholic children of diverse ethnic backgrounds who had transitioned to Protestant schools, 'thus facilitating a prudent and inoffensive effort to bring back these children to their schools, and them, and their families, if it so be, to their church and to their faith'.[146] Despite being instructed to continue working on the 'foreign problem', Bossy was eventually informed that 'although considerable merit was found in [his] expose, it was financially impossible for the Commission to consider [his] candidacy for the proposed office of Special Foreign Representative' due to 'certain difficulties, chiefly financial'.[147] Thus, a year had passed and Bossy had been offered no compensation for his work. In spite of that, in the winter of 1936 he decided to send another and more detailed report on the communist threat against the 'foreign children' schooled by the MCSC. In it, Bossy announced an upcoming 'list of the names, addresses, places of meetings and other details' of foreign pupils attending Catholic schools that were attending communist meetings or showed sympathy towards communism in other ways.[148] As he saw it, 'the cause of Christian civilization' was at stake; and that cause depended on the salvation of what he called the 'New Canadians'.[149]

In 1936, editor of *L'École Sociale Populaire* Jesuit Joseph P. Archambault decided to assist Bossy in his endeavour to be employed by the MCSC to help preserve 'the Catholic element in the foreign (i.e., non-French and non-English speaking) population of Montreal', as Archambault put it.[150] Searching for support, Archambault established contact with Albert A. Gardiner, Assistant General Passenger Traffic Manager for the Canadian National Railways, to discuss the situation. Gardiner had been talking publicly about the 'foreign problem' and the need to help integrate Catholic immigrants at least since 1934.[151] He lamented seeing that Montreal was still treating Catholic immigrants as 'foreigners', neglecting them and making no effort to learn from them. He argued that although 'foreigners' by origin, they were nonetheless 'brothers in faith'. As Gardiner saw it, Montreal had to help these immigrants become good Canadians, integrating them as coreligionists.[152] Like Bossy and Archambault, who had just published an anti-communist pamphlet entitled *Sous la Menace Rouge* (Under the Red Threat), Gardiner believed that communism was a 'virus' that could be prevented 'in and through the schools', and that communism was overall more effective among non-French and non-English speakers – immigrants.[153] After Archambault introduced him to Bossy, Gardiner took '[his] cause with great energy' and, partly because of his experience as an instructor and his ability to speak multiple languages, he agreed that Bossy should be employed in a special capacity to tackle the problem, possibly in Catholic as in non-Catholic schools.[154] Both Gardiner and Archambault agreed that, in order for Bossy to effectively look after 'the interests of the foreign children in the matter of instruction' and 'bring [New Canadians] over to the right side', he needed the full support of the MCSC.[155]

Bossy's chances of being employed by the MCSC as a 'Special Representative' seemed to increase even more in 1936, when conservative populist politician Maurice Duplessis became Quebec's new premier. After forty years of Liberal rule, the Union Nationale (a new party formed from a merger between the Action Libérale Nationale and Quebec's Conservative Party) won with 56.8% of the popular vote. Upon seizing power, Duplessis pledged loyalty to the French-Canadian Catholic clergy, promising the Church and Quebec to fight against communism and protect the social teachings of the Church.[156] In view of the new political setting, Bossy was hoping that the MCSC would give him the chance to join 'the general and necessary fight against Communism in which matter Mr. Duplessis has taken so spirited and so splendid a stand'.[157] Gardiner too believed that Bossy's work would give Duplessis 'an opportunity to put into effect an important work in accordance with his avowed and announced position against Communism and ... find a useful and proper play for Bossy's fitness to take part in this work'.[158] It looked like Archambault envisaged Bossy's application 'in the same light: that is, as a useful contribution in the anti-Communist campaign'.[159]

In September 1936, Tom J. Coonan, former president of *The Montreal Beacon* (before John J. Fitzgerald) and now Minister without portfolio in Maurice Duplessis' cabinet, called president of the Classocracy League of Canada Edward LaPierre.[160] Apparently, Coonan was a sympathizer of the CLC, and he was well acquainted with LaPierre as well as Fitzgerald, with whom he had travelled, and even Bossy, with whom Coonan had already discussed the communist threat 'especially among the foreign population'.[161] When Coonan called LaPierre, he thanked 'the Classocrats' for their exchange of letters and telegrams, and spoke about 'the good will and great energy of the Cabinet' to bring about change. During the call, LaPierre mentioned Bossy's struggle in trying to get a position with the MCSC. Coonan assured LaPierre that he would help Bossy '[secure] a position' with the MCSC, starting with offering his name as referee in Bossy's new application to the commission.[162] Jack Mead, who had introduced Bossy to Fitzgerald back in 1934 and was now RCMP Superintendent, also offered Bossy his name as referee.[163]

With the support of Coonan and Mead, 'men who are, due to their experience, real authorities to judge of its merits', Bossy decided to write his letter of application to the MCSC for the new position.[164] In it, he insisted that 'the menace of anti-religious and anti-patriotic Communism is more obvious than ever', and that 'consultations with social-minded and high-placed personages concerning this very real danger have ... moved [him] ... to reopen the question raised in [the 1935] memorandum'.[165] Having a provincial minister and a RCMP official as referees seemed to be of great assistance, as on November 15, 1936, Bossy was finally employed by the MCSC as 'as representative concerning foreign problems' to gather 'accurate statistical information regarding pupils of foreign nationalities enrolled in both Catholic and Protestant schools'.[166] His first task: organizing a religious and civic campaign to mobilize 'our foreign Catholics'. With the approval of the Catholic Church, Bossy proposed the formation of a movement that 'combined [the] Christian foreign forces of this city [of Montreal]', and that was dedicated to the 'salvation and good citizenship of thousands of neglected and forgotten strangers-citizens within our gates'.[167]

Up to that moment, the voice of the 'New Canadians' seemed to be missing from the anti-communist Christian movement that was taking place throughout the province of Quebec. On October 25, 1936, under the auspices of coadjutor archbishop of Montreal Georges Gauthier[168], a demonstration taking place simultaneously in Montreal and Quebec City mobilized 'hundreds of thousands' of French-Canadian Catholics against communism.

34 *Christian Revolutions*

In Montreal, where according to the liberal newspaper *La Presse* (The Press) '100,000 manifestants' participated, the main speakers included the secretary of l'Université de Montréal Edouard Montpetit; the MLA (Member of the Legislative Assembly) Mercier Gérard Thibeault; and the president of the Catholic unions Philippe Girard. All of them spoke in French, followed by the intervention of Counselor Léo McKenna, who spoke in English on behalf of the few English Catholics who joined.[169] In Quebec City, reportedly 15,000 participants rallied with Cardinal Jean-Marie-Rodrigue Villeneuve and Premier Duplessis to publicly declare war against communism – a war that Duplessis had already started by passing the 'Padlock Law', which 'made it illegal to publish or distribute literature tending to propagate communism ... and allowed the ... closing of any house or hall used for propagating communism'.[170] There was no doubt, claimed Joseph-Papineau Archambault, that 'the province of Quebec does not want communism'.[171]

Jesuit William X. Bryan lamented that the French-Canadian Catholics were apparently better informed about the red threat than the English-speaking Catholics – whose only representation during the double demonstration had been Counselor McKenna.[172] English Catholics must mobilize along with the French-Canadian Catholics, he said, and fight against communism and the abuses of capitalism.[173] For such a fight, unity was crucial: 'We were successively described as Francophones and Anglophones. We are, simply, Canadians'.[174] Yet, while the French Canadians were massively mobilizing and the English Catholics were mostly absent, the 'foreign-speaking' Catholic communities didn't seem to attend at all – at least their presence wasn't reported. In an attempt to address that problem, coadjutor archbishop Georges Gauthier established contact with Bossy, who was working at the MCSC as 'special representative'.

Gauthier offered Bossy the position of secretary of a new 'Committee of the Foreign-Parish Clergy', a committee which would be in charge of organizing a religious and civic anti-communist demonstration led by faithful (Catholic) 'New Canadians'. The demonstration would take place at the Notre Dame Basilica in Montreal.[175] On October 30, 1936, the committee met for the first time for the purpose of preparing a 'public Catholic manifestation of anticommunistic [sic] nature of all foreign-speaking Catholics in Montreal similar to that of French-Catholic manifestation recently held in the metropolis' and in Quebec City. At the meeting, Bossy presented his plan as symbolizing 'cooperation in action and unity in the attitude towards communism adopted by Catholics all over the world'.[176] Content with Bossy's ideas, the ethnic parish representatives signed a final statement that read: 'For all the spiritual and temporal benefits extended to us by our adopted country we most willingly purpose to reciprocate utilizing our native abilities and ingenuities for the upbuilding [sic] and general welfare of Canada'.[177]

The 'grand ceremony' would be celebrated on December 6, 1936, and would count on the public speeches of William X. Bryan, Joseph-Papineau

Archambault, Albert A. Gardiner, Victor Doré, and Georges Gauthier. Priests of descent other than French or English would also speak.[178] The rally would be composed by 'various colonies of the metropolis which are of Catholic faith', which would include German, Lithuanian, Polish, Slovak, Syrian, Ukrainians, Greek, and Italian.[179] Reportedly, 'several thousand foreign language Catholics' were brought together not only to position themselves against communism, but also to express their loyalty to Canada and its government and institutions, as well as the Catholic Church.[180] Gauthier was the first to speak, but not before he publicly congratulated Bossy, introduced as an employee of the MCSC, and blessing his work.[181] These 'foreigners', said Gauthier in French, know more about the communist menace than anyone else, which is why they now rally to 'claim that this country must remain Christian for it to be good to live there'. More importantly, he continued, these 'foreigners' are living proof of the mighty force of 'Redemption' by which nations and nationalisms may be overcome towards the creation of an 'army of brothers'.[182] Having come to 'a land whose true greatness is based upon and may only be sustained by its adherence to Christian ideals', they have brought with them 'the inestimable gift of the Catholic Faith'.[183] But victims of unemployment, Archambault intervened, Canadian immigrants have become the main targets of communism, which 'speaks their tongue and promises a new state in which ... no-one will suffer, in which everyone will work and live without fear of tomorrow'. He proclaimed:

> Catholics of all languages ... the time has come to unite us all, in a vast army where each battalion will keep its leaders, its language, its traditions, but will fight shoulder to shoulder, under the same authority, according to the same commands, for the triumph of the same cause.[184]

Victor Doré followed. It was in the schools, he said, that communism could be defeated. It was in the schools that Anglophones, Francophones, and 'New Canadians' could become brothers. Canadians of 'foreign language', said Doré, must trust and help the (Catholic) school so that it can play a role in raising foreign children to become Canada's pride.[185]

The 'historic novelty'[186] of the religious and civic demonstration of the Catholic foreigners in Montreal was highlighted by *L'Illustration Nouvelle*, which was the semi-official publication of Duplessis' Union Nationale (edited by Canadian fascist leader Adrien Arcand);[187] the nationalists *Le Devoir* and *La Tribune*; and by the liberal *Le Canada*.[188] It was reported that up to 15,000 people attended the demonstration.[189] To Bossy, this was great news. On the one hand, the mobilization had effectively worked as a test to measure the strength of the Canadian Catholic 'foreigners'. On the other, these numbers might guarantee that the ad hoc organizing committee for December 6, 1936, would not rush to dissolve. In fact, Bossy expected that the committee would embrace the responsibility to permanently oversee the 'New Canadians'

Christian and patriotic loyalty while also working towards the improvement of their economic conditions. And indeed, in 1937, the New Canadians Committee was institutionalized.[190] Ultimately, Bossy told Gauthier, the goal was to organize and secure the Christian faith of the 'New Canadians' in order for them to mobilize along with the French and English Canadians, facilitating unity among 'all milieus of our citizenry: French, English and foreign'. Ensuring the Christian and civic allegiance of the 'foreign' Canadian would be the first step towards a much-desired Christian revolution.[191]

Conclusion

This chapter demonstrates that even though the impact of Walter J. Bossy's proposal for a Canadian classocratic state in 1934 and 1935 was rather negligible, it constituted a stepping stone for him to build connections that would be key to his eventual recruitment by the MCSC in 1936 to act as guardian and representative of those communities perceived as belonging to the 'New Canadians'. It also reveals that, by 1936, Bossy envisioned Canada as a nation composed of three elements that needed to cooperate in order to protect Canada from the communist threat.

It also stresses the role that ethnicity and religion had in shaping Bossy's project of nation building in the early 1930s. Specifically, it shows that, while highlighting the existence of a plural Canada that must strive for the common good, Bossy excluded groups of East Asian, African, and Jewish descent, as well as non-Christian communities, from his vision. In conclusion, as Bossy was starting to develop a trichotomic view of Canada, he was also proposing new parameters of exclusion on the basis of origin and faith. In doing so, Bossy was advancing a plan that promoted white and Christian supremacist ideals to mould a new state. A new Canada defined by an unprecedented form of illiberal multi-culturalism.

Notes

1. *The Montreal Beacon*, June 29, 1934, p. 5.
2. Bossy's full name was Vladislav Lizislav Jacenty Bossy, see "Interview", April 1972, p. 1, file Bossy, Walter J., Biographical Material, 1912–1972, vol. 1, MG30 C72, LAC.
3. Originally a Polish village, Yaslo or Jasło was annexed by Austria in 1772 and made part of the province of Galicia. The town was regained by Poland in 1918, after the First World War.
4. Edward LaPierre, "Biographical Notice of Walter J. Bossy", file Bossy, Walter J., Biographical Material, 1912–1972, vol. 1, MG30 C72, LAC; "Interview", April 1972, p. 2, file Bossy, Walter J., Biographical Material, 1912–1972, vol. 1, MG30 C72, LAC.
5. J. Tarnovych, *Volodymyr Bossy: 40 Rokiv na fronti Ukrayinskoyi Spravy, 1914–1954* [Walter Bossy: 40 Years at the Forefront of the Ukrainian Cause] (Toronto: Lypynski Ukrainian Educational Institute, 1954), 14, cited in: Paul Michael Migus, "Ukrainian Canadian Youth: A History of Organizational Life in Canada: 1907–1953" (Master's thesis, University of Ottawa, 1975), 88.

Christian Revolutions 37

6. "Interview", April 1972, p. 4, file Bossy, Walter J., Biographical Material, 1912–1972, vol. 1, MG30 C72, LAC; Robert Gagnon, *Histoire de la Commission des écoles catholiques de Montréal* (Montreal: Boréal, 1996), 186. Gagnon states that Bossy was unable to understand French, something that Bossy's personal papers prove untrue, as he undeniably engaged regularly in correspondence in French, as well as read French-Canadian literature and periodicals. It would seem that, even though he often received help with his writing (both in English and in French), by 1931 Bossy was able to understand both.
7. "Interview", April 1972, p. 7, file Bossy, Walter J., Biographical Material, 1912–1972, vol. 1, MG30 C72, LAC.
8. No substantive modern study on the Pavlo Skoropadsky Hetmanate or a biography of the Hetman is available. For an introduction to the problem and to the literature on the subject, see: A. Maliarevskii, *P. Skoropadskii Getman vseia Ukrainy* (Kiev: 1918), an official biography cited in Hans Joachim Torke and John Paul Himka, *German-Ukrainian Relations in Historical Perspective* (Edmonton: University of Alberta Press – Canadian Institute of Ukrainian Studies, 1994), 81. See also: John Stephen Reshetar, *The Ukrainian Revolution, 1917–1920* (Princeton: Princeton University Press, 1952), 143–207; or Taras Hunczak, "The Ukraine under Hetman Pavlo Skoropadsky", in *The Ukraine, 1917–1921: A Study in Revolution* (Cambridge: Cambridge University Press 1977), 61–81.
9. Rhonda Hinther and Jim Mochoruk, eds., *Re-Imagining Ukrainian Canadians: History, Politics, and Identity* (Toronto: University of Toronto Press, 2010), 175.
10. Ivan Lysiak Rudnytsky, *Essays in Modern Ukrainian History* (Cambridge: Harvard University Press, 1987), 31–2.
11. Orest Subtelny, *Ukraine: A History* (Toronto: University of Toronto Press, 2009), chapter 19. Viacheslav Lypynsky (1882–1931) was a prominent figure in Ukrainian political life. He was a Ukrainian ambassador to Austria during Skoropadsky's Hetmanate and thereafter (1918–1919) and the leader of the Hetmanite movement in the 1920s. He was the founder of the state school in Ukrainian historiography and political thought and author of a number of influential historical, political-theoretical, and ideological works. See: Torke, Himka, *German-Ukrainian Relations in Historical Perspective*, 83.
12. Hinther and Mochoruk, eds., *Re-Imagining Ukrainian Canadians*, 175.
13. Ibid., 175. For more information on Walter J. Bossy and the Hetmanite movement, see: Orest T. Martynowych, *Ukrainians in Canada: The Interwar War* (Canadian Institute of Ukrainian Studies Press, 2016); or Manoly R. Lupul, *A Heritage in Transition. Essays in the History of Ukrainians in Canada* (Toronto: McClelland and Stewart, 1982): the Hetmanites' 'commitment to the principles of hierarchy and authority and their positive evaluation of the church' were particularly appealing to the Catholic clergy in Canada (p. 156).
14. Hinther and Mochoruk, eds., *Re-Imagining Ukrainian Canadians*, 180. Even though there seems to be a consensus among Ukrainian-Canadian scholars that the Soviet Union planned for the extermination of the Ukrainian 'nation' during the interwar years – and this is how Bossy saw it – there are several scholars that reject that interpretation. See, for instance: David R. Marples, *Heroes and Villains: Creating National History in Contemporary Ukraine* (Budapest: Central European University Press, 2007); Timothy Snyder, *Bloodlands: Europe Between Hitler and Stalin* (New York: Basic Books, 2012); Robert Conquest, *The Harvest of Sorrow: Soviet Collectivisation and the Terror-Famine* (New York: Random House, 2018).
15. Ivan Lysiak Rudnytsky, "Viacheslav Lypynsky: Statesman, Historian, and Political Thinker", in *Essays in Modern Ukrainian History* (Edmonton: Canadian Institute of Ukrainian Studies Press, 1987), 437–46; Danylo Husar Struk, ed., *Encyclopedia of Ukraine*, vol. III (Toronto: University of Toronto Press, 1993), 246–7.

16. J. Pelenski, ed., "The Political and Social Ideas of Vjaceslav Lypyns'kyj", special issue of *Harvard Ukrainian Studies*, vol. 9, no. ¾ (1985); Rudnytsky, "Viacheslav Lypynsky", in *Essays in Modern Ukrainian*, 437–46; Alexander J. Motyl, "Viacheslav Lypyns'kyi and the Ideology and Politics of Ukrainian Monarchism", *Canadian Slavonic Papers*, vol. 27, no. 1 (March 1985): 31–48.
17. Alexander J. Motyl, "Viancheslav Lypyns'kyi and the Ideology and Politics of Ukrainian Monarchism", *Canadian Slavonic Papers*, vol. 27, no. 1 (March 1985): 32.
18. Richard Bellamy, *Modern Italian Social Theory: Ideology and Politics from Pareto to the Present* (Stanford: Stanford University Press, 1987), 34–5.
19. Patrick Dunleavy, *Theories of the State: The Politics of Liberal Democracy* (Basingstoke: Macmillan Education, 1987), 136–8.
20. Ibid., 138–40.
21. Vsevolod Holubnychy, *Soviet Regional Economics: Selected Works of Vsevolod Holubnychy* (Edmonton: Canadian Institute of Ukrainian Studies, University of Alberta, 1982), 134, 135, 138.
22. Anton S. Filipeko, ed., *A Social and Solidarity Economy: The Ukrainian Choice* (Cambridge: Cambridge Scholars Publishing, 2017), 40.
23. Martha Bohachevsky-Chomiak, *Ukrainian Bishop, American Church: Constantine Bohachevsky and the Ukrainian Catholic Church* (Washington: Catholic University of America Press, 2018), 210–1.
24. This insight is from a 1931 tour that Bossy undertook around Canada to talk about bolshevism and 'the Muscovites'. In it, he preached that the Soviets were aiming at universally destroying Christianity through atheism. See: *La Presse*, May 28, 1931, p. 16. As we will see, Bossy will be contradictory in his discourses on integral Christianity, for example seeking the support of Protestants while blaming them for the bolshevization of immigrants.
25. Leo XIII, *Rerum Novarum; On the Rights and Duties of Capital and Labour* (May 15, 1891).
26. Matthew Feldman and Marius Turda, eds., "Conclusion," in *Clerical Fascism in Interwar Europe* (London: Routledge, 2008).
27. The Italian Corporate State was based on the outlawry of social warfare in favour of class collaboration; and on the inclusion of the producers' organizations into the national state. Fascism regarded labour and the incorporation into syndicates, guilds or corporations 'a social duty': 'For every profession one organization, and only one, is legally recognized by the state'. Thus, under Fascism, '[a]ll members of a given profession are represented by the officially recognized organization of that group', which Bossy would later appropriate as 'Class Councils'. See: Carmen Haider, "The Italian Corporate State", *Political Science Quarterly*, vol. 46, no. 2, (June 1931): 228–30; "Déclaration, thèse, statuts", *L'École Sociale Populaire*, July and August 1935, nos. 258–9, pp. 26–8; *La Presse*, March 9, 1936, p. 9.
28. Craig R. Prestiss, *Debating God's Economy: Social Justice in America on the Even of Vatican II* (Pennsylvania: Pennsylvania University Press, 2008), 202.
29. Laura Cerasi, "From corporatism to the 'foundation of labour': notes on political cultures across Fascist and Republican Italy", *Dossie. Corporatismos: experiencias históricas e suas representaçoes ao longo do século XX*, vol. 25, no. 1 (Jan./Abr., 2019): 247–8; Maurizio Cau, "An inconvenient legacy: corporatism and Catholic culture from Fascism to the Republic", *Dossie. Corporatismos: experiencias históricas e suas representaçoes ao longo do século XX*, vol. 25, no. 1 (Jan./Abr. 2019): 225. Post-war Italian Christian Democratic formations would recast corporatism on a democratic basis. The idea of 'spiritual union' of nations and the myth of Christendom has been explored specifically in post-war Europe to explain European integration. See, for example: Philip

M. Coupland, "Western Union, 'Spiritual Union', and European Integration, 1948–1951", *Journal of British Studies*, vol. 43, no. 3 (July 2004): 371–2, which explains that 'by claiming that there was no higher authority than the state, [totalitarianism] denied the sovereignty of the values and laws that the church held to be God-given, transcendent, and universal'.
30. Pius XI, *Quadragesimo Anno, On Reconstructing the Social Order* (May 15, 1931), 81, 84. See also: Bernard V. Brady, *Essential Catholic Social Thought*, 2nd ed., (New York: Orbis Books, 2017).
31. Pius XI, *Quadragesimo Anno*, 36, 110.
32. *Le Devoir*, November 13, 1911, pp. 1–2. In this book, all the French-written sources are translated by the author.
33. Michiel Horn, *The League for Social Reconstruction: Intellectual Origins of the Democratic Left in Canada 1930–1942* (Toronto: University of Toronto Press, 1980).
34. Patricia Dirks, *Failure of l'Action Libérale Nationale* (Montreal: McGill-Queen's University Press, 1991).
35. Janine Stingel, *Social Discredit: Anti-Semitism, Social Credit, and the Jewish Response* (Montreal: McGill-Queen's University Press, 2000).
36. Gregory Baum, *Catholics and Canadian Socialism: Political Thought in the Thirties and Forties* (Toronto: James Lorimer Ltd., 1980), 78–9, 88–90; Jean Hamelin and Nicole Gagnon, *Histoire du catholicisme québécois*, Tome I: 1898–1940 (Montreal: Boréal Express, 1984), 35–8. See also: Andrée Lévesque, *Virage à Gauche Interdit: Les communistes, les socialistes et leurs ennemis au Québec, 1929–1939* (Montréal: Boréal Press, 1984).
37. "Interview", April 1972, pp. 1–5, file Bossy, Walter J., Biographical Material, 1912–1972, vol. 1, MG30 C72, LAC. See also: To the Principal from Director of Studies of the MCSC J. M. Manning, March 4, 1937, file MCSC Correspondence 1936–1939, vol. 9, MG30 C72, LAC, which mentions Bossy being employed as a teacher in the MCSC's schools for 'many years'; also "Les catholiques étrangers sont ici trop isolés", *La Presse*, August 28, 1937, which mentions that Bossy had been employed by the MCSC since 1931 focusing on 'students speaking a language other than French or English' (p. 30). The following letter from the secretary of the MSCS states that Bossy was employed in 1932 'as a special teacher': "A qui de droit" (To Whom it May Concern) from Roméo Desjardins, secretary of the MSCS, April 28, 1937, file MCSC Correspondence 1936–1939, vol. 9, MG30 C72, LAC.
38. "Interview", April 1972, p. 6, file Bossy, Walter J., Biographical Material, 1912–1972, vol. 1, MG30 C72, LAC.
39. "Interview", April 1972, p. 7, file Bossy, Walter J., Biographical Material, 1912–1972, vol. 1, MG30 C72, LAC.
40. "Interview", April 1972, p. 7, file Bossy, Walter J., Biographical Material, 1912–1972, vol. 1, MG30 C72, LAC: 'Meade [sic] met me he become [an] almost daily friend of mine coming to my house to Ahuntsic [neighbourhood in Montreal] calling me here and there and so on'. Although the first letter exchanged between F. J. Mead and Walter J. Bossy dates August 14, 1933, the first letter that mentions a 'cheque' in exchange for espionage work dates January 2, 1934. See: file Correspondence Mead, F.J. 1933–1958, vol. 2, MG30 C72, LAC.
41. On the Hetmanite movement's sympathies for Hitler, see: T. Dann to RCMP Commissioner, December 14, 1937, file 94-A-00180, vol. 38, RG146, LAC. On Bossy's particular sympathies for Hitler, see: file Ukrainian vol. 14, MG30 C72, LAC.
42. "Officer in RCMP Honored at Dinner", file Correspondence Mead, F.J. 1933–1958, ca. June 1938, vol. 2, MG30 C72, LAC.

43. "Officer in RCMP Honored at Dinner", file Correspondence Mead, F.J. 1933–1958, ca. June 1938, vol. 2, MG30 C72, LAC; "Interview", April 1972, p. 7, file Bossy, Walter J., Biographical Material, 1912–1972, vol. 1, MG30 C72, LAC: 'Mead brought me in contact with the Irishman, John J. Fitzgerald whose publishing [was] the only [English] Catholic newspaper in Montreal. The Montreal Beacon'.
44. Bossy calls Fitzgerald 'Irishman' in: "Interview", April 7, 1972, file Bossy, Walter J., Biographical Material, 1912–1972, vol. 1, MG30 C72, LAC. See also: *Un Mouvement, Une Oeuvre, Walter J. Bossy, 25 ans au service des Néo-canadiens (1925–1950)*, 17, file New Canadians Service Bureau, vol. 5, LAC. This booklet confirms the fact that Fitzgerald was the Editor of *The Montreal Beacon* when he met Bossy in 1934.
45. John J. Fitzgerald, "Citizens", file Fitzgerald Correspondence 1945, vol. 3, MG30 C72, LAC. Information on Fitzgerald's origins and life can be found in: "Trade Board ex-secretary dies at 67", *Sherbrooke daily record*, October 21, 1960, 3. On the Irish influence upon Loyola College, see: Kathleen O'Brien and Sylvie Gauthier, "Montréal: Re-Imagining the Traces", *The Canadian Journal of Irish Studies*, vol. 26, no. 1 (Spring 2000): 32. See also: Robert J. Grace, *The Irish in Quebec. An Introduction to the Historiography* (Toronto: University of Toronto, 1993), 105, which narrates the inauguration of Loyola College in Montreal in 1896 as an achievement for those English-speaking 'Irish desirous of pursuing their education beyond high school'.
46. Fitzgerald to Muszynski, March 21, 1944, file Correspondence Fitzgerald J. J. 1944, vol. 3, MG30 C72, LAC. On the Self-Determination for Ireland League in Eastern Canada, see: Patrick Mannion, "The 'Irish Question' in St. John's, Newfoundland, and Halifax, Nova Scotia, 1919–1923", *Acadiensis*, vol. 44, no. 2, (summer/autumn 2015): 46.
47. Fitzgerald to Swift, March 27, 1947, file Correspondence J. J. Fitzgerald 1947, vol. 3, MG30 C72, LAC.
48. Art Cawley, "The Canadian Catholic English-Language Press and the Spanish Civil War", *CCHA Study Sessions*, vol. 49 (1982): 25–51, 28.
49. Fitzgerald to Swift, March 27, 1947, file Correspondence J. J. Fitzgerald 1947, vol. 3, MG30 C72, LAC.
50. Walter J. Bossy, *A Call to All Socially Minded Christian Canadians* (Montreal: The Classocracy League of Canada, 1934), 7. My emphasis.
51. Bossy, *A Call*, 7. In the foreword, Fitzgerald explains that he helped produce Bossy's work, and no doubt this refers especially to his assistance in terms of grammar and composition, as will often occur thereafter.
52. *The Prairie Messenger*, February 6, 1935, p. 2. On William X. Bryan, see: Frederick E. Crowe, *Lonergan* (MN: Liturgical Press, 1992), 4; George Seldes, *The Catholic Crisis* (New York: Julian Messner, 1945), 80.
53. *Western Catholic*, April 3, 1935, page (?), file CLOC Clippings, vol. 14, MG30 C72, LAC.
54. *Prairie Messenger*, February 6, 1935, p. 2.
55. *Winnipeg Free Press*, August 4, 1934, p. 9.
56. Krumpelmann to *The Montreal Beacon*, March 16, 1935, file Classocracy League of Canada Correspondence 1934–1937, vol. 8, MG30 C72, LAC.
57. To be precise, Bossy's articles were published in *The Montreal Beacon* on May 18, 1934; June 15, 1934; and June 29, 1934. See: *The Montreal Beacon*, June 29, 1935, p. 10. In "Interview", April 1972, file Bossy, Walter J., Biographical Material, 1912–1972, vol. 1, MG30 C72, LAC, Bossy states that his first articles on Classocracy were reprinted in 27 Catholic newspapers. In March 1935, Bossy mentions that Fitzgerald has 'five English Catholic papers, more

or less supporting Classocracy', but I have found no such papers. See: Bossy to Fitzgerald, March 30, 1935, file Correspondence Fitzgerald, J. J., 1935–1937, vol. 3, MG30 C72, LAC.
58. Bossy, *A Call*, 9.
59. In Canada, as in the rest of western liberal democracies of the interwar period, 'civilization' often equaled 'Christianity' or Christian values and ideals. For the Canadian case in particular, see, for example: James Walker, *"Race", Rights and the Law in the Supreme Court of Canada* (Toronto: Osgoode Society for Canadian Legal History, 2006).
60. Bossy, *A Call*, 14.
61. Ibid., 40.
62. Ibid., 41.
63. Bossy, *A Call*, 11, 40, 43. The perception that class or societal differences based on labour is 'natural', which leads to the 'racialization' of class, has been explored, for example, by: David R. Roediger, *The Wages of Whiteness. Race and the Making of the American Working Class* (London: Verso, 1991); Judith Walkowitz, *City of Dreadful Delight: Narratives of Sexual Danger in Late-Victorian London* (Chicago: The University of Chicago Press, 1992). All these references refer to social Darwinism as the application of the natural sciences, specifically to Darwin's theories of evolution and survival, to explain (and justify) socio-economic and ethnic differences. In the late nineteenth century, social Darwinism was similarly used by progressive, liberal and leftist intellectuals, in Canada and abroad, to suggest that the cooperation between social groups (against class struggle) was the way forward for common progress to occur. For more on social Darwinism and progressive politics in Canada, see: Allen George Mills, *Fool for Christ: The Political Thought of J.S. Woodsworth* (Toronto: University of Toronto Press, 1991), 68–9; Anthony Mardiros, *William Irvine: The Life of a Prairie Radical* (Toronto: James Lorimer Ltd., 1979), 106, 178; Marlene Shore, *The Science of Social Redemption: McGill, the Chicago School, and the Origins of Social Research in Canada* (Toronto: University of Toronto Press, 1987). See also: "The Classocracy League of Canada. Order, Justice, Toil. Christian, Corporate, Monarchical", January 30, 1936, file CLOC, vol. 8, MG30 C72; and "Déclaration, thèse, statuts", *L'École Sociale Populaire*, July and August 1935, nos. 258–9, pp. 59–60.
64. Bossy, *A Call*, 11.
65. Ibid., 21.
66. Bossy, *A Call*, 34. In page 33 of *A Call*, Bossy speaks in a more elaborate manner of Canada being strategic in keeping the 'yellow race' away through its Pacific frontier. See also: "Report", February 22, 1939, vol. 9, file MCSC Correspondence file 1936–1939, LAC, in which 'Jews and Asiatics' are not considered 'Christian foreigners' and so are not to be protected from the 'Red threat'.
67. "Vandal", *Cambridge Dictionary* online, 2020. Visited on September 15, 2020.
68. Bossy, *A Call*, 9.
69. Ibid., 43.
70. Ibid., 30.
71. Ibid., 31–2.
72. Bossy, *A Call*, 18. After the First World War, the Communist International (Comintern) promulgated a doctrine of 'Communist internationalism' inspired by Leninist analysis that perceived the Russian Revolution as the first blow of a 'World Revolution' that would transform international society root and branch. Thus, possibly Bossy associated 'internationalism' with 'world revolution'. See: "Internationalism" in Silvio Pons and Roberto Service, *A Dictionary of 20th-century Communism* (Princeton: Princeton Reference, 2012), 423.

42   *Christian Revolutions*

73. Jeffrey Herf, *The Jewish Enemy* (Harvard: Harvard University Press, 2006), 310–1.
74. Jean Blondel, ed., *Comparative Government: A Reader* (US: Macmillan Education, 1969), 197.
75. Philip Morgan, *Fascism in Europe, 1919–1945* (London: Routledge, 2003), 161. The (contradictory) conspiracy that Jewish communities controlled both capitalism and communism was exploited widely by radical-right literature throughout the nineteenth and twentieth centuries. The former idea goes back to the biblical writings on apostle Judas Iscariot handing over Jesus Christ to the Romans in exchange for 30 coins. The latter relates to the fact that communism became an attractive political alternative to Jewish communities because it promoted secularism as well as internationalism, which allowed them to obtain a sense of belonging denied to them under European Christian nation-states. See, for example: David Niremberg, *Anti-Judaism: The Western Tradition* (New York: W.W. Norton & Company, 2013).
76. Bossy, *A Call*, 11.
77. Ibid. My emphasis.
78. Ibid., 19.
79. Ibid., 18–9.
80. Bernard Lazare, *Antisemitism: Its History and Causes* (New York: Cosimo Classics, 2006), 140; Charles A. Small, ed., *Global Antisemitism: A Crisis of Modernity* (Leiden: Martinus Nijhoff Publishers, 2013), 232. See also: Hyam Maccody, *Antisemitism and Modernity: Innovation and Continuity* (London: Routledge, 2006), 29.
81. For an in-depth understanding of Ukrainian-Jewish relations in the nineteenth and twentieth centuries, see: Howard Aster and Peter J. Potichnyj, *Ukrainian-Jewish Relations in Historical Perspective* (Edmonton: University of Alberta Press – Canadian Institute of Uktainian Studies, 1990), especially pages 111 to 158 on Ukrainian-Jewish antagonisms in the Galician region in the late nineteenth century to understand the context in which Bossy grew up.
82. Volodymyr Bosyi (Walter J. Bossy), *Rozval Europy i Ukraina* (Montreal: Nakladom vyd. Katolytska Ukraina, 1933), 45, 78, 138–9.
83. *Ukrainski visty*, November 4, 1936. Translated into English by Orest Martynovych in Hinther and Mochoruk, *Re-Imagining Ukrainian Canadians*, 191.
84. In the 1940s, Bossy switched from a restricted form of pluralism to 'universalism', resolving to tolerate (and convert) rather than encourage the persecution of Jews. In the above-cited interview for LAC taken in April 1972, Bossy declared that he has 'never been enemy of Jews, I always study the Jews' and also that 'Hitler made me so mad that I turned and defended the Jews', referring to Hitler's occupation of Bohemia and Moravia in March 1939. According to Bossy, once he began defending the Jews he received 'letters and letters', among which there was one from Arcand, threatening him. Bossy stated that the RCMP (Frederick J. Mead) warned him that Arcand was trying to kill him, and the RCMP helped Bossy hide from him. See also: Bossy to Mead, June 23, 1939, file Correspondence Mead, F.J. 1933–1958, vol. 2, MG30 C72. On Bossy's postwar meeting with Jacques Maritain and his repudiation of anti-Semitism, see *Ukrainskyi robitnyk*, October 2, 1953.
85. See: Jean-François Nadeau, *The Canadian Führer: The Life of Adrian Arcand* (Montreal: Lux Éditeur, 2010).
86. *Ukrains'kyi robitnyk*, October 2, 1953, file Ukrainian, vol. 14, MG30 C72, LAC. This file contains some information in Ukrainian on Bossy's acquaintance with Arcand. I thank professor Orest Martynowich for providing me with such information in April 2019. In the interview of April 1972, Bossy

Christian Revolutions 43

stated that Adrien 'Arcand, the leader of [the] neo-fascist groups' hated him, and even 'planned to kill' him, because 'I always study the Jews to see what is the reason or mystery for hating Jews'. Bossy adds that during the war 'Hitler made me so mad, that I turned and defended Jews'. Despite these allegations, Arcand's fonds at LAC (MG30-D91) provide no proof of him ever planning to harm or conspire against Bossy. More on Walter J. Bossy and antisemitism in Chapters 4 and 5 of this monograph.

87. See: file Jewish, vol. 14, MG30 C72, LAC.
88. *Le Clé du Mystère* (n.d.), 7, 19, Morisset Library, University of Ottawa, Adrien Arcand Collection (microform), FC 2924.1.
89. Ibid., 9.
90. Ibid., 14.
91. Ibid., 18.
92. Ibid., 20.
93. Ibid., 21.
94. Bossy to Fitzgerald, July 28, 1937, file Correspondence Fitzgerald, J. J., 1935–1937, vol. 3, MG30 C72, LAC.
95. Eugene Sanctuary, *Are These Things So?* (New York: E.N., 1934), page previous to Table of Contents.
96. Sanctuary, *Are These Things So?*, 221–2, 224
97. Hinther and Mochoruk, *Re-Imagining Ukrainian-Canadians,* 183. There is no proof that Arcand ever invited Bossy to any of the events he organized.
98. Terence J. Fay, *A History of Canadian Catholics* (Montreal: McGill-Queen's University Press, 2002), 207; *Le Programme de Restauration sociale expliqué et commenté* (Montreal: École Sociale Populaire, 1934). Among the main proposals of *Le Programme* was the establishment of a corporatist society of professional organizations, as originally advocated by Leo XIII (p. 5).
99. Bossy, *A Call*, 12, 14.
100. Ibid., 15.
101. Ibid., 16.
102. Bossy to Fitzgerald, March 30, 1935, file Correspondence Fitzgerald, J. J., 1935–1937, vol. 3, MG30 C72, LAC.
103. Fitzgerald to Bossy, January 6, 1935, file Correspondence Fitzgerald, J. J., 1935–1937, vol. 3, MG30 C72, LAC.
104. In September 2019, I visited R. B. Y. Scott papers at The United Church of Canada Archives in Toronto, and specifically consulted Box Number 1 of 5, Scott, R.B.Y., 1899–1987, Correspondence, 1926–1984, and did not find any correspondence between him and any member or sympathizer of the Classocracy League of Canada. Likewise, in December 2019, I visited Francis Reginald (Frank) Scott Fonds at LAC (MG30 D211) and found no proof of any connections between the classocrats and Scott, or anything that demonstrated that Scott had been interested in the Classocracy League of Canada.
105. Dorothy Day, *All the Way to Heaven: The Selected Letters of Dorothy Day* (New York: Image Books, 2012), 71.
106. Eugene Forsey, "Quebec On the Road to Fascism", *Canadian Forum*, vol. XVII, no. 203 (December 1937): 298–300; *The McGill Daily*, vol. 35, no. 081, February 11, 1946; "CCF National Council, 1937–38", in *Cooperative commonwealth federation. The CCF marches on. Full report*, presented to McGill University Library by Prof. F.R. (Francis Reginald) Scott in 1938. In a letter from Bossy to Fitzgerald, March 30, 1935, file Correspondence Fitzgerald, J. J., 1935–1937, vol. 3, MG30 C72, LAC, Bossy mentions Sheridan being grouped with other Irish in Montreal to discuss Classocracy. Also, in *Le Nationaliste*, May 29, 1921, Madeleine Sheridan appears listed in 'Montreal subscribers to

44   *Christian Revolutions*

Irish Relief' (p. 5), giving 15$, which is a considerably high amount at the time. These two references, apart from her last name and religious affiliation, suggest she was of Irish descent and belonged to the upper class.
107. *Social Forum*, June 1936, p. 4.
108. On the one hand, the introduction of minimum wages in the interwar years that were ostensibly directed to protect women and children gave firms further incentive to hire men in manufacturing. On the other, at a time of widespread unemployment there was a state-led priority to employ those who were considered to be the 'breadwinners'. On this issue, see: Nicole M. Fortin, and Michael Huberman, "Occupational Gender Segregation and Women's Wages in Canada: An Historical Perspective", *Scientific Series,* Montreal (March 2002): 8; Nancy Christie, *Engendering the State: Family, Work, and Welfare in Canada* (Toronto: University of Toronto Press, 2000).
109. On the theory that 'class' and 'gender' are formed simultaneously, see: Joan Scott, *Gender and the Politics of History* (Columbia: Columbia University Press, 2018), particularly Chapters 2–4; Barbara Taylor, *Eve and the New Jerusalem: Socialism and Feminism in the nineteenth century* (Harvard: Harvard University Press, 1993); and Anna Clark, *The Struggle for the Breeches: Gender and the Making of the British Working Class* (Berkeley: University of California Press, 1995). On 'class' and 'race' formed simultaneously, see: Ann Stoler, *Race and the Education of Desire: Foucault's History of Sexuality and the Colonial Order of Things* (Durham: Duke University Press, 1995); Bettina Bradbury, *Working Families* (Toronto: University of Toronto Press, 2007); and Roediger, *The Wages of Whiteness*.
110. Sheridan to Bossy, Nov. 14/1935, file CLOC, vol. 8, MG30 C72, LAC.
111. Gary Dorrien, *Social Ethics in the Making: Interpreting an American Tradition* (UK: Wiley-Blackwell, 2011), 305; Nancy L. Roberts, *Dorothy Day and the Catholic Worker* (New York: State University of New York, 1984), 4; James Chappel, *Catholic Modern: The Challenge of Totalitarianism and the Remaking of the Church* (Harvard: Harvard University Press), 136.
112. Day, *All the Way to Heaven*, 71.
113. Day to Sheridan, ca. March 1934, and Day to Sheridan, September 12, 1934, in Day, *All the Way to Heaven*, 71, 80–1.
114. *La Presse*, Novembre 18, 1935, p. 26.
115. Katharine E. Harmon, *There Were Also Many Women There: Lay Women in the Liturgical Movement in the United States: 1926–59* (Minnesota: A Pueblo Book, 2013), 180.
116. Day, *All the Way to Heaven*, 67.
117. Baum, *Catholics and Canadian Socialism*, 161–2.
118. Day to de Hueck, April 11, 1934, in Day, *All the Way to Heaven*, 72–3.
119. Paula Maurutto, "Private Policing and Surveillance of Catholics: Anticommunism in the Roman Catholic Archdiocese of Toronto, 1920–1960", *Labour/Le Travail* (Fall 1997): 121, 117. The presence of ethnic minorities in the Canadian Communist Party was so high that it became known as the 'immigrant party'. See: Stephen Endicott, *Raising the Workers' Flag*, 28.
120. Paula Maurutto, "Governing Charities: Church and State in Toronto's Catholic Archdiocese, 1850–1950", dissertation (York University, 1998), 187.
121. John J. Fitzgerald, "Vote Christianity", ARCAT, MN AP02.01, McNeil Papers. The article was to be published in the first edition of *The Friendship House News*, a monthly paper by the Canadian Worker published at St. Francis Catholic Friendship House and printed by the Christian Brothers of De la Salle at St. John's Industrial School (1934).
122. John J. Fitzgerald, "Vote Christianity", ARCAT, MN AP02.01, McNeil Papers.

123. Walter J. Bossy, "Memorandum", p. 15, submitted to the Comité D'Aide Aux Etrangers Catholiques, file Neo-Canadian Activities – New Canadian Friendship House 1937, vol. 4, MG30 C72, LAC.
124. "Déclaration, thèse, statuts", *L'École Sociale Populaire*, July and August 1935, nos. 258–9, pp. 30; *L'Action Catholique*, July 22, 1935, p. 1.
125. Jean-Claude St-Amant, "La propagande de l'École sociale populaire en faveur du syndicalisme catholique 1911–1949", *Revue d'histoire de l'Amérique française*, vol. 32, no. 2 (September 1978): 209.
126. *L'Action Catholique*, July 22, 1935, p. 1; *Le Soleil*, July 23, 1935, p. 9; *Le Nouvelliste*, July 23, 1935, p. 2; *Le Devoir*, July 31, 1935, p. 8; *Le Progrès du Saguenay*, August 8, 1935, p. 6; and *Le Bien Public*, August 29, 1935, p. 12.
127. "Order, Justice, Toil. Christian, Corporative, Monarchical", The Classocracy League of Canada, January 30, 1936, file CLOC, vol. 8, MG30 C72, LAC.
128. "Déclaration, thèse, statuts", *L'École Sociale Populaire*, July and August 1935, nos. 258–9, pp. 30.
129. Ibid., 7–9, 32.
130. In fact, it didn't mention anyone, which might be partly because even though the group presented itself as fully formed, the only people who officially supported (or considered themselves to be members of) the CLC were RCMP Colonel Jack Mead; editor of *The Montreal Beacon* John J. Fitzgerald; Edward LaPierre – more on him below; and William X. Bryan, an ardent supporter who was promoting the classocratic state over the Catholic Half Hour radio program at the CBS-affiliate CKAC, a French-Canadian radio station of Montreal owned by *La Presse* and 'the only French-language broadcasting station of significant power' at the time. On CKAC, see: Arthur Siegel, *Politics and the Media in Canada* (Toronto: McGraw-Hill Ryerson, 1983), 163. See extracts from the Catholic Half Hour radio program on October 21, and November 4, 1934, at CKAC radio station here: "Déclaration, thèse, statuts", *L'École Sociale Populaire*, July and August 1935, nos. 258–9, pp. 57–8.
131. Bossy to Fitzgerald, March 30, 1935, file Correspondence Fitzgerald, J. J., 1935–1937, vol. 3, MG30 C72, LAC.
132. Ibid.
133. Ibid.
134. Bossy to Fitzgerald, March 30, 1935, file Correspondence Fitzgerald, J. J., 1935–1937, vol. 3, MG30 C72, LAC; Fifth Census of Canada, 1911, province of Quebec, district number 183, Poll 37 in Ste. Marie Montreal, row 35; *L'Illustration Nouvelle*, March 27, 1936, p. 10; *Le Devoir*, March 21, 1936, p. 6; Paul-André Linteau, René Durocher, Jean-Claude Robert, *Histoire du Québec contemporain: de la Confédération à la crise, 1867–1929* (Montreal: Boréal Express, 1979), 560–6.
135. The following letter indicates that by March 1935, LaPierre and Bossy had been in close contact for six months: Bossy to Fitzgerald, March 30, 1935, file Correspondence Fitzgerald, J. J., 1935–1937, vol. 3, MG30 C72, LAC. The following file gives information on LaPierre's position at the time: file Correspondence La Pierre, Edward 1935–1971, 1935, vol. 2, MG30 C72, LAC. The three men (Fitzgerald, Bossy, and LaPierre) seem to consecutively run *The Montreal Beacon* between 1934 and 1935, as mentioned in: Bossy to Fitzgerald, March 30, 1935, file Correspondence Fitzgerald, J. J., 1935–1937, vol. 3, MG30 C72, LAC. Apparently, as the same document indicates, by 1935 Fitzgerald controlled (financially?) 'five English Catholic papers ... more or less supporting Classocracy' all over Canada.
136. Bossy to Fitzgerald, March 30, 1935, file Correspondence Fitzgerald, J. J., 1935–1937, vol. 3, MG30 C72, LAC.

137. *L'Illustration Nouvelle,* March 3, 1936, p. 6; *La Presse,* March 7, 1936, p. 51; Fitzgerald to LaPierre and Bossy, July 24, 1937, file Correspondence Fitzgerald, J. J., 1935–1937, vol. 3, MG30 C72, LAC, mentions the patronage of Bryan and Archambault towards these talks.
138. *La Presse,* March 9, 1936, p. 9; *Le Devoir,* March 21, 1936, p. 6.
139. Edward LaPierre (Executive of the National Council), The Classocracy League of Canada. Order, Justice, Toil. Christian, Corporative, Monarchical, January 30, 1936, file CLOC, vol. 8, MG30 C72.
140. LaPierre defined revolution as 'the replacing of one state-system by another in a comparatively short period of time'.
141. Mark McGowan and Brian P. Clarke, *Catholics at the Gathering Place* (Toronto: The Canadian Catholic Historical Association, 1993), 223. It is safe to assume that Bossy contributed in everything published under the name of the Classocracy League of Canada. On *The Social Forum*: the paper had been also inspired by the weekly meetings that Catherine de Hueck organized under the same title of "Social Forum", in which 'socially concerned Catholics came together to express their disapproval of the present system and their hope in the regenerative power of a new, radical ethic'. According to Gregory Baum, Jacques Maritain himself often attended these meetings. See: Baum, *Catholics and Canadian socialism,* 162. Maritain was teaching in Toronto at the Pontifical Institute of Medieval Studies between 1933 and 1934, see: Julie Kernan, *Our friend, Jacques Maritain: A Personal Memoir* (New York: Garden City, 1975), 88–9.
142. *Social Forum,* June 1936, page (?), vol. 14, MG30 C72, LAC. Supposedly, by July 1936 LaPierre was also working 'on the history of CLOC [Classocracy League of Canada]', as he informed Bossy, but I have found no other record of such an endeavour. See: LaPierre to Bossy, July 20, 1936, file Correspondence La Pierre, Edward 1935–1971, vol. 2, MG30 C72, LAC.
143. Fitzgerald to Bossy, January 6, 1935, file Correspondence Fitzgerald, J. J., 1935–1937, vol. 3, MG30 C72, LAC.
144. The petition or memorandum and its content is referred in a letter from Bossy to Archambault, October 10, 1935, file MCSC Correspondence file 1936–1939, vol. 9, MG30 C72, LAC; and also in a letter from Bossy to Victor Doré, October 21, 1936, file MCSC Correspondence Sent For Position, 1935–1936, vol. 9, MG30 C72, LAC. See also: Bossy to Archambault, October 10, 1936, file MCSC Correspondence 1936–1939, vol. 9, MG30 C72, LAC. Here Bossy mentions that he should be employed in a special capacity, looking 'after the interests of the foreign children in the matter of instruction, information for the Commission and Christian citizenship', and mentions that he sent a memorandum in October 1935 to Victor Doré in that regard.
145. Bossy to Doré, October 21, 1936, file MCSC Correspondence Sent For Position, 1935–1936, vol. 9, MG30 C72, LAC.
146. Report from Bossy to Doré, December 31, 1936, file MCSC Correspondence file 1936–1939, vol. 9, MG30 C72, LAC. See also:
Gagnon, *Histoire de la Commission des écoles catholiques de Montréal,* 186, which confirms the information provided by Bossy's personal papers at MG30 C72, LAC, regarding his responsibilities at the MCSC vis-à-vis 'foreign Catholic students' in 1936.
147. Letter dated October 15, 1936, from Bossy to 'the distinguished members of the Catholic School Commission', in file MCSC Correspondence Sent For Position, 1935–1936, vol. 9, MG30 C72, LAC. Bossy mentions his 'association with this Committee ... greatly facilitates the work envisaged', but by December 1936 he was not officially been employed by the MCSC. See: Bossy to Coonan, October 17, 1936, file MCSC Correspondence 1936–1939, vol. 9, MG30 C72, LAC.

148. Bossy to Doré, December 31, 1936, file MCSC Correspondence 1936-1939, vol. 9, MG30 C72, LAC.
149. Bossy to Coonan, October 17, 1936, file MCSC Correspondence 1936-1939, vol. 9, MG30 C72, LAC.
150. Walter J. Bossy, "Memorandum", p. 1, 1937, vol. 4, file Neo-Canadians Activities – New Canadians Friendship House ca. 1936, MG30 C72, LAC.
151. Gardiner's 1934 speech was over the radio station CKAC. About CKAC, see: Paul-André Linteau, René Durocher, Jean-Claude Robert, François Ricard, eds., *Quebec Since 1930* (Toronto: James Lorimer&Company, 1991), 123. Although officially a French-speaking station, by 1940, 34% of its programs were in English. See details on Gardiner's occupation here: *Publications de la Chambre de commerce française au Canada*, July–August 1934, p. 15. See John J. Fitzgerald mentioning Gardiner's enthusiastic support for Bossy here: Fitzgerald to Gardiner, October 20, 1936, file Correspondence Fitzgerald, J. J., 1935–1937, vol. 3, MG30 C72, LAC. See the report about Gardiner's radio speech here: *Le Devoir*, January 16, 1934, p. 4. Military records indicate that Albert Gardiner was a Methodist born in 1898.
152. *Le Devoir*, January 16, 1934, p. 4.
153. Gardiner to Archambault, October 7, 1936, file MCSC Correspondence Sent For Position, 1935–1936, vol. 9, MG30 C72, LAC.
154. Bossy to Archambault, October 10, 1936, vol. 9, file MCSC Correspondence file 1936–1939, MG30 C72, LAC.
155. Ibid. See also: Bossy to Coonan, October 17, 1936, vol. 9, file MCSC Correspondence file 1936–1939, MG30 C72, LAC, in which Bossy refers to the support of Archambault and Gardiner in his endeavour.
156. *La Presse*, October 26, 1936, p. 1.
157. Bossy to Coonan, October 17, 1936, vol. 9, file MCSC Correspondence file 1936–1939, MG30 C72, LAC.
158. Gardiner to Archambault, October 7, 1936, file MCSC Correspondence Sent for Position, 1935–1936, vol. 9, MG30 C72, LAC.
159. Bossy to Coonan, October 17, 1936, vol. 9, file MCSC Correspondence file 1936–1939, MG30 C72, LAC.
160. T.J. Coonan as president of *The Montreal Beacon* indicated here: *The Beacon*, March 7, 1935, p. 6, file Classocracy League Correspondence 1934–1937, vol. 8, MG30 C72, LAC. About Coonan's position as a member of Duplessis' 1936 cabinet, see: André Lavoie, ed., *Répertoire des parlementaires québécois, 1867–1978* (Quebec: Bibliothèque de la Législature, 1980).
161. Fitzgerald mentioned to Coonan that he still 'retain[s] very happy memories of [their] boat trip to Quebec'. See: Fitzgerald to Coonan, October 20, 1936, file Correspondence Fitzgerald, J. J., 1935–1937, vol. 3, MG30 C72, LAC. See also: Bossy to Coonan, October 17, 1936, file MCSC Correspondence file 1936–1939, vol. 9, MG30 C72, LAC.
162. About Coonan's call, see: LaPierre to Bossy, September 6, 1936, vol. 8, file Classocracy League Correspondence 1934–1937, MG30 C72, LAC. See also: Fitzgerald to Bossy, October 20, 1936, file Correspondence Fitzgerald, J. J., 1935–1937, vol. 3, MG30 C72, LAC, and Fitzgerald to Coonan, October 20, 1936, file Correspondence Fitzgerald, J. J., 1935–1937, vol. 3, MG30 C72, LAC. All these letters mention the efforts to find support for Bossy to be employed at the MCSC as a 'special representative'.
163. Bossy to 'the distinguished members of the Catholic School Commission', October 15, 1936, file MCSC Correspondence Sent For Position, 1935–1936, vol. 9, MG30 C72, LAC.

164. Fitzgerald to Coonan, October 20, 1936, file Correspondence Fitzgerald, J. J., 1935–1937, vol. 3, MG30 C72, LAC; Bossy to 'the distinguished members of the Catholic School Commission', October 15, 1936, file MCSC Correspondence Sent For Position, 1935–1936, vol. 9, MG30 C72, LAC.
165. Bossy to 'the distinguished members of the Catholic School Commission', October 15, 1936, file MCSC Correspondence Sent For Position, 1935–1936, vol. 9, MG30 C72, LAC.
166. "A qui de droit" (To Whom it May Concern) from Roméo Desjardins, secretary of the MSCS, April 28, 1937, file MCSC Correspondence 1936–1939, vol. 9, MG30 C72, LAC; Bossy to Fitzgerald, ca. 1936, file Correspondence La Pierre, Edward 1935–1971, vol. 2, MG30 C72, LAC; Doré to Bossy, January 8, 1937, file MCSC Correspondence 1936–1939, vol. 9, MG30 C72, LAC. This new charge was also announced in *Le Devoir*, December 5, 1936, p. 1.
167. Letter of Approval from His Excellency [presumably Coadjutor Archbishop of Montreal Mgr. Gauthier], October 1937, file Neo-Canadian Activities, New Canadian Federation Correspondence 1937–1941, vol. 4, MG30 C72, LAC; Bossy to Gardiner, July 14, 1937, file MCSC Correspondence Sent About Memorandum 1937, vol. 9, MG30 C72, LAC.
168. Georges Gauthier was coadjutor archbishop between 1923 and 1939, and became Archbishop of Montreal in 1939. Gauthier condemned the CCF because he believed that it might foment class war. See: Bruce Nesbitt, *Conversations with Trotsky: Earle Birney and the Radical 1930s* (Ottawa: University of Ottawa Press, 2017), 257.
169. *Le Devoir*, October 9, 1936, p. 3; *Le Devoir*, October 26, 1936, p. 1; *La Presse*, October 26, 1936, p. 1.
170. *L'Action Catholique*, October 26, 1936, p. 3; Judy Fudge and Eric Tucker, *Labour Before the Law: the Regulation of Workers' Collective Action in Canada, 1900–1948* (Toronto: Oxford University Press, 2001), 212.
171. *L'Ordre Nouveau*, November 5, 1936, p. 1.
172. *Le Devoir*, October 26, 1936, p. 3.
173. *La Presse*, October 26, 1936, p. 1.
174. *Le Devoir*, November 9, 1936, p. 1.
175. Walter J. Bossy, "Memorandum", p. 4, 1937, file Neo-Canadians Activities – New Canadians Friendship House ca. 193, vol. 46, MG30 C72, LAC; Bossy to Doré, December 31, 1936, file MCSC Correspondence file 1936–1939, vol. 9, MG30 C72, LAC. See also: *Un Mouvement, Une Oeuvre, Walter J. Bossy, 25 ans au service des Néo-Canadiens (1925–1950)* (Montreal: Bureau du Service des Néo-Canadiens, 1950), 18, file New Canadians Service Bureau, vol. 5, MG30 C72, LAC (also in: ARC-E 1, S46, T4, 5441, Montreal Catholic School Commission Archives). This short book explains that in 1936, 'at the invitation of His Exc. Mgr. Georges Gauthier, coadjutor archbishop of Montreal, Mr. Bossy organized their anti-communist rally with the cooperation of the national priests.'
176. "Records. Preliminary Meeting of the Foreign-Speaking Catholic Parish Priests of Montreal, QUE", file Neo-Canadian Activities Foreign Speaking Catholic Parish Priests Meeting, Montreal 1936, vol. 4, MG30 C72, LAC. Present at the meeting were coadjutor archbishop of Montreal Georges Gauthier (Honorary President); Chancellor of Arch-Diocese in Montreal Canon Valois; Checho-Slovak priest Felicko (Chairman); German priest Adalbert Debelt (Vice-Chairman); Polish priests Stephen Musielak, Thaddeus Osewsky, Bernard (Treasurer) and Blaise; Ukrainian priests J. Tymochko and Jean (Press Agent); Hungarian priest Nicolaus Wesselenje; Lithuanian priest J. Bobinas (Secretary); and Walter J. Bossy (Acting Secretary). 'Italians, Syrians and Other [Catholics] not yet represented in this committee' would be invited in

subsequent meetings. Italian priest Benedetto Maria, for example, would participate in the second meeting. See: "Second Meeting of the Foreign-Speaking Catholic Parish Priests of Montreal, QUE", file Neo-Canadian Activities Foreign Speaking Catholic Parish Priests Meeting, Montreal 1936, vol. 4, MG30 C72, LAC.
177. "Of The Fourth Meeting of the Foreign-Speaking Catholic Parish Priests of Montreal, QUE", file Neo-Canadian Activities Foreign Speaking Catholic Parish Priests Meeting, Montreal 1936, vol. 4, MG30 C72, LAC.
178. Bossy to Maurice Julien, September 25, 1937, file Neo-Canadian Activities, New Canadian Federation Correspondence 1937–1941, vol. 4, MG30 C72, LAC.
179. *La Tribune,* December 5, 1936, p. 9.
180. Fitzgerald to Gauthier, March 1, 1937, file Correspondence Fitzgerald, J. J., 1935–1937, vol. 3, MG30 C72, LAC, mentions the patronage of Gauthier. The number of foreigners refers in particular to those who allegedly 'filled the great Notre Dame Church', and it is indicated by Bossy here: Bossy to Armand Dupuis, August 18, 1939, file MCSC Correspondence 1936–1939, vol. 9, MG30 C72, LAC.
181. *Un Mouvement, Une Oeuvre,* 18, file New Canadians Service Bureau, vol. 5, LAC, MG30 C72, LAC. On how Bossy was introduced by Gauthier: *L'Illustration Nouvelle,* December 4, 1936, p. 7. This article also includes the program, and so the events and parishes, involved in the demonstration.
182. Full quote: 'They are, moreover, a living proof of the all-powerful force of the Redemption which, beyond the barriers of languages and nations, creates an army of brothers [...]'. See: *Le Devoir,* December 7, 1936, p. 2.
183. Speech signed as 'Demonstration. Foreign Catholic Populations. Notre Dame Church, Montreal, Que., December 6th 1936', file Allegeance Day Plans Publicity, Speeches, 1938, vol. 4, MG30 C72, LAC.
184. *Le Devoir,* December 7, 1936, p. 2.
185. Ibid.
186. This is in fact inaccurate. *The Book of New Canadians* (1930), written by a schoolteacher named D. J. Dickie, mentions the 'All-Canadian Festival', which allegedly took place in Winnipeg in summer of 1928. The festival brought together 'New Canadians from fifteen countries of Northern Europe ... to illustrate the national arts and culture which they are contributing to Canadian life'. Although Bossy was living in Winnipeg at the time, there is no proof of him being involved in the festival. However, the possibility of him knowing or learning about (or from) the festival stands. In particular, it is striking that the festival included addresses as well as evening ethnic concerts and dances in a similar fashion to the New Canadians Allegiance Day festival organized by Bossy in 1938 (p. 62). It is also worth adding that participants to the festival Dickie was referring to had allegedly come to Canada from 'Norway, Sweden, Denmark, Iceland, Germany, France, Belgium, Jugo-Slavia, Czecho-Slovakia, Roumania [sic], Finland, Hungary, Ukrainia [sic], Poland and Russia', almost exactly the same ethnic groups that Bossy chose to mobilize as 'New Canadians' in 1938. See: *The Raymond Recorder,* July 20, 1928, p. 2; *Stony Plain Sun,* July 12, 1928, p. 8.
187. Jean-François Nadeau, *The Canadian Führer: The Life of Adrien Arcand* (Toronto: James Lorimer & Company Ltd., 2010), 130; Stanley R. Barrett, *Is God a Racist?* (Toronto: University of Toronto Press, 1987), 23.
188. The historic novelty of the event is highlighted here: "Une manifestation religieuse des Catholiques étrangers ici", *L'Illustration Nouvelle,* December 4, 1936, p. 7; "La première cérémonie du genre à Montréal", *Le Devoir,* December 7, 1936, p. 2. Other references include: "Emouvante manifestation des

étrangers à l'église N.-Dame", *L'Illustration Nouvelle*, December 7, 1936, p. 5, discourse of Félix C. Felicko, president of the organizing committee. Felicko spoke in English, but his speech was translated in situ by 'Father Bobinas', see: *Le Canada*, December 5, 1936, p. 10.
189. Bossy would claim that 'about 2,500' people attended that demonstration. See: "Interview", April 1972, p. 6, file Bossy, vol. 1, MG30 C72, LAC. However, *Un Mouvement, Une Oeuvre*, 18, file New Canadians Service Bureau, vol. 5, MG30 C72, LAC, mentions that 15,000 people participated in this demonstration.
190. Bossy to Bryan, June 11, 1937, file Correspondence La Pierre, Edward 1935–1971, MG30 C72, vol. 2, MG30 C72, LAC; Bossy to Julien, September 25, 1937, file Neo-Canadian Activities, New Canadian Federation Correspondence 1937–1941, vol. 4, MG30 C72, LAC.
191. Bossy to Gauthier, June 12, 1937, file Neo-Canadian Friendship House, ca. 1936, vol. 4, MG30 C72, LAC.

3 Allegiances

> There [are] perhaps one thousand reasons why I cannot assume the role of a leader in the Canadian-national movement, but I certainly can inspire such a movement.
>
> Walter J. Bossy, July 30, 1937[1]

New Canadians Friendship House

After the 'test mobilization of the foreign elements of [Montreal]' in December 1936, Bossy wrote to classocracy sympathizer William X. Bryan saying that, given the existing capacity for foreign mobilization against communism, more work should be put towards the organization of the foreign element.[2] Yet, effective organization could not happen without the social and economic advancement of these immigrant groups. Indeed, he believed that the 'most practical' way to reach out to Canadian immigrants with a nation-wide socio-political purpose was to help the 'many different foreign speaking groups' improve their well-being first.[3] Above all, the goal was to prevent their radicalization. Thus, Bossy was determined to pursue 'anti-communist action amongst the foreigners'; an action that would be defined by a 'Catholic spirit' that is 'social' and focuses on the 'welfare of individuals, families and groups partly for their own sake and partly for the sake of the larger community'.[4] In addition, it would be inspired by the 'classocratic plan of combating Communism', and the ultimate goal of establishing an integrated corporatist Canadian (and white) Christian state.[5] Indeed, Bossy understood the 'salvation' of what he described as *the foreign element* to be the first step in the accomplishment of his larger plans for a reactionary nation-building project.[6]

Wanting to begin with the 'physical and economic' amelioration of immigrant communities, Bossy proposed the establishment of a 'New Canadian Friendship House' (NCFH) inspired by the Friendship Houses created by Catherine de Hueck in Toronto and Combermere, and by Dorothy Day in New York.[7] The NCFH would constitute a 'temporary refuge' for 'New Canadians', providing them with a soup kitchen, a reading room and a popular school, the expenses of which could be covered by implementing

DOI: 10.4324/9781003283348-3

the 'adoption' system proposed by Jesuit Joseph P. Archambault in *Sous la Menace Rouge* (Under the Red Threat, 1936).[8] In his pamphlet, Archambault explained that during the First World War wealthier cities had 'adopted' those which had suffered more, bringing comfort and help: 'Why not apply this method to our foreign groups?' Archambault proposed that French-Canadian Catholic organizations and parishes patronize foreign Catholic groups. With cooperation between French Catholics and foreign Catholics 'we would all benefit', thereby fostering social unity, and diminishing the red threat 'which threatens to gangrene [Montreal]'.[9]

Even though Bossy stated that the NCFH project extended to 'all foreign groups', it was limited on a religious and an ethnic basis.[10] To begin with, the project aimed to protect only Christian Canadians, as it emerged from the urgency of preserving an already existing 'Catholic element in the foreign (i.e., non-French and non-English speaking) population' and 'of drawing back to the ... Christian principles those of the foreign population already infected by Communist propaganda'.[11] As the 'successful religious and civic manifestation of Catholic foreign groups held in Notre Dame Church on Dec. 6th, 1936' had shown, a common faith could foster cooperation between different ethnic groups coexisting in Canada, 'country of their choice and adoption'.[12] This was why Bossy believed the character of his project should be 'integrally Catholic in spirit'. Only in appearance would such a project 'seem to be wider than Catholicism'.[13] In terms of ethnicity, even though the NCFH was supposed to 'extend to all foreign groups', it specifically addressed 'the Teutonic, Scandinavian and Slavic Elements of the Foreign Population of Montreal.' Belgians and Italians, explained Bossy, would be an 'exception [as they] are easily assimilated into the French-Canadian milieu on account of the Belgians' fluency in the French language and the facility of the Italians in learning French.' In such cases, assimilation ensured amelioration.[14] On what Bossy considered to be 'sound grounds', the plan 'does not include [...] Hebrews, Chinese, Japanese and other Asiatics, nor negroes' either.[15] Based on the type of literature that Bossy was consuming at the time, including the works of antisemites and fervent anti-communists Adrien Arcand and former US intelligence officer Walter B. Odale[16] (more on him below), these prejudices stemmed from the conspiratorial idea that Jewish, Asian, and Black communities had communist tendencies, or were part of a worldwide communist scheme, and therefore constituted a danger to Canada and to Christian civilization as a whole.[17]

In August 1937, *La Presse* congratulated Bossy on his NCFH project. Lamenting that 'foreign Catholics are too isolated here' and often ended up joining the communist ranks, the newspaper recognized in the NCFH the way by which to keep the foreign population on 'the right path'. The NCFH, explained the French-Canadian newspaper, would enable 'foreign-speaking' residents to bond as a group and to learn about Canada and their French and English coreligionists. The Slav and Germanic Catholic communities, it went on, represent 'a force that must be made immediately useful for good'. At the NCFH, mothers would receive financial help to better take care of their children, to whom bursaries could also be directed so that they could 'attend High Schools, Boy Scouts and Girl Guides [...]'. For the men, the NCFH could offer 'French and English lessons, and ... a library will make available to these foreigners works or translations of works of Catholic propaganda, and of social order based on Christianity, etc.' *La Presse* asked for assistance from both English- and French-speaking Canadians so that the project could get started.[18] Similarly, *Le Devoir* insisted that something had to be done with this 'mass of foreign origin' which was allegedly more prone to revolutionary action. The ethnic parish priests could not cope with the multiple needs of their flocks, it argued, and consequently the 'strangers are not grouped, but scattered', further exposing them 'to revolutionary propaganda'.[19] The paper insisted that means be mobilized to support the NCFH, for the 'problem of foreigners [...] touches on most questions regarding a moral and material order which should interest us. It has been neglected so far. But there's always time to try to regain lost ground'.[20] Equally, *L'Illustration Nouvelle*, applauded the 'new Canadian House of Friendship' as a means to assist 'aliens of German, Scandinavian and slave origin in Montreal'.[21]

In September 1937, Montreal journalist and Political Science Professor at Sir George Williams University Herbert F. Quinn, author of *The Bogey of Fascism in Quebec* (1938) and *The Union Nationale* (1963), wrote in the federalist *The Montreal Daily Star* about 'the formation [in Montreal] of an organization to look after the material and moral needs of our citizens of foreign origin'. 'Walter J. Bossy', he explained, is 'the moving force in this movement'. His project is the answer to 'the plight of our citizens of foreign origin' who, not unlike what the French Canadians had done through the St. Jean Baptiste Society, were mobilizing to obtain national recognition. Quinn explained that 'there has been a great degeneration in the morale of [the "foreign"] section of our citizens, and a strong tendency to lean towards Communism'. The NCFH, he established, would help address this tendency. The question was, however: would the movement receive the 'necessary moral and financial help from the people of Montreal, our governmental authorities, our service clubs, and other associations'? 'What are we going to do about it?'[22]

Quinn and Bossy were, in fact, friends. Only recently, Quinn had sent Bossy a copy of his *The Bogey of Fascism in Quebec*, where he had tried to 'point out to some of our English speaking friends that the danger of Fascism triumphing in this province is negligible, despite the fact that to read some of the American magazines today you would think that this province was in the hands of a Dictator.'[23] Some American magazines were indeed interpreting the 'political, social and religious developments in the province of Quebec' as a sign of fascist advancement. The ecumenical American magazine *Christian Century*, for instance, published an article in November 1936 addressing the 'Fascist' demonstrations in Montreal

54 *Allegiances*

and Quebec City on occasion of the Feast of Christ the King against communism.[24] According to the newspaper, the event 'awakened memories for some who had experienced the days just before Mussolini in Italy or the days just before Hitler in Germany.' The paper mentioned the presence and speeches in Montreal of coadjutor archbishop Georges Gauthier, of acting mayor Léo McKenna, and of Jesuit William X. Bryan, and highlighted their denunciation of communism and 'a call to all the faithful to join in a crusade for its extermination'. Just as in Montreal, narrated the magazine, in Quebec cardinal Jean-Marie-Rodrigue Villeneuve and premier Maurice Duplessis insisted that there could be no compromise 'between us and communism'. The *Christian Century* asked: 'Does Catholicism Menace Free Speech?'[25] But to Herbert F. Quinn, the revival of Catholicism in Quebec was simply a sign of an increasing provincial nationalism.[26] And nationalism, he said to Bossy, was exactly what Canada needed.[27]

In October 1937, Gauthier wrote to Bossy acknowledging his campaign towards the organization of 'our foreign-Catholics and finally for the establishment of a "New Canadian Friendship House" for them in Montreal'. The project, he said, 'meets with my whole-hearted approval'. Gauthier was hoping that the city would respond generously to Bossy's appeal, for the 'salvation and good citizenship of thousands of neglected and forgotten strangers-citizens within our gates' depended on it.[28] Bossy received 'quite a few very encouraging letters' like Gauthier's, as well as 'assurances from numerous charitable and fraternal associations, prominent businessmen and political and religious leaders, of their interest and willingness to co-operate in this venture'. This is why he resolved to start his endeavour by establishing a New Canadian Citizens Federation (NCF), for which the establishment of NCFHs at a national level would be but 'one of the aims'.[29]

Bossy envisaged the formation of a NCF as part of his plans for the establishment of a corporatist state in Canada. He believed that for national unity to occur, the 'three different groups, i.e. the English, French and Foreign speaking ... should be, separately, organized'. In fact, establishing a NCF was his way of organizing what he called the 'third group' according 'to one plan, along one line'. So, he would address this specific project with a 'classocratic scope' and 'as a Classocrat'.[30] In sharing his plans with Classocracy League of Canada (CLC) leader Edward LaPierre, Bossy said that he found himself finally 'in a position to begin [addressing] the foreign field of action of the Classocracy League of Canada'. The New Canadians project was ultimately to be utilized 'for our sacred cause only. May God bless our endeavours'.[31] Yet, Bossy suspected that it would not be that easy to obtain nationwide support for the establishment of a NCF. Based on his short experience as a leader of the CLC, he was suspicious that his ethnic background might jeopardize once again his nationalist endeavours. Thus, this time, he thought that publishing his biography in advance might help Canadians trust him.[32]

If he were 'a rich foreigner or a Jew' or 'a pure Englishman', Bossy lamented, he 'would not need any published introduction'. But, 'in this American world ... advertisement decides about the purchase of goods'.[33] Bossy expected the biography to be first published in English, a French version to be later published by Archambault in *L'École Sociale Populaire*. In his biography, Bossy's Ukrainian background would be seen only as related to his new Canadian identity.[34] Although it looks like Bossy's biography was never published, existing drafts written by LaPierre and Bossy himself are revealing. Entitled *One of Our New-Canadians*, the short biography introduced Bossy and the 'New Canadians', the group and movement he thought he represented. In the document, 'New Canadians' as a signifier was explicitly defined and composed by 'Scotch-Canadians, Irish-Canadians, German-Canadians, Polish-Canadians, Ukrainian-Canadians, Italian-Canadians [as well as] smaller groups of Icelandic, Scandinavian or other European origins.'[35] The document explained that 'The Canadian Nation is a conglomeration of many different nationalities who ... have in the first place brought with them from their native countries their culture and their beautiful specific customs and thus have enriched the organism of their adopted country – Canada.'[36] Supposedly, *One of Our New-Canadians* constituted a call to 'every Canadian citizen to foster and facilitate this natural synthetic process' of amalgamation. In spite of this, in his narrative, Bossy excluded Indigenous communities, explicitly indicating that the new Canadian nation would be defined solely by 'settlers'. And, from among those settlers, only 'Continental European' customs would be desirable in the creation of a multi-cultural Canada. In particular, Bossy hoped that, with time, 'these various [European] strains will coalesce and merge, and so produce a rich and original Canadian nationality, distinguishable from all other contemporary nationalities, and distinguishable likewise from any of the various elements that compose it'.[37]

But exactly how distinct Canada would be from other nationalities is unclear. As a matter of fact, Bossy's wish to promote the racial intermixing of whites while severely restricting access to such an amalgamation is no different from nativist approaches to the American idea of 'the melting pot'.[38] On the other hand, his proposal was different in that he envisaged that amalgamation as resulting from the collective contribution of European cultures rather than from the cultural assimilation of European whites into 'the pre-existing cultural and social molds modeled on Anglo-Protestants'.[39] Specifically, *One of Our New-Canadians* insisted that every European 'national strain has some constructive factor in his culture and tradition to contribute to the ultimate national individuality of Canada'. To 'New Canadians' as well as to English- and French-speaking Canadians, Bossy demanded an end to 'clinging jealousy and exclusively to an imported national culture which is bound to undergo a change and insisting upon a hyphenated designation that connotes this narrower outlook.' Bossy was suggesting *cultural integration*. Even though he wouldn't use such a term until the postwar period (when he would insist upon cultural integration as much as religious assimilation), this early assessment constitutes a precedent to the postwar idea that some sort of multi-culturalism would lead to a 'far more glorious and realistic' sense of unity and belonging than traditional Canadian binationalism.[40]

Fundraising

When he presented his proposal (in English) on the New Canadians Friendship House (NCFH) to coadjutor archbishop Georges Gauthier in June 1937, Bossy stated that the NCFH would act as a 'centre of distribution of sound Catholic and patriotic doctrine and organization'. The cause was one and the same: 'Christianity and Canadianism'.[41] The idea that national and religious unity, specifically Christian unity, are interdependent is at the core of Christian nationalism. Christian nationalism, as Andrew L. Whitehead and Samuel L. Perry put it, 'represents a unique cultural framework' often – but not always – tied to hopes for authoritarian, ethnocentric and radically prejudiced governance.[42] Defenders of Christian nationalism seek to 'defend particular group boundaries and privileges using Christian language'.[43] Precisely, in Bossy's reports on the 'problem of Catholic foreign children'[44] to the Montreal Catholic School Commission (MCSC), he established parallels between Canadian citizenship and Christian 'intellectual and moral formation'.[45] It was his view that Canadian *tradition* and Christian *spirit* were one and the same which led him to further believe that 'Catholicizing and Canadianizing' was too an equivalent endeavour.[46]

Canadian *Catholic* nationalism in particular is not without precedent. The 'Catholic fundraising society for preserving the faith of immigrants and native peoples', the Catholic Church Extension Society (CCES), for instance, claimed that 'religious duties and patriotic endeavour' must not work at cross purposes.[47] Originally founded in the United States, the society had an independent Canadian Extension Society based in Toronto. While the society's board largely reflected a Toronto-based support, it also had token representation from Quebec in the persons of Archbishop L. N. Bégin, premier Louis-Alexandre Taschereau, and Bishop Joseph-Alfred Archambault.[48] However, the success of the CCES in Quebec was jeopardized by its underlying mission: the cultural imperialism characterized by anglicization. It was precisely the CCES' indifference to Franco-Ontarian appeals on bilingual schools that caused Bégin and Archambault to resign from the society in 1910.[49] As opposed to the CCE, which caused French Canadians to feel alienated, Bossy sought to give them a leading role in the Christianization of Canada:

> [T]he French-Canadian Catholic group should for the sake of their common Catholic faith and for the future of Quebec and indeed of the whole Canada [...] set up channels whereby the life-giving doctrines of

Catholic sociology, so clearly and eloquently set forth in the French tongue, can eventually reach an ethnic group that stands in such need of sound social doctrine and guidance.[50]

Bossy also proposed the translation of 'French Catholic social literature into several languages', arguing that only by speaking to the 'foreigner' in his own tongue could he be 'rescued, or saved, from the false "mysticity" [sic] of Communism and inspired to generous and fruitful social action'. In the guidance of the immigrant communities, 'French and Catholic inspiration should predominate'.[51] Bossy was not the first to argue that Catholicism in North America could only thrive through the preservation of ethnic diversity, the guidance of French Canada, and the use of Christianity as a bonding tool for cultural cooperation. In the early twentieth century, the French-Canadian Archbishop of the multicultural ecclesiastical province of St. Boniface, Adélard Langevin, led a long and controversial campaign in western Canada for the survival and expansion of Catholic culture through denominational education and against the assimilation of immigrant communities of descent other than French or British. Not unlike Bossy, Langevin believed that assimilation and the cultural homogeneity promoted by the British Canadian political elites led to the loss of faith, and that therefore cooperation was more desirable. Furthermore, Langevin also looked at French Canadians as the group that could inspire such cooperation, for they 'alone had valued and encouraged cultural diversity' against English-speaking Catholics efforts to foster assimilation – as in the case of the Catholic Church Extension Society.[52]

In interwar Canada, the belief that French culture had a crucial role in protecting Christian civilization in North America became also crucial to radical-right movements like that of Adrien Arcand's Parti National Social Chrétien (National Social Christian Party, later National Unity Party). As a young student, Arcand developed 'a strong sense of belonging to a Christian civilization shaped by old France'.[53] However, 'the cult of strength and hierarchy put forward by Arcand as an operating principle was attained through the constant use of the English language.'[54] Indeed, Arcand saw the British Empire as a community of nations in which Canada could participate 'on the basis of equal partners in solidarity'.[55] The main difference between Arcand and Bossy's visions, though, was that while the former argued that only those of English and French extraction could regard themselves as *Canadians*, the latter aimed to incorporate the rest of (white) Europeans living in Canada into the national identity under a common Christian framework.[56] Bossy's view was more aligned with what Jeannine Hill Fletcher calls 'Christian theologies of supremacy', which think theologically about the project of building a nation. In doing so, Bossy's 'race discourse' was 'underwritten by Christian theology' rather than by pseudoscientific explanations of difference or social Darwinism, for example, as was the case for Arcand.[57]

Without a doubt, Bossy believed that Catholicism must prevail over Protestantism, and so it is only natural that he highlighted the 'spiritual values symbolized by French Canada' and 'the vitality of French-Canadian Catholicism' vis-à-vis the rest of Canada.[58] However, the possibility of Bossy's using Francophilia as a means to simply obtain the (financial) support of a highly ethnicized Catholic Church, rather than as an expression of admiration, must be seriously considered. For one thing, Bossy began referring to the leading role of the French Catholics only when he resolved to massively organize 'the foreign Catholics of various nationalities' into a 'constructive Christian social movement'. For that to happen, Bossy needed 'preliminary financial support' or 'minimal funds' from what he called 'the outstanding, patriotic and socially minded Canadian citizens', for which he reached out to the French-Canadian Catholic Church hierarchy and Quebec's premier Maurice Duplessis, for example, urging them to 'adopt the Catholic foreign population'.[59] Thus, allowing the French Canadians to have a leading role in such movement would secure the establishment of centres for the education, mobilization, and incorporation of the Catholic 'foreigners'.

That Francophilia was an opportunistic stance becomes even more likely when one considers that, precisely by mid-1937, while they were trying to spread their plans for national reconstruction and raise funds in Quebec, John J. Fitzgerald and Bossy were also actively seeking support from English-speaking individuals 'of personal means' in Ontario.[60] In this regard, Bossy 'expect[ed] very much from the action [of] Mr. Laprès', who would work with Fitzgerald to find support in that province.[61] A naturalized 'alien' from Cheboygan, Michigan, Joseph-Arthur Laprès was 'a distinguished member' of Montreal's 'Catholic Standing Committee', the Catholic Committee of the Council of Public Instruction, which was composed of clergy as well as Catholic laymen and members of the teaching profession.[62] A sales manager for Canada Cement and a representative of the Canadian Manufacturers' Association in Montreal, Laprès served too as president of the Society for Crippled Children and a member of the Board Room of the Montreal City & District Saving Bank. He was also a supporter of the Classocracy League of Canada.[63] Laprès was particularly concerned about class consciousness constituting an obstacle for the successful establishment of a classocratic state, which could only be sustained by the total elimination of class conflict. This is why he and Fitzgerald began working on a plan to promote 'industrial peace' in Ontario and in Quebec as a step prior to suggest reform along the lines of European cultural cooperation.[64]

In line with the interwar message of the Catholic Church, their plan was to specifically counter the communist influence in the unions 'within the frame of social harmony and Christian respect for all classes'.[65] Laprès and Fitzgerald's project addressed 'the threat to Industrial Peace', the most 'disturbing factor in the present economic situation in Canada, and especially in the provinces of Ontario and Quebec'. Such a disturbance was being promoted by 'Communistic elements' and was penetrating the industrial and social spheres of both employers and employees.[66] Their use of the term 'industrial peace' is significant. In the early thirties, 'industrial peace' was directly associated with the suppression of worker's rights and, more particularly, their right to strike. In Italy, Fascist leader Benito Mussolini aimed to 'bring about industrial peace and an end to class warfare', thus 'eliminat[ing] the need for strike action'. To *il Duce*, industrial peace was also a necessary step in 'the political and economic integration of Italy under Fascist leadership', an integration he saw only possible through totalitarian corporatism: 'How can there ever be industrial peace until all workers are under government control – and all government under a Duce? I accept!'.[67] Laprès and Fitzgerald's view was certainly influenced by totalitarian understandings of power as well. To begin with, their project considered the scrutiny of all channels through which communist propaganda might influence the workers. This included 'every possible labour organization'; 'the leading newspapers of Toronto or Montreal'; and student 'leagues and societies'.[68] In order to achieve industrial peace, they argued, '*aggressive* counter activities' had to be implemented and '*centralized* ... so that *every* element of the population may be *directed* to promoting a constructive Canadianism [against] destructive Communism'.[69] There is little doubt that fascism was a main source of inspiration to Laprès and Fitzgerald's plans for industrial peace which, just like in Fascist Italy, was conceived as a necessary step for the effective development of an economically and politically integrated, centralized, aggressively anti-communist, and corporatist state. Fitzgerald argued that those works which had inspired him the most in regard to achieving industrial peace were *Americanism or Communism?*[70]; "I Was a Communist Agitator"; and *Winning Better Conditions With the C.I.O.*

Published in 1935 by American anti-communist Walter B. Odale, *Americanism or Communism?* blamed communism for 'every conceivable social problem, from the disintegration of family life to labour unrest to the growing crime rate'.[71] The book praised fascism as a nationalist movement against communism, which was dominated by 'aliens' that had 'acquired but little of our ideology and speak English with a foreign accent, if at all.'[72] It also related communism with the 'hatred of God and all forms of religion; destruction of home and family life; confiscation of all private property [...]; class hatred; social equality and intermarriage of all races'.[73] In short, Odale was arguing that communism represented all that America was not.[74] To Odale, just like to Mussolini, the suppression of communism and the boost of nationalism were only possible through violent anti-communism and the reorganization of society based on professional groups under an integrated state. So, in order to protect the American worker against the dangers of communism, Odale suggested the use of the American Federation of Labour (AFL) for the promotion of 'patriotism, national pride, and every sense of well-being which civilized people enjoy through being an integral part of their own government'.[75] An international labour union, and the largest union grouping in the United States at the time, the AFL was founded and dominated by craft unions, whereby workers were organized based on the particular trade, or guild, to which they belonged.

"I Was a Communist Agitator" was a 1937 confession by former anti-communist John Hladun, aka Jack Logan.[76] Hladun, 'a Canadian farm boy' whose devout Greek Catholic parents had arrived in Canada from Austria-Hungary in 1896, was recruited by the Ukrainian Labour-Farmer Temple Association (ULFTA)[77] at the age of 16. He was soon summoned to Moscow 'to be instructed in making armed war against the Canadian government and [...] against the social and political institutions for which [Canada] stood'. The Comintern had placed in him the hope that he would become 'one of the great leaders of the revolutionary movement in Canada and the world'. At the International Lenin University, Hladun studied 'the technique of treason'.[78] He was instructed in how to 'shape our struggle for domination of the Canadian labor movement'; how to 'use my position in the Ukrainian Canadian social and cultural organization to which I belonged back in Winnipeg to advance the influence of the Party'; and 'what tactics we were to pursue in promoting an open break between French and English Canada.'[79]

Hladun returned to Canada in 1930, when he began working for the ULFTA and the Communist Party's Ukrainian section, allegedly wrecking unions and exploiting the jobless: 'Our policy was simply to pump the men full of Marxism, Leninism, revolution and the Soviet Union, and hope that nothing would be done about the domestic conditions we were inveighing against'.[80] Hladun began rejecting 'the golden doctrine of Communism' when he realized that Russia, allegedly the enemy of capitalism, was in fact a capitalist state; that the workers did not own the goods they produced; that freedom there meant only 'freedom to conform'; and that class prisoners were in fact victims of a persecutor state.[81] He left the Communist Party of Canada (CPC) in 1933.[82] Hladun said that while some want to fight communism, too many fail to do so because 'they make no real effort to understand it'.[83] This is why three years after he left the CPC he wrote a series of 11 articles for the *Winnipeg Free Press* entitled "I Was a Communist Agitator", in which he explained his experience.[84]

One last important source for the development of Fitzgerald and Laprès' plans for industrial peace was *Winning Better Conditions With the C.I.O.*, issued by the American Committee for Industrial Organization (CIO) in March 1937. Unlike the AFL, the CIO organized workers by industry rather than by craft.[85] It exhibited 'both the pageantry and idealism of a great liberation movement and the determination to foster responsible, contractual unionism in the mass production sector'.[86] In Canada, the CIO awakened 'new hopes for a genuine labour movement' that by 1937 was demanding an 8-hour day, better wages and working conditions, a seniority system and the recognition of collective bargaining.[87] What the CIO was fighting for was the overall amelioration of workers, whom Odale pointed out were prone to radicalization if they were denied a 'sense of well-being' – especially foreigners or immigrant communities. As Fitzgerald saw it, the CIO presented useful guidelines towards the pacification of the workers through the implementation of better conditions and through patriotism.

Fitzgerald ordered several copies of *Americanism or Communism?*, "I Was a Communist Agitator", and *Winning Better Conditions With the C.I.O.*, and asked Laprès 'to select a group of men numbering from six to ten who would agree to have a series of three conferences with Walter Bossy' on the relationship between 'foreigners' and the communist threat. The idea was to inform these 'men of personal means' about the conditions of unrest that were sweeping the country, and have them contribute financially to the establishment of Bossy's New Canadians Federation (NCF).[88] Although meetings did indeed occur, these seem to have produced no results.[89] With no significant support for the suppression of class consciousness and the establishment of Bossy's NCF, Fitzgerald resolved to focus back to the Classocracy League of Canada (CLC) and its opportunities as a movement or, possibly, a political party: 'Classocracy should launch out immediately and expect from its supporters a complete spirit of sacrifice'. What they needed was a new 'Classocracy office' in Montreal, and a paper that turned workers into 'inspired Classocrats': *The Canadian Classocrat*.[90] But first, they needed money. Perhaps Jesuit William X. Bryan, Bishop Archambault, or Minister T. J. Coonan, early supporters of Bossy's, would help organize picnics, boat trips, and card parties to increase contributions – considered Fitzgerald. Hopefully, Laprès would be able to 'secure free quarters' through the Catholic Standing Committee, to which Fitzgerald sent several copies of Hladun's story for inspiration.[91]

As the vice-president of the City Improvement League (CIL), a local organization concerned as much about city planning as about moral and social 'degeneration', Laprès sought additional support.[92] Specifically, he approached the president of the CIL Thomas Taggart Smyth, an Irish Canadian who was also the chairman of the Catholic Standing Committee and, most importantly, a reactionary at the front of the Canadian branch of the transnational organization Friends of National Spain.[93] Laprès pointed out to Smyth that 'in the person of Mr. Walter Bossy the School Commission has a man who is ... eminently qualified to work with, and for, the Commission towards the practical application of the [Christian] principles ...'.[94] Even though no official form of cooperation between the CIL and the CLC was ever established, Thomas Taggart Smyth did become a significant source of financial support to Bossy's New Canadians subsequent projects until the 1950s.[95]

Smyth's support was not enough, however. With a view to expanding their influence in regard to social reconstruction, Laprès suggested assisting Edward LaPierre in obtaining the position of secretary of the Catholic Standing Committee.[96] This would allow him to 'extend his connections with the prominent people and to influence them'. While LaPierre should never use 'the word "Classocracy"', as the leader of the movement he would 'in time convince everybody concerned [of] the usefulness of Classocracy.' Should he not succeed in becoming a Secretary of the Committee, then the opening of a CLC office and other works would have to be subsidized by themselves.

In a way, though, the CLC had already expanded. Indeed, Fitzgerald's permanent establishment in Blind River, Ontario, had been the first step towards the CLC becoming a nationwide party or movement. As Bossy put it: '...you are now a citizen of Ontario while we are citizens of Quebec. That means: two main provinces are invaded by Classocrats.'[97] In Montreal, the classocracy sympathizers would strive 'to inspire and influence' the existing political parties until these '(although blindly) tend towards classocratic plan for social justice and occupational hierarchy'. Hopefully, they would soon present their own 'manifesto and political program for the election'.[98] In Ontario, Fitzgerald would become 'a strong man behind the present weak [provincial] government', gradually rallying around him 'a group of most able politicians'. In Quebec and in Ontario, said Bossy, the classocrats began mobilizing as one 'Christian Front'.[99] And then, things got even better. In July 1937, LaPierre was appointed Acting Secretary of the Catholic Standing Committee.[100]

Allegiance day

As Myra Rutherdale and Jim Miller argue, commemoration legitimizes 'acceptable Canadian representations'.[101] It allows for the institutionalization of ideas on who is inside and outside the nation, or who can be considered a 'citizen'.[102] In other words, commemoration is not only about establishing a collective identity, but also and perhaps more importantly about legitimizing its existence. It is also a way of extending a relationship of power vis-à-vis the state, thereby forcing its recognition as an integral part of the larger community. In 1938, this is all Bossy wanted for the 'New Canadians':

> New Canadians throughout Canada are coming to realize more and more the meaning, the rights and duties of Canadian citizenship. At the same time they are becoming conscious of their own collective strength and of their moral and cultural value as citizens and nation builders.[103]

In order to demand that 'New Canadians' be acknowledged as legitimate components of the Canadian nation and the Canadian identity, Bossy decided to organize what he called an Allegiance Day. The object of the New Canadians Allegiance Day was 'the nationwide institution of a regularly recurring annual demonstration of allegiance to His Majesty, the King, on the part of his most faithful subjects, the "New" Canadians.'[104] Accordingly, the celebration would take place on June 9, the king's birthday, at Lafontaine Park in Montreal.[105] The purpose was for this to be an annual celebration (to take place on the same day)[106] in which the 'New Canadians' would celebrate their identity as a collective group, but also as Canadians and loyal servants of the British crown. The 'New Canadians', the king's 'most faithful subjects', would honour what monarchy represents, that is the transcendence of 'all divergences of race or language or creed of faction', and the equality between Old and 'New Canadians'.[107] But there was more to that. To Bossy's mind, in organizing a New Canadians Allegiance Day he was also fulfilling the Montreal Catholic School Committee's instructions for him (now as the MCSC's Auxiliary Assistant for Foreign Classes) to combat communism among the 'foreign' population of Montreal. This is why he specifically called upon the Christian ethnic communities and 'The Foreign pupils of Protestants and Catholic schools' to join this 'patriotic demonstration'. Bossy described his plan as wishing to mobilize *'all* New Canadians of *all* Christian denominations' to 'counteract this subversive [communist] propaganda'.[108]

Canadians 'from within all *three ethnic groups* French, British and Continental European, and not from the "New Canadian" element exclusively ... as is sometimes mistakenly held' had joined the communist ranks, and so it was the goal of such a demonstration to challenge any suspicion towards the New Canadians' loyalty based on prejudice.[109] The demonstration was not only a way to 'proclaim our strength in numbers, and our value in nation-building, as well as our ... civic equality and unity with the bulk of the population, the French and British stock', but also an organized reaction against communism, 'a definite menace to our Christian civilization'.[110] With these goals in mind, an Initiating Committee of 'New Canadians Allegiance Day' was formed with Edward LaPierre as secretary-treasurer, Bossy as organizer, and Jean-Joseph Penverne as president. Penverne was a lawyer from Montreal and a member of the Conservative Party of Canada and, according to LaPierre, and an 'inspiring speaker'.[111] He was also a new Canadian from Britanny, France.[112]

On June 9, 1938, over 3000 adults and 500 children took part in this 'patriotic demonstration' led by the 'New Canadians', which *Le Devoir* described as *'the third element* of the Canadian population after the French element and the English element'. '[E]ven if we hardly hear of them,' continued the French-Canadian newspaper, 'they have 2,000,000 souls ... they have contributed their part to the development of the country'.[113] The celebration was conducted in both English and French, and it took place in the city of Montreal only.[114] There, Penverne inaugurated Allegiance Day by stating in French that the 'New Canadians' 'wish not only to express their loyalty to the King but also their faith in the institutions, traditions, and laws of Canada, and their desire to join their efforts to those of a peaceful and prosperous nation'. It would be a big mistake, he claimed, 'to refuse to consider these people as brothers. These young children that you see gathered are the hope of Canada and in a few years you will see them taking an active part in the functioning of the institutions of the country'.[115] Disregarding the fact that Christian Protestants might have too attended the call (as he supposedly wished), Bossy saluted the 'New Canadians' 'inestimable gift of the *Catholic* Faith, ripened and richened in most cases because your people had held it against centuries of oppression or against the even greater danger of insidious efforts to lead you astray.' It was by their consistent practice of the Christian principles, he said, that they would 'find a new home' in Canada, 'a land the broad expanse of which is marked with the sign of the Cross and by the bleeding feet of Catholic apostles'.[116]

What Bossy did not say at the demonstration was that, in fact, he believed that Catholic groups should take the lead in the fight against communism – and in the process of nation-building. 'For too long', he said in a letter to president of the MSCS Armand Dupuis, 'Protestant influences have predominated in this great mass [of New Canadians], but it is not too late'.[117] Thus, to him, Allegiance Day was not just an act of Christian cooperation and unity against both prejudice and alleged subversive forces, but also a means to increase the influence of Catholicism among ethnic minorities. In spite of that, it is worth noticing that (unlike the Notre Dame demonstration of 1936) members of the Catholic clergy refrained from actively participating in Allegiance Day. However, we know that the 'campaign conducted by Mr. Walter J. BOSSY for organizing our foreign-Catholics ... in Montreal' to continue the work which began in December 1936 met with the approval of both Bishop Joseph P. Archambault and archbishop coadjutor Georges Gauthier a year earlier.[118] According to Bossy, who spoke in French at the event, difficulties to involve foreign clergy in activities following the demonstration at Notre Dame arose from them having 'already an increase in work in the holy ministry that they exercise among numerous and often distributed parishioners'.[119] In other words, apparently they were too busy. Although perhaps their interest in such endeavours had simply diminished.

Despite that lack of official religious support, a denominational bias characterized Allegiance Day – as did an ethnic bias. Even though Bossy's appeal to the institution of an Allegiance Day claimed to be 'all-inclusive' in character, and representing all 'Children of the Great Migration – of all origins', it was only and specifically addressed to 'Belgian, Bulgarian, Czechoslovakian, Danish, Dutch, Finnish, German, Greek, Hungarian, Italian, Lithuanian, Norwegian, Polish, Rumanian, Russian, Swedish, Syrian, Ukrainian, [and] Yugo-Slav.'[120] It is important to note that, although Bossy didn't deem it necessary to work towards the amelioration of Belgian and Italians due to their alleged capacity to easily adapt among French Canadians, as seen above, he considered them to part of the 'New Canadian' community, and consequently expected them to be represented at every event he organized. This included the New Canadians Allegiance Day and Committee, and the unsuccessful 'first international film festival', which Bossy planned to take place between November 1938 and March 1939.[121]

Perhaps the most interesting incorporation here is that of Syrians. Why Syrians (a generic term then applied to immigrants from today's Syria and Lebanon) qualified as 'New Canadians' under Bossy's eyes, and therefore as Europeans or white, is unclear. On the one hand, Bossy's papers from the early postwar period reveal that, to him, 'Syrians' ('Armenians, Lebanese and Syrians') belonged neither to the 'Foreign Colonies' ('The Black Neighbourhood', 'The Jewish Diaspora', and 'Chinatown') nor to the 'New Canadians', but were somewhere in between.[122] This was explained based on their economic success and their religious and cultural affinity: '[They] occupy an exceptional, privileged place in the industrial life of the city. Orthodox or Catholics of the Greek rite, all usually speak French and have transferred their unfailing love for France to New France.'[123] On the other hand, historian of ethnicity Sarah Gualtieri argues that, in the twentieth century, Syrian immigrants to North America gained their right to 'whiteness' among certain circles on religious and racial grounds. Specifically, they insisted on their 'connection to the Holy Land and to Christianity'[124], and on their Semitic origin, which they argued was 'a branch of the white race'.[125] If either of these arguments were true to Bossy, then the contradictory decision of including Syrians while explicitly excluding the Jewish community from his 'New Canadians' 'movement' further demonstrates Christian supremacy and antisemitism being essential to Bossy's understanding of social reform in Canada.

At Allegiance Day, Bossy explained that the 'New Canadians', who come 'from various countries of the old world (the "Christendom" of mediaeval and early modern history)', have 'often mistakenly referred to as "foreigners"'. In fact, he said, they had 'colonized'[126] Canadian soil just as the French and the British had, thereby contributing 'in diverse ways and in varying degrees, to that specific social and cultural phenomenon which is Canadian nationhood'. Ignoring this, he thought, was simply 'shortsighted and unfair'.[127] In fact, the 'New Canadians', who had been given 'the rights and privileges of Canadian citizenship', had not abused such rights by 'indulging in sedition [or] in parasitism' – like others had, he implied. Rather, they had 'lived up to the duties of pioneering citizenship'. And thanks to their efforts and their work, Bossy argued, the sovereignty of King George VI had been consolidated. In spite of that, he continued, thus far the only Canadian voices raised to express 'love and loyalty' to the monarch had been the English and the French Canadian, 'which might have led observers outside the country to come to the conclusion that the whole population of Canada consists of but two language groups'. Indeed, the 'New Canadians' had 'failed to add our own voice to the rich harmony of national rejoicing'.[128] Such an omission conveyed a 'distortion of the historical, ethnical and social fact that the population of Canada includes, besides the universally recognized English-speaking and French-speaking Canadians, two million "New Canadians"'.[129] Montreal's mayor, Adhémar Raynault, who had 'very generously donated a personal contribution towards the expenses involved in the inaugural demonstration', referred to the 'thousands of fellow citizens of European origin' who wished to 'openly express their faith in their adopted country, their respect for existing laws and their submission to the reigning King'.[130] He further expressed his hopes that the event 'will establish a tradition which will be followed year after year, not only in Montreal, but throughout the Dominion of Canada'.[131]

John Murray Gibbon, author of *Canadian Mosaic* (1938), applauded Montreal's Allegiance Day as a 'colorful pageant of New Canadians' and a celebration of 'Folk', and he connected it to a similar demonstration that took place a month later, on July 1 (Dominion Day) at Exhibition Park in Toronto.[132] The New Canadians 'Folk Festival' in Toronto rallied around 25,000 people, including 'Ukrainians, Macedonians, Dutch, Danish, Germans, Spanish, Mexicans, Japanese, Finnish, Polish and Greeks', who united 'to pay their respects to Canada'.[133] A total of '26 different races' joined the festival, which consisted of a parade, dances, music, and an art display.[134] Toronto Mayor Ralph C. Day (Liberal Party) claimed that the event was 'without precedent in Canada.'[135] Diversity was certainly better reflected in such an event that at the one that took place just about a month earlier in Montreal. Nonetheless, the purpose of the two events, namely challenging binationalism, was not too different, which explains why Gibbon assumed they were related events. Just like Bossy, even though Toronto Mayor Day aimed to celebrate the New Canadians Folk Festival in Toronto annually, the event seems to have been a one-off.[136] The reasons for this remain unclear, although scholars such as R. D. Francis describe other events for the recognition of minorities' cultural heritage in summer 1939 as 'unheard by a Canadian public totally preoccupied by the entry of Canada into World War II'.[137]

After Allegiance Day on June 9, 1938, in Montreal, LaPierre, Bossy, and Penverne resolved to form a permanent committee 'to consolidate and extend our Allegiance Day Movement'. Meetings took place with a view to ultimately establishing an organization to represent and protect the 'New Canadians' as *the third ethnic group* of our country's population'.[138] It was not until February 1939, however, that the New Canadians Federation (NCF) was born under the slogan: 'We are no longer "foreigners", but co-builders of Canadian unity'.[139] The NCF aimed to improve the status of all those Canadians 'whose ancestors came from European countries other than Great Britain, Ireland[140] and France'.[141] The NCF represented the union of 'closed communities' organized 'for the sake of Canadian unity'. It aimed 'to place and to keep before representative and responsible "Old" Canadians the vital social, economic and educational problems of their fellow "New" Canadians, while fostering in the latter a sense of self-help through mutual assistance' as well as 'to cooperate with all organizations and movements that tend to enhance the general status of New Canadians'. Doing so was a 'necessary patriotic and sociological effort.'[142] By March 1939, the New Canadians Federation had already purchased an office in Montreal situated at 1220 University Street for $2,100,000.[143]

As Bossy saw it, national recognition of the 'New Canadians' had to start in the province of Quebec. If the 'New Canadians' were able to cooperate on the basis of common social, political, and economic grievances as well as common descent, cooperation between them and French Canadians could be achieved on the basis of common faith and a shared sense of alienation. '[A] union of minorities' was desirable, believed Bossy, to 'greatly enhance their power to safeguard and vindicate their common religious and patriotic interests.'[144] French Canadians did not realize the value of uniting their efforts with the 'New Canadians' so that their own social power is strengthened. Indeed, 'French-Canadians do next to nothing to attract newcomers', he thought. To Bossy, the reason for that was that French Canadians were prejudiced.[145] Collaborator of *Le Bien Public* Louis Durand (nom de plume Léon Dufrost[146]) applauded Bossy's efforts to promote the collaboration between French and 'New Canadians', and compared them to efforts for the Americanization of 'foreigners who came to the United States to settle there permanently'. Citing *L'Action Française*, Durand praised such tactics as of 'high national thought, a lesson we can apply at home'. In the process of Americanization, Durand wrote, the role of the host community was crucial, encouraging the immigrant 'to recognize his value, to help him by giving him a good example, by mingling with his life, by making him participate in his own'. More importantly, by allowing the 'New Canadians' into their cultural milieu, French Canadians 'could hope to one day attain political predominance in Canada'.[147]

That the successful integration of immigrant communities could be seen as an opportunity for French Canada to achieve political superiority in Canada at large had been previously explored by French-Canadian nationalist and founder of Quebec's L'Action Française (French Action) Lionel Groulx. Throughout the 1930s, Groulx argued that while immigration was a 'vast problem', it also represented an opportunity for the French Canadians to consolidate their position and have 'the majority in numbers in Canada'. This could be done by integrating the foreigner into the French-Canadian nation so as to create 'a new breed of French Canadians'. Just like Bossy, Groulx believed that the adequate means to foster acculturation was education and amalgamation, which Groulx saw as a political tool by which to assimilate the foreigner while strengthening French Canada.[148] The main difference between Groulx's vision and that of Bossy, however, was that while the former believed that French Canada should stay French Canadian after the successful incorporation of foreigners, the latter saw that incorporation as part of a larger process of diversification within a common Christian framework.

J. N. Korchinsky, a Ukrainian editor based in Toronto, described Bossy's vision as bringing spiritual unity in cultural diversity, the wish to 'promote national unity, based on the autonomy of groups, mutual aid, respect for laws and traditions, fidelity to the Christian ideal'. Bossy 'wants to make Canada a living mosaic, a harmonious country, made up of different but

68   *Allegiances*

fraternal peoples'.[149] Similarly, Franco-Ontarian Jesuit Guy Courteau celebrated the work of 'a well-known new Canadian, Mr. Walter-J. Bossy', who 'has never ceased to communicate to French Canadians, on behalf of new immigrants and 'New Canadians' of old stock, an urgent call for rapprochement and mutual aid'. He wondered if the next step would be promoting the collaboration between Catholics, Protestants, and Jews.[150]

But no further steps were taken, as the Second World War brought all of Bossy's projects to a halt. After the conflict broke out, he abandoned the New Canadians Federation project to work exclusively as an instructor officer at Canadian Officers Training Corps (COTC) at Loyola College. Two of his sons served overseas: one in the air force, the other in the navy. A third one entered the ranks of the reserve army.[151] The 'New Canadians' would have to wait.

The Ukrainian question

Bossy had been involved in the Hetmanite movement since he first came to Canada in 1924. In fact, upon his arrival he founded the Canadian Sitch Association, later United Hetman Organization (UHO), a conservative monarchist political organization officially supported by the Ukrainian Catholic Church. Having witnessed chaos in revolutionary Ukraine while fighting against the Bolsheviks between 1916 and 1920, Bossy concluded that 'Ukrainian Canadians needed an organization capable of inculcating duty, discipline, and obedience to spiritual and secular authority'. Through the UHO, he promoted allegiance to Berlin-based Hetman Pavlo Skoropadsky, a landowner and general who had ruled Ukraine with the backing of the German army in 1918.[152] In doing so, Bossy hoped Ukrainians would achieve independent statehood in Europe and harmony in North America. During the 1920s, Ukrainian Canadians who were equally 'tired of political and denominational bickering' and who 'yearned for a strong authority' joined Bossy's call. The UHO quickly became the only non-communist Ukrainian 'mass organization' in Canada.[153]

During the 1930s, the Soviet and Polish repression of Ukraine radicalized many Ukrainian Canadians who were desperate to find support for their country's independence. At the time, the only country that seemed willing and powerful enough to intervene was Nazi Germany. Its aggressive anti-communism and apparent support for self-determination made of Hitler a potential hero to any anti-communist Ukrainian Canadian.[154] In 1936, Michael Hethman, Bossy's successor as UHO Quartermaster General who had just spent more than six months in Berlin, published several articles in *Ukrainskyi robitnyk* advocating Ukrainian cooperation with Nazi Germany.[155] The support for such cooperation among Hetmanites was made obvious when Danylo Skoropadsky visited Canada between late 1937 and early 1938 as part of his 'tour of two months' around North America.[156] During this tour, German pro-Nazi groups hosted him while Skoropadsky

Allegiances 69

'expressed his admiration for the German people's triumphant efforts to build a better life for themselves by launching a domestic and external struggle against Bolshevism'.[157]

In Quebec City, the Catholic newspaper *L'Action Catholique* hosted 'His Highness' in the presence of the Cardinal-Archbishop Jean-Marie-Rodrigue Villeneuve. The newspaper shared with its readers the 'tragic history' of Ukraine and highlighted the anti-Bolshevik tradition of the Skoropadsky family.[158] When visiting Montreal, where Skoropadsky stayed with Bossy, the local newspapers likewise highlighted 'the painful history of Ukraine and the Skoropadsky family'. Ukrainian separatism was overall supported by the local newspapers, which understood independence as the liberation of the territory from Bolshevism.[159] According to Skoropadsky, if someone had to be admired for the destruction of Bolshevism that was Nazi leader Adolf Hitler, whom he described as 'the Greatest Man of the Century'. In Montreal, the most outspoken admirer of Hitler and notorious antisemite Adrien Arcand toasted the Ukrainian prince at a banquet organized by Bossy in one of the Ukrainian Catholic parishes. Like Skoropadsky and Arcand, Bossy 'was certain that Hitler would save the Christian world from the Jewish menace'.[160] Not unlike many Christians at the time, Bossy believed there was a connection between Judaism and communism, and therefore thought that antisemitism was justified so long as it served the purpose of combating Bolshevism.[161] Such an idea was neither new nor unique. Between 1917 and 1923, the belief that 'Jews were responsible for Bolshevism' was used to 'justify the mass slaughter of Jews in Ukraine by the anti-Bolshevik counterrevolutionaries'.[162] In the interwar period, coding the Jews as 'Communist-allied enemies of the Catholic family' was 'the mainstream' among Catholics.[163] Sticking to that belief until the end of the Second World War, during the conflict Bossy still cooperated with RCMP officer and classocracy sympathizer Jack Mead, reporting as usual on suspected communist elements in Montreal. Unsurprisingly, Bossy's recurrent method used to identify subversive communists essentially consisted in tracing (or imagining) Jews.[164]

In his private correspondence with Mead, Bossy reveals that, upon his visit, 'His Highness [Skoropadsky] imposed on me a great deal of work'. This was possibly related to obtaining Ukrainian Canadian support for cooperation with Nazi Germany towards Ukraine's independence.[165] But in Europe things did not look good. Hungary seemed to be developing a growing interest in the easternmost section of Czechoslovakia, the Carpatho-Ukraine.[166] Aware of that interest, Hitler announced that Carpatho-Ukraine should be granted, at least provisionally, 'home-rule under Prague'. Rather than a selfless sympathy towards Ukraine's national consciousness, Hitler's own interest in the region was based on the idea that denying a common frontier between Hungary and Poland would benefit Germany's ambitions to expand beyond the Czechoslovakian Carpathians.[167] On the other hand, Poland wanted the support of Germany in ensuring that the Carpatho-Ukraine

70 *Allegiances*

went to Hungary in order to keep away the Ukrainian nationalist minority so menacing to the Poles. Germany considered Poland's interests in the south-east because Hitler could ask for the Danzig in exchange. But no formal deal ever took place and, in late 1938, Hungary attempted to occupy the Carpatho-Ukraine. Faced with that move, Hitler did nothing. By March 1939, the Carpatho-Ukraine was Hungarian and Hungary Hitler's ally.[168] To Bossy, the collapse of Carpatho-Ukraine 'made our dreams and hopes disappear ... like soap bubbles.' 'Herr Hitler' had 'betrayed' Ukraine, and now Bossy found himself 'politically confused and patriotically disgusted'.[169] Shortly after the Carpatho-Ukraine fell to Hungary, Hitler decided to invade Poland and, with that move, the West shook. The Second World War had begun.

'The Future looks dark to me', wrote Mead to Bossy on September 12, 1939, 11 days after the German invasion of Poland. The 'Force' might go to war, he said.[170] Bossy was 40 years old, and he wished to 'enlist in active military service' to fight against the Nazis just like Mead was about to do, and insisted (to Mead and several other RCMP officers) that his experience as 'lieutenant in the Austrian Army [and] as a captain ... in the Ukrainian Army ... against Red Russians' could be of use in the upcoming conflict.[171] In spite of his enthusiasm, Bossy was advised 'to put that wish at the back of [his] mind, and to concentrate on [his] own field of Propaganda'.[172] Precisely towards that aim, in December 1940 the RCMP helped Bossy and other Ukrainian monarchists found *Narodnia gazeta* (People's Gazette), an anti-Soviet weekly which would be issued in Winnipeg.[173] Sent to subscribers of the former Ukrainian Labour Farmer Temple Association (ULFTA) organ *Narodna hazeta* (People's Newspaper), which had been 'crucial to the dissemination of communism and socialism among the Ukrainians', *Narodnia gazeta* sought to turn Ukrainian communists into 'patriotic Canadian minded'.[174]

There was one particular organization that reacted badly to the foundation of *Narodnia gazeta*: the Ukrainian Canadian Committee (UCC). The UCC, formed in November 1940, was an 'ad hoc committee of influential citizens within the nationalist segment of the Ukrainian Canadian community' intended to represent and coordinate the Ukrainian Canadian community during the war effort. When the UCC was constituted, the individual Ukrainian-Canadian organizations 'agreed to join ... to coordinate their activities' under 'united representation'.[175] To the presumably all-encompassing UCC, independent Ukrainian-Canadian organizations and organs – including the communist ones – constituted a threat to the unity of the Ukrainian community. That's why the appearance of *Narodnia gazeta* left the UCC 'very much puzzled'. Bossy lamented that 'these people', who were exclusively concerned with Ukraine, would never be able to understand 'what great work we have started'. While the UCC 'will argue that this paper creates disunity among Ukrainians', said Bossy, they were in fact the ones causing disunity for they are 'not a bit concerned with the Canadian

Unity'. In fact, Bossy considered *Narodnia gazeta* a 'weapon to wield against [their] non-Canadian action'. So, he concluded, 'the reason of their opposition is and will be purely from selfish and limited to the Ukrainian problem motives.' The *Narodnia gazeta* would only join the UCC provided that the organization concentrates 'its efforts 100% for Canada and not 100% for the Ukrainian intrigues into which neither I nor our paper will allow itself to be involved'.[176]

Teodor Datzkiw, the new 'head of the monarchist United Hetman Organisation (UHO) in Canada', was an editor of the newspaper *Kanadiiskyi farmer* (Canadian Farmer) for five years before joining *Narodnia gazeta*.[177] Datzkiw was in Winnipeg taking care of the anti-communist and Ukrainian nationalist weekly when he wrote in alarm to Bossy (who remained in Montreal) saying that 'representative for the UNF [Ukrainian National Federation of Canada] on the UCC executive' Wasyl Swystun had 'embarked on a campaign against us'.[178] Apparently, Swystun thought that *Narodnia gazeta* was a 'provocation to the Ukrainians', for it was 'disrupting the much desired unity of the Ukrainians in Canada at the present moment'. It looked like Swystun would take the necessary steps 'in order to have the "People's Gazette" stopped'. Against such claims, Bossy argued that what really mattered was not the unity of Ukrainians but that of Canadians. And for that to happen mobilizing Ukrainian Canadians for European matters exclusively, which was what the UCC was doing, was certainly not helpful. As Bossy saw it, the most dangerous element for the disunity of Canada was not his newspaper but communism, powerful as ever due to its gaining protection under the democratic system. He insisted that the largest and 'most powerful' Communist Party section in Canada was dominated by Ukrainians. Therefore, Ukrainian-Canadian unity essentially constituted a danger against, rather than a step towards, Canadian unity.[179]

Bossy believed that while the communists seemed to be reorganizing in the name of liberty against Nazism, they were in fact 'united with the Nazis in a common effort' against civilization. Their becoming even more empowered through the support of the rest of their ethnic community only meant that a 'revolution, or at least serious upheavals', could still take place in Canada. But 'Ottawa knows', said Bossy to Datzkiw, 'that the [Ukrainian Canadian Committee] is nothing but a political tool of all those Ukrainian political leaders in Canada who above all are interested in the Ukraine of Europe'. It is also known, he continued, that 'Ukrainians are going with Britain in this war conditionally, i.e. if Britain will help in the liberation of Ukraine.' Given this, Bossy affirmed that Ottawa was not interested in 'how strongly and sincerely the Ukrainians in Canada are getting united' but in 'how to lessen the very insecurity arising from the Communist-Nazi co-operation in Canada'. With that, he concluded, 'our own people' could help. *Narodnia gazeta* would take care of 'transforming' the potentially revolutionary elements of the Canadian community 'into Canadian patriot[s]'. For 'except a few hundred hardened Communists who have passed into underground activities, the remaining tens of thousands are simply ordinary people ...'. *Narodnia gazeta* would give them the 'proper nourishment, show them the mistakes of their leaders and the consequences therefrom, and these people will be saved'.[180]

Bossy thus gave the *Narodnia gazeta* the mission of turning Ukrainian communist supporters into 'Canadian Laborites, interested in the future welfare of Canada'. That is what 'Ottawa' wanted from *Narodnia gazeta*, and that is why it had sponsored it with its 'own presses'. Only 'the spirit of Christian, Canadian patriotic and Social-Democratic ideals' should prevail among Ukrainian Canadians. Only 'loyalty to the labour cause and affection [to] the King!'. For such a task, *Narodnia gazeta* would work as a 'disinfecting' tool, 're-educating the Leftist ... force into good citizens in a sincere and intelligent manner'. That way, 'former Communists [would] relinquish their allegiance to Moscow and become loyal to Canada'.[181] Mead had 'absolute faith in [Bossy]', but he quickly observed that his friend was perhaps too passionate in criticizing the Ukrainian community and organizations associated with the UCC. The idea was that *Narodnia gazeta* pointed to the 'mistakes' some Ukrainians had made 'in sympathizing with this or any other alien movement to the detriment of the country'. However, Mead did not think attacking those former supporters would gain their trust in any way. And this was, after all, what the newspaper had to be used for in order to convert radicalized Ukrainian Canadians into loyal citizens.[182]

To this mild criticism, Bossy responded that he was not a 'business-man', but 'a Christian Canadian at war with Evils'.[183] Shortly thereafter, Mead decided to send Bossy a list of 'policy changes'. He asked Bossy to eliminate 'all controversial matters that may be prejudicial ... or offensive to patriotic-minded Ukrainians'. No other Ukrainians should be ridiculed in the content, thereby '[m]aintaining a respectful attitude towards all Ukrainian organizations and their leaders in Canada'. Mead believed that the aggressive editorial policy Bossy had followed so far was not anticipating any 'miraculous transition from Communism to Socialism'. The current approach made of the original goals something implausible. Therefore, a new policy should be designed to focus on 'purely instructive and constructive' content that highlighted 'the virtues of British democracy', 'Canadian citizenship', etc. Readers should be reoriented and rehabilitated, rather than confronted, '[f] or it was through their ignorance of these features in Canadian citizenship that most of them had been misled by radical demagogues'.[184]

A week later Bossy answered Mead stating that he agreed '100%' with the changes.[185] Three days after writing that letter, however, Bossy presented his resignation. He informed Mead that 'two days earlier' one of the 'local regiments' proposed him 'a Commission to join the Army'. Having received numerous letters of rejection for the position of Lieutenant, Bossy was instead offered a role 'in the capacity of Sergeant-Instructor' for the course 1940–1941 at the Loyola Contingent of Canadian Officers Training Corps (COTC).[186] Bossy trusted his job at the COTC would ultimately be to form men 'on the meaning of democracy and the reason why they were fighting', namely 'the forces of Christianity' in a 'new Crusade' against the 'anti-Christ of Nazism and Communism'.[187] After 'sound consideration', Bossy had decided to accept the proposal, which 'of course, automatically obliges me to sever all my connections with the People's Gazette'. Bossy argued that he 'prefer[red] to act and to feel only as a Canadian' and that was why he had decided to 'help Canada in a most realistic way – with the machine-gun unit'.[188] Mead answered the 'letter of resignation' with surprise, and confessed he 'did not expect it'. Mead, Bossy's old friend, the one who introduced Bossy to John J. Fitzgerald so that the Classocracy League of Canada could be constituted, thanked him 'for the work that you have done' and said he was 'very[,] very sorry that you were not able to see the thing through'.[189]

It wouldn't be until March 1943 that Bossy wrote to Mead again, this time asking the colonel to secure a copy of American Catholic bishop John F. Noll's *Civilization's Builder and Protector*, which both he and Fitzgerald had read.[190] Fitzgerald found Noll's book particularly encouraging given 'the work we have in hand'.[191] Essentially, *Civilization's Builder and Protector* urged bringing back the essence of the Middle Ages in order to stop social decay.[192] Specifically, as an antidote against modern decadence, class struggle and unrestrained capitalism Noll suggested the recovery of the medieval guilds.[193] The book concluded that only a guild system would ensure that all nations strive towards a common interest beyond 'their nationalism'; a common interest rooted in 'a common religion obligating all to love one another'.[194] From such interest, a new 'patriotism' rooted in a shared spirituality will be constituted.[195] Back in 1935, when *A Call to Socially Minded Christians Canadians* was published, 'the voice of the [*Montreal*] *Beacon* was unique', wrote Fitzgerald. Now, he observed, 'it has many echoes … the masses are ready'.[196]

Conclusion

This chapter shows that Bossy's allegiances between 1937 and the early 1940s resulted from a combination of personal sympathies and opportunism. Above all, he mostly focused on promoting his New Canadians project in Montreal and among French Canadians, publicly stressing their shared religious affiliation and minority status. In reality, however, Bossy knew that financial support from Quebec would only take place if he guaranteed that a collaboration between French Canadians and the 'New Canadians' would lead the former to increase their overall national influence. It is thus difficult to say whether Bossy ever thought of French Canada as a cultural and religious ally, or whether he was simply seeking to obtain enough regional support to fund his own political goals.

Chapter 3 also suggests that the minority status which Bossy experienced throughout his life both within and outside Canada could have been a major contributing factor to his embracing approaches to statecraft like classocracy, which *in theory* could help overcome ethnic and class conflict through cultural integration. Indeed, Bossy was born in Poland among a Ukrainian minority to an ethnically mixed marriage; migrated to an overwhelmingly French-speaking Canadian province; was friend to English-speaking Catholics mostly; and dedicated his life in Canada to the general improvement of 'New Canadians' as well as to the future of his Ukrainian community in Canada and abroad. That he had a blurred identity and conflicting loyalties is no wonder. And yet, it is possible that Bossy's complex identity was precisely what allowed him to strive for a system that could seemingly be more inclusive. By validating both Bossy's allegiance towards Canada, and his allegiance towards Ukraine, this chapter gives Bossy's political thought a chance to be transnational, and his identity a chance to be unfixed.

Notes

1. Bossy to Fitzgerald, July 30, 1937, file Correspondence Fitzgerald, J. J., 1935–1937, vol. 3, MG30 C72, LAC.
2. Bossy to Bryan, June 11, 1937, file Correspondence La Pierre, Edward 1935–1971, vol. 2, MG30 C72, LAC.
3. Ibid.; Bossy to Laprès, June 7, 1937, file Correspondence Laprès, J. A. 1937–1940, vol. 2, MG30 C72, LAC. The idea that the challenge of immigration must be dealt with through 'practical Christianity' is a crucial idea in the Canadian Social Gospel and is described as the pragmatic application of the Gospel principles. See, for example: John S. Moir, *Christianity in Canada: Historical Essays* (Yorkton: Redeemer's Voice Press, 2002), 21.
4. Bossy to the Comité D'Aide Aux Étrangers Catholiques, file Neo-Canadian Activities – New Canadian Friendship House, 1937, p. 10, vol. 4, MG30 C72, LAC.
5. Bossy to Bryan, June 11, 1937, file Correspondence La Pierre, Edward 1935–1971, vol. 2, MG30 C72, LAC.
6. Edward LaPierre seems to have 'elaborated' Bossy's original memorandum, according to Bossy's papers. See: Bossy to LaPierre, July 15, 1937, file Correspondence La Pierre, Edward 1935–1971, vol. 2, MG30 C72, LAC. From this letter we also know that RCMP colonel Jack F. Mead assisted Bossy 'in the preparation of the English copy'. See also: Bossy to Mead, July 16, 1937, file Correspondence Mead, F. J. 1933–1958, vol. 2, MG30 C72, LAC.
7. Bossy to the Comité D'Aide Aux Etrangers Catholiques, file Neo-Canadian Activities – New Canadian Friendship House, 1937, pp. 10, 15, vol. 4, MG30 C72, LAC; John J. Fitzgerald, "Vote Christianity", MN AP02.01 (McNeil Papers) ARCAT, an article that was to be published in the first edition of *The Friendship House News* (1934).
8. Bossy to the Comité D'Aide Aux Étrangers Catholiques, file Neo-Canadian Activities – New Canadian Friendship House, 1937, p. 13, vol. 4, MG30 C72, LAC.
9. Joseph P. Archambault, *Sous la menace rouge* (Montreal: École Sociale Populaire, 1936), 10.
10. For one thing, the memorandum was directed to the Comité D'Aide Aux Étrangers Catholiques, that is the Aid Committee for *Catholic* Foreigners. See Bossy's reference to 'all foreign groups' in p. 6 of it. For more on the Canadian Communist Party and the immigrant experience in it, see: Stephen Endicott,

Raising the Workers' Flag: The Workers' Unity League of Canada, 1930–1936 (Toronto: University of Toronto Press, 2012); Paula Maurutto, "Private Policing and Surveillance of Catholics: Anti-communism in the Roman Catholic Archdiocese of Toronto, 1920–1960", *Labour/Le Travail* (fall 1997): 113–36; Norman Penner, *Canadian communism: the Stain years and beyond* (Toronto: Methuen, 1988); Donald Avery, *Dangerous Foreigners: European Immigrant Workers and Labour Radicalism in Canada, 1896–1932* (Toronto: McClelland and Steward, 1979).

11. Bossy to the Comité D'Aide Aux Etrangers Catholiques, file Neo-Canadian Activities – New Canadian Friendship House, 1937, p. 1, vol. 4, MG30 C72, LAC.

12. Bossy to the Comité D'Aide Aux Etrangers Catholiques, file Neo-Canadian Activities – New Canadian Friendship House, 1937, p. 4, vol. 4, MG30 C72, LAC; Bossy to Maurice Julien, September 25, 1937, file Neo-Canadian Activities, New Canadian Federation Correspondence 1937–1941, vol. 4, MG30 C72, LAC.

13. Bossy to the Comité D'Aide Aux Etrangers Catholiques, file Neo-Canadian Activities – New Canadian Friendship House, 1937, p. 10, vol. 4, MG30 C72, LAC.

14. Bossy to the Comité D'Aide Aux Etrangers Catholiques, file Neo-Canadian Activities – New Canadian Friendship House, 1937, pp. 1, 6, vol. 4, MG30 C72, LAC.

15. Bossy to the Comité D'Aide Aux Etrangers Catholiques, file Neo-Canadian Activities – New Canadian Friendship House, 1937, p. 6, vol. 4, MG30 C72, LAC. It is worth mentioning that at the time it was not uncommon for charities and similar organizations to be sectarian. On the history of Black or African-Canadian cooperation, social welfare, and charities in Montreal, see: Carla Marano, "For the Freedom of the Black People: Case Studies on the Universal Negro Improvement Association in Canada, 1900–1950", dissertation (University of Waterloo, 2018); David Este, Christa Sato, Darcy McKenna, "The Coloured Women's Club of Montreal, 1902–1940. African-Canadian Women Confronting Anti-Black Racism", *Canadian Social Work Review*, vol. 34, no. 1 (August 29, 2017): 81–99. On charities, antisemitism, and Jewish organized benevolence and philanthropy in Montreal, see: Gerald J. J. Tulchinsky, *Taking Root: The Origins of the Canadian Jewish Community* (Toronto: Lester Publishing, 1992), 111–2; and also Bettina Bradbury, Tamara Myers, eds., *Negotiating Identities in 19*th *and 20*th *Century Montreal* (Vancouver: University of British Columbia, 2005), 179–80, 197. On the Montreal Chinese community and its internal structures of solidarity, see for example: Kwok B. Chan, *Smoke and Fire: The Chinese in Montreal* (Hong Kong: Chinese University Press, 1991).

16. Odale was also the head of Portland's secret police unit Red Squad, dedicated to investigating 'radical activity'. See: Paula Abrams, *Cross Purposes: Pierce V. Society of Sisters and the Struggle Over Compulsory Public Education* (Michigan: The University of Michigan Press, 2009), 66.

17. For more details on the literature by Adrien Arcand that Bossy was consuming at the time, see Chapters 2 and 4. In 1937, Bossy read Walter B. Odale, *Americanism or Communism?* (Cambridge: Harvard University Press, 1935), which argued specifically that each 'year a certain number of American negroes are sent to the Soviet Union, where they are schooled in the doctrines of Communism, and then sent back' (pp. 27–8). On Canadian Jews being considered enemies of Christian nations and Christianity, see: Alan Davies, ed., *Antisemitism in Canada: History and Interpretation* (Waterloo: Wilfrid Laurier University Press, 1992), 153–4; L. Ruth Klein, ed., *Nazi Germany, Canadian Responses: Confronting Antisemitism in the Shadow of War* (Montreal:

76 *Allegiances*

McGill-Queen's University Press, 2012), 221. On prejudices against Canadians of African or Asian descent, see: James Walker, *"Race", Rights and the Law in the Supreme Court of Canada* (Waterloo: Wilfrid Laurier University Press, 2006), 15; Timothy J. Stanley, "White Supremacy, Chinese Schooling, and School Segregation in Victoria: The Case of the Chinese Students' Strike, 1922–23", *Historical Studies in Education*, vol. 2, no. 2 (fall 1990): 44. It is worth highlighting that such prejudices were present in both sides of the political spectrum in Canada. For example, contemporary Canadian and social democrat James S. Woodsworth believed that 'people of colour were ... potentially if not actually depraved'. '[T]he Chinese, Japanese and Hindus' and the 'black' were 'detrimental to our highest national development, and hence should be vigorously excluded'. To Woodsworth, 'the expression "This is a white man's country" has a deeper significance than we sometimes imagine'. See: J. S. Woodsworth, *Strangers Within Our Gates* (Toronto: F.C. Stephenson, 1909), 279; Mariana Valverde, *The Age of Light, Soap, and Water: Moral Reform in English Canada 1885–1925* (Toronto: University of Toronto Press, 2008), 119.

18. *La Presse*, August 28, 1937, p. 30.
19. *Le Devoir*, September 27, 1937, p. 1. Emphasis in the original.
20. Ibid.
21. *L'Illustration Nouvelle*, September 2, 1937, p. 4.
22. Herbert F. Quinn to Editor of *The Montreal Daily Star*, September 20, 1937, file Neo-Canadian Activities, New Canadian Federation Correspondence 1937–1941, vol. 4, MG30 C72, LAC.
23. Quinn to Bossy, January 23, 1939, file Neo-Canadian Activities, New Canadian Federation Correspondence 1937–1941, vol. 4, MG30 C72, LAC. Quinn's "The Bogey of Fascism" was published in the *Oeuvre des Tracts* in December 1938, no. 234.
24. *The Christian Century*, November 25, 1936, p. 1560. On the demonstration, which took place on October 25, 1936, see, for example: Jacques Lacoursière, *Histoire populaire du Québec: 1896–1960* (Montreal: Septentrion, 1997), 232.
25. *The Christian Century*, November 25, 1936, p. 1561.
26. Herbert F. Quinn, "The Bogey of Fascism", *Oeuvre des Tracts*, no. 234 (December 1938): p. 1.
27. Quinn to Bossy, October 22, 1940, Neo-Canadian Activities, New Canadian Federation Correspondence, 1937–1941, vol. 4, MG30 C72, LAC.
28. Letter of approval from 'His Excellency', copy to Joseph P. Archambault from Walter J. Bossy, October 1937, file Neo-Canadian Activities, New Canadian Federation Correspondence 1937–1941, vol. 4, MG30 C72, LAC.
29. Bossy to Fitzgerald, July 30, 1937, file Correspondence Fitzgerald, J. J., 1935–1937, vol. 3, MG30 C72, LAC; Bossy to the National Employment Commission, ca. 1938, Allegeance Day Correspondence Sent 1938, vol. 4, MG30 C72, LAC.
30. Bossy to Fitzgerald, July 30, 1937, file Correspondence Fitzgerald, J. J., 1935–1937, vol. 3, MG30 C72, LAC.
31. Bossy to LaPierre, July 15, 1937, file Correspondence La Pierre, Edward 1935–1971, vol. 2, MG30 C72, LAC. See also: undated (ca. 1937), unsigned, directed to a 'Sir', file Neo-Canadian Activities, New Canadian Federation Correspondence, 1937–1940, vol. 4, MG30 C72, LAC.
32. Bossy to Fitzgerald, July 30, 1937, file Correspondence Fitzgerald, J. J., 1935–1937, vol. 3, MG30 C72, LAC.
33. Bossy also wanted to publish brochures addressing relevant issues such as the formation of a 'Canadian Christian Youth Movement'; the creation of 'study clubs to permeate the educational system with our ideas'; a 'National Code' defining 'the Canadian patriotism'; and 'Classocracy and the Jew'. I have found none of such brochures among Bossy's papers or anywhere else.

Allegiances 77

34. Bossy to Fitzgerald, July 30, 1937, file Correspondence Fitzgerald, J. J., 1935–1937, vol. 3, MG30 C72, LAC.
35. John J. Fitzgerald (in fact, Bossy and LaPierre), "One of Our New-Canadians", 1937, pp. 1–5, file Bossy, Walter J. Biographical Notes, 1912–1972, vol. 1, MG30 C72, LAC.
36. Ibid.
37. Ibid.
38. The melting pot is a metaphor for a heterogeneous society gradually becoming more homogeneous. It has been used by some to characterize the United States since the eighteenth century. The theory has been rejected by proponents of liberal multiculturalism, who suggest nurturing diversity instead. Nativist approaches to the melting pot include excluding 'undesirable' groups (European or not) from the melting pot.
39. David A. Hollinger, "Amalgamation and Hypodescent: The Question of Ethnoracial Mixture in the History of the United States", *The American Historical Review*, vol. 108, no. 5 (December 2003): 1366.
40. John J. Fitzgerald, "One of Our New-Canadians", 1937, pp. 1–5, file Bossy, Walter J. Biographical Notes, 1912–1972, vol. 1, MG30 C72, LAC.
41. Bossy to Gauthier, June 12, 1937, file Neo-Canadian Friendship House ca. 1936, vol. 4, MG30 C72, LAC.
42. Andrew L. Whitehead, Samuel L. Perry, *Taking America Back for God* (Oxford: Oxford University Press, 2020), 19–20.
43. Ibid., 21.
44. His work included visiting schools to verify statistics or to inspect special classes; interviewing the pupils; calling upon foreign parish priests to submit or to amplify lists; and calling upon families who require personal attention in the important matter of having their children sent to Catholic (MCSC) schools. See: Bossy, "Second Report, from January 1st to June 30th, 1937" to Victor Doré, General Chairman of the MCSC, file MCSC Correspondence file 1936–1939, vol. 9, MG30 C72, LAC.
45. Bossy was appointed Director of Foreign Classes in November 1936 by the Administrative Board of Montreal Catholic School Commission. See: Bossy to the MCSC, March 15, 1946, file MCSC Foreign Classes Administration 1937–1946, vol. 10, MG30 C72, LAC. Bossy was asked to take such a position by the Archbishop of Montreal Gauthier and the Committee of Foreign Catholic parish priests established that year. See: "An outline of creation and development of this special service Dept. –Since: November 1936 until June 1943", file MCSC Foreign Classes Administration 1937–1946, vol. 10, MG30 C72, LAC. In this file, the lists of districts, schools, teachers, and students inspected by Bossy between 1936 and 1943 are available. See details on 'foreign textbooks' noticed by Bossy in the above-mentioned "Second Report, from January 1st to June 30th, 1937" submitted to Mr. Victor Doré.
46. Bossy, "Second Report, from January 1st to June 30th, 1937" to Victor Doré, General Chairman of the MCSC, file MCSC Correspondence file 1936–1939, vol. 9, MG30 C72, LAC.
47. George Daly, *Catholic Problems in Western Canada* (Toronto: Macmillan, 1921), 85; Mark McGowan, "Toronto's English-Speaking Catholics, Immigration, and the Making of a Canadian Catholic Identity, 1900–1930", in Terrence Murphy and Gerald Stortz, eds., *Creed and Culture. The Place of English-speaking Catholics in Canadian Society 1750–1930* (Montreal: McGill-Queen's University Press, 1993), especially page 206.
48. Murphy, Stortz, eds., *Creed and Culture*, 219.
49. Ibid., 228–9.

50. Bossy to Gauthier, June 12, 1937, file Neo-Canadian Friendship House ca. 1936, vol. 4, MG30 C72, LAC.
51. Ibid. Bossy will maintain that 'the French-Canadians should become the sponsors and protectors and apostles' of 'this great body of fellow-Catholics and fellow-Canadians' to the detriment of English and Protestant influences which have generally dominated. See: Bossy to Armand Dupuis, August 18, 1939, file MCSC Correspondence file 1936–1939, vol. 9, MG30 C72, LAC.
52. Roberto Perin, "Adélard Langevin", *Dictionary of Canadian Biography*, vol. 14 (Toronto: University of Toronto/Université Laval, 2003). See also: Roberto Perin, "Saint-Boniface au coeur d'un catholicisme continental et pluraliste", *SCHEC, Études d'histoire religieuse*, vol. 85, nos. 1–2 (2019): 23–38.
53. Jean-François Nadeau, *The Canadian Führer: The Life of Adrian Arcand* (Montreal: Lux Éditeur, 2010), 29, 196.
54. Nadeau, *The Canadian Führer*, 168.
55. Ibid., 213–5.
56. Ibid., 215.
57. Jeannine Hill Fletcher, *The Sin of White Supremacism: Christianity, Racism, & Religious Diversity in America* (London: Orbis, 2017).
58. *Un Mouvement, Une Oeuvre, Walter J. Bossy, 25 ans au service des Néo-Canadiens (1925–1950)* (Montreal: Bureau du Service des Néo-Canadiens, 1950), 18, file New Canadians Service Bureau, vol. 5, MG30 C72, LAC.
59. Bossy to Gauthier, June 12, 1937, file Neo-Canadian Friendship House ca. 1936, vol. 4, MG30 C72, LAC; Bossy to Maurice Julien, September 25, 1937, file Neo-Canadian Activities, New Canadian Federation Correspondence 1937–1941, vol. 4, MG30 C72, LAC; Bossy to A. A. Gardiner, July 14, 1937, file MCSC Correspondence Sent About Memorandum 1937, vol. 9, MG30 C72, LAC.
60. Fitzgerald to Laprès, May 5, 1937, file Correspondence Laprès, J. A. 1937–1940, vol. 2, MG30 C72, LAC; Bossy to Laprès, June 7, 1937, file Correspondence Laprès, J. A. 1937–1940, vol. 2, MG30 C72, LAC.
61. Bossy to Bryan, June 11, 1937, file Correspondence La Pierre, Edward 1935–1971, vol. 2, MG30 C72, LAC.
62. LaPierre on behalf of the Catholic Standing Committee to Adolph L'Archevêque Pedagogical Council, of the Catholic School Commission in Montreal, November 20, 1937 (?), file Correspondence La Pierre, Edward 1935–1971, vol. 2, MG30 C72, LAC.
63. "The Naturalization Act, 1914", *Department of the Secretary of State* (1921), no. 0022, p. 330. See also *Sessional Papers of the Parliament of the Dominion of Canada* (1921), vol. 57, no. 8, p. 330. The death date and professional position may be found in: *Pit and Quarry*, vol. 49, no. 2 (1957), p. 56. Birth date and other details, like the fact that he was a Catholic French-Canadian born in Valleyfield (Quebec) and that his wartime occupation was working as a nurse, here: "Attestation Paper" from Military Records (LAC), no. 3155896 (retrieved in July 2019). On Laprès' positions at the time, see: LaPierre on behalf of the Catholic Standing Committee to Adolph L'Archevêque Pedagogical Council, of the Catholic School Commission in Montreal, November 20, 1937 (?), file Correspondence La Pierre, Edward 1935–1971, vol. 2, MG30 C72, LAC; *Industrial Canada*, vol. 47, nos. 1–6 (1946), p. 87. The *Proceedings of Annual Convention of the Association of Highway Officials of the North Atlantic States*, 1939, mentions Laprès being Sales Manager for Canada Cement Co in Montreal at the time. *The Rotarian* (April 1949) mentions J. Arthur Laprès as the Past President of the Rotary Club, in p. 47. The Letter from John (as signed) to Laprèss [sic], marked as "Personal", May 5, 1937, file Correspondence Laprès, J. A. 1937–1940, vol. 2, MG30 C72, LAC, infers that Laprès had

Allegiances 79

met Edward LaPierre and Walter J. Bossy through John J. Fitzgerald with the object of learning more about their Classocratic project. Beginning with summer 1937, Laprès would regularly meet with Bossy, La Pierre, and Mead in Montreal to discuss their plans for anti-communist action based on the Classocratic ideal, as shown by: Bossy to Fitzgerald, July 14, 1937, file Correspondence Fitzgerald, J. J., 1935–1937, vol. 3, MG30 C72, LAC. By the end of July 1937, Bossy was including the name of 'Arthur' along with that of Mead, Edward, and John when referring to 'our group'. See: Bossy to Fitzgerald, July 30, 1937, file Correspondence Fitzgerald, J. J., 1935–1937, vol. 3, MG30 C72, LAC. On Laprès being a member of the Board Room of the Montreal City & District Savings Bank, see: *The Municipal Review of Canada* (1949), vols. 45–7. Laprès will later become the president of H. J. O'Connell Ltd. road contractors and the representative of organized employers for the Canadian Construction Association. See: *The Labour Gazette*, vol. 52, no. 4, p. 427; and *Engineering and Contract Record*, vol. 67, no. 1, p. 120.

64. Fitzgerald to Laprès, May 5, 1937, file Correspondence Laprès, J. A. 1937–1940, vol. 2, MG30 C72, LAC; Bossy to Laprès, June 7, 1937, file Correspondence Laprès, J. A. 1937–1940, vol. 2, MG30 C72, LAC.
65. Terence J. Fay, *A History of Canadian Catholics* (Montreal: McGill-Queen's University Press, 2002), 239.
66. Memorandum Re Organization to Promote Industrial Peace in Ontario and Quebec, May 5, 1937, p. 1, file Correspondence Laprès, J. A. 1937–1940, vol. 2, MG30 C72, LAC.
67. David Evans, *Mussolini's Italy* (Pennsylvania: McGraw-Hill Companies, 2005); Jules Archer, *Twentieth-Century Caesar: Benito Mussolini* (NZ: Bailey Bros and Swinfen, 1972); Robert Edwin Herzstein, *Western Civilization: From the seventeenth century to the present* (Boston: Houghton Mifflin, 1975), 632.
68. Memorandum Re Organization to Promote Industrial Peace in Ontario and Quebec, May 5, 1937, p. 1, file Correspondence Laprès, J. A. 1937–1940, vol. 2, MG30 C72, LAC.
69. Memorandum Re Organization to Promote Industrial Peace in Ontario and Quebec, May 5, 1937, file Correspondence Laprès, J. A. 1937–1940, vol. 2, MG30 C72, LAC, 2, 3.
70. The idea of looking at the United States to better tackle with Canadian specificities was not uncommon. See, for example, J. S. Woodsworth's *Strangers Within Our Gates* (1909): 'Much may be learned from the United States, where conditions similar to our own have existed for some years' (page 6).
71. On Walter B. Odale, see: Paula Abrams, *Cross Purposes: Pierce v. Society of Sisters and the Struggle Over Compulsory Public Education* (Michigan: University of Michigan Press, 2009), 66–7.
72. Walter B. Odale, *Americanism or Communism?* (Portland: Priv. Printed, 1935), 30, 47. In the United States as elsewhere, anti-Communism related Communism with the 'foreign' element mainly due to the former's internationalist nature and its Moscow-oriented character. Associations between communism and the immigrant communities may thus be first established by perceiving both as *foreign*, thereby ascribing radical political tendencies to ethnicities perceived as alien. On anti-communism and the immigrant experience in Canada, see: Donald Avery, *Dangerous Foreigners: European Immigrant Workers and Labour Radicalism in Canada, 1896–1932* (Toronto: McClelland and Steward, 1979); Lita-Rose Betcherman, *The Swastika and the Maple Leaf: Fascist movements in Canada in the thirties* (Toronto: Fitzhenry & Whiteside, 1978); Stephen Endicott Lyon, *Raising the Workers' Flag: The Workers' Unity League of Canada, 1930–1936* (Toronto: University of Toronto Press, 2012); Andreé Levesque, *Virage à Gauche Interdit: les communistes, les socialistes et*

leurs ennemis au Québec, 1929–1939 (Montréal: Boréal Express, 1984); Robin Martin, *Shades of Right: nativist and fascist politics in Canada, 1920–1940* (Toronto: University of Toronto Press, 1992); Norman Penner, *Canadian Communism: the Stalin years and beyond* (Toronto: Methuen, 1988).
73. Odale, *Americanism or Communism?*, 42.
74. Specifically, Odale stated that 'For Communists, pinks, liberals, and other admirers and defenders of the Soviet System to claim that they are representative of true Americanism is just about as logical as the idea of riding two horses that are going in opposite directions. It simply cannot be done.' See: Odale, *Americanism or Communism?*, 47.
75. Odale, *Americanism or Communism?*, 44.
76. Hladun's confession would be retrieved once again in the wake of the Igor Gouzenko affair. The article "They Taught Me Treason", published in *Macleans* by John Hladun on October 1, 1947, elaborates on his early confession entitled "I Was a Communist Agitator" published in 1937. As I was unable to find the original confession, I relied on this later version for my analysis.
77. The ULFTA was a Canadian national organization with strong ties with the 'Old Continent' whose mission was to 'give moral and material aid to the Ukrainian working people and to the labour cause in general through ... educational, cultural, and mutual aid activities'. See: Ukrainian Labour Temple Association, "Constitution" (adopted at the First Convention of the ULTA, 16–18 January 1920, Winnipeg), cited in Rhonda Hinther and Jim Mochoruk, eds., *Re-Imagining Ukrainian Canadians: History, Politics, and Identity* (Toronto: University of Toronto Press, 2010), 336. Notice point 10: 'To give every necessary aid to Ukrainian workers and farmers who live in Canada, as well as those who arrive in Canada or are leaving Canada'.
78. *Macleans*, "They Taught Me Treason", John Hladun, October 1, 1947, pp. 7, 76. Apparently, the perfect English in which Hladun expresses himself in this article is the result of in-depth editing by *Maclean's* editor Blair Fraser, which hid Hladun's 'semi-articulate sentences in broken English'. See: Stephen Endicott (2012), 344.
79. *Macleans*, "They Taught Me Treason", John Hladun, October 1, 1947, p. 76.
80. Ibid., p. 83.
81. Ibid., p. 21.
82. Ben Gold, appellant v. United States of America, appellee: in the United States Court of Appeals for the District of Columbia Circuit, no. 12, 352: brief for appellant, p. 116.
83. *Macleans*, "They Taught Me Treason", John Hladun, October 1, 1947, p. 76.
84. Ben Gold, appellant v. United States of America, appellee: in the United States Court of Appeals for the District of Columbia Circuit, no. 12, 352: brief for appellant, p. 116. Hladun narrated how he had explained to the Russians that the Canadian government was giving five dollars a week for groceries as relief, to which the Communists had shouted: 'Why do you come here telling us stories about privation and the economic crisis in America? Your workers are living in a paradise. We miners are supposed to be first-class labor, but we do not get half the food that your unemployed get. Do you know what we eat? Cabbage soup! Then more cabbage soup!'. See: *Macleans*, "They Taught Me Treason", John Hladun, November 1, 1947, p. 52.
85. Fitzgerald to Bossy, June 2, 1937, file Correspondence Fitzgerald, J. J., 1935–1937, vol. 3, MG30 C72, LAC.
86. Robert H. Zieger, *The CIO, 1935–1955* (US: The University of North Carolina Press, 1995), 22. See also: Committee for Industrial Organization, *The C.I.O. What It Is and How It Came to Be. A Brief History of the Committee for Industrial Organization* (October 1937), 5–6.

87. Research Committee of the League for Social Reconstruction (authors of *Social Planning for Canada*), *Democracy Needs Socialism* (Toronto: Thomas Nelson: 1938), 82; Irving Abella, "Oshawa Strike", *The Canadian Encyclopedia*, (February 7, 2006).
88. Fitzgerald to LaPierre and Bossy, July 24, 1937, file Correspondence Fitzgerald, J. J., 1935–1937, vol. 3, MG30 C72, LAC; Fitzgerald to Laprès, May 5, 1937, file Correspondence Laprès, J. A. 1937–1940, vol. 2, MG30 C72, LAC; Bossy to Laprès, June 7, 1937, file Correspondence Laprès, J. A. 1937–1940, vol. 2, MG30 C72, LAC; Fitzgerald to Bossy, June 2, 1937, file Correspondence Fitzgerald, J. J., 1935–1937, vol. 3, MG30 C72, LAC. Fitzgerald ordered ten copies of 'the CIO booklet', and 'three additional copies of "Communism or Americanism"'. See: Fitzgerald to Bossy, June 2, 1937, file Correspondence Fitzgerald, J. J., 1935–1937, vol. 3, MG30 C72, LAC.
89. Bossy to Laprès, June 23, 1937, file Correspondence Laprès, J. A. 1937–1940, vol. 2, MG30 C72, LAC.
90. Fitzgerald to LaPierre and Bossy, July 24, 1937, file Correspondence Fitzgerald, J. J., 1935–1937, vol. 3, MG30 C72, LAC. On June 11, 1937, file Correspondence LaPierre, vol. 2, LaPierre notes that he received $5.00 from Bossy and $10.00 from Fitzgerald towards 'The Canadian Classocrat'. The journal was to be released weekly, as explained in: Bossy to Fitzgerald, July 30, 1937, file Correspondence Fitzgerald, J. J., 1935–1937, vol. 3, MG30 C72, LAC. The League's previous office, situated at 6274 De Normanville Str. (La Petite-Patrie, Montreal), may have been too expensive, which would explain why Fitzgerald was asking Laprès 'to secure free quarters'.
91. Fitzgerald to LaPierre and Bossy, July 24, 1937, file Correspondence Fitzgerald, J. J., 1935–1937, vol. 3, MG30 C72, LAC.
92. Laprès was the vice-president of the City Improvement League in 1926 and until 1950 at least, as indicated in: Gabriel Rioux, "Le milieu de l'urbanisme à Montréal (1897–1941): histoire d'une 'refondation'", dissertation, (Université Panthéon-Sorbonne – Paris I; Université du Québec à Montréal. Département d'histoire, 2013), 332 (Appendix E).
93. LaPierre to Bossy, November 13, 1938, file Neo-Canadian Activities, New Canadian Federation Correspondence 1937–1941, vol. 4, MG30 C72, LAC. On Smyth's descent, see: *Le Devoir*, June 16, 1964, which indicates that Smyth was buried in St. Patrick's Basilica of Montreal, the 'National Church for the Irish population of Montreal'. See: Robert J. Grace, *The Irish in Quebec: An Introduction to the Historiography* (Quebec: Institut québécois de Recherche sur la Culture, 1993), 98, which indicates that Rome declared St. Patrick a 'national parish' for the 'Hibernienses' (Irish Catholics) of Montreal in 1874; Jean-Pierre Wallot, Pierre Lanthier, Hubert Watelet, *Constructions identitaires et pratiques sociales* (Ottawa: Presses de l'Université d'Ottawa, 2002), 205, 216; Camille Harrigan, "Storied Stones : St. Patrick's Basilica. History, Identity, and Memory in Irish Montréal, 1847–2017", Master's thesis (Concordia University, 2018). Taggart Smyth was also the General Manager of the Montreal City and District Savings Bank, the 'first successful one of its kind [that] had a conspicuous [French and English] Irish-Catholic core in its directorate' from its beginnings – although the presence of Anglicans, Presbyterians and Unitarians among the early honorary directors and managing directors shows a clear cooperation among different Irish religious groups. It was a bank that functioned in both French and English and was from the outset a bank for '... the industrious classes, and not a Bank of Deposit for the wealthy'. See: *Le Devoir*, November 9, 1938, p. 3; Grace, *The Irish in Quebec*, 92, 103–4; John Irwin Cooper, "The Origins and Early History of the Montreal City and District Savings Back 1846–1871", *CCHA Report*, 13, 460

82 *Allegiances*

(1945): 15–25. Cooper argues that the bank may be considered 'a benefit society' (p. 16). Finally, Smyth was also member of the Université de Montréal's Council, as shown in: *Le Devoir*, November 9, 1938, p. 3. On Smyth being the leader of the Canadian branch of the Friends of National Spain, see: Bàrbara Molas, "Transnational Francoism: The British and the Canadian Friends of National Spain", *Contemporary British History*, vol. 35, no. 2 (August 4, 2020): 165–86.

94. LaPierre on behalf of the Catholic Standing Committee to Adolph L'Archeveque Pedagogical Council, of the Catholic School Commission in Montreal, November 20, 1937 (?), file Correspondence La Pierre, Edward 1935–1971, vol. 2, MG30 C72, LAC. It is in file 'Fitzgerald Correspondence of 1937' that Bossy mentions LaPierre becoming secretary of 'the Committee', see: vol. 3, MG30 C72, LAC. See also: Bossy to LaPierre, August 16, 1937, file Correspondence Fitzgerald, J. J., 1935–1937, vol. 3, MG30 C72, LAC. Interestingly, the Dutch Canadian Club in Montreal also encouraged the cooperation between the New Canadians movement and the CIL, see: LaPierre to Bossy, November 13, 1938, file Neo-Canadian Activities, New Canadian Federation Correspondence 1937–1941, vol. 4, MG30 C72, LAC.
95. See: "Liste de souscripteurs du Bureau des Néo-Canadiens" 1951, file New Canadians Service Bureau Lists of Contributors 1948–1952, vol. 6, MG30 C72, LAC; and "Liste de souscripteurs du Bureau des Néo-Canadiens" 1948, 1949–1950, 1951, file New Canadians Service Bureau Lists of Contributors 1948–1952, vol. 6, MG30 C72, LAC.
96. What is said is that 'according to our [Mead, Laprès, Bossy, and LaPierre] last night's conversation, [Edward] has a good chance to become a secretary of the Committee'. The only person that could have helped LaPierre obtain that position was Laprès, given that he was the only Classocrat who already was a prominent member of such a committee. See: Bossy to Fitzgerald, July 30, 1937, file Correspondence Fitzgerald, J. J., 1935–1937, vol. 3, MG30 C72, LAC.
97. Bossy to Fitzgerald, July 30, 1937, file Correspondence Fitzgerald, J. J., 1935–1937, vol. 3, MG30 C72, LAC.
98. Ibid.
99. Ibid.
100. Ibid.
101. Myra Rutherdale and Jim Miller, "'It's Our Country': First Nations' Participation in the Indian Pavilion at Expo 67", *Journal of the Canadian Historical Association / Revue de la Société historique du Canada*, vol. 17, no. 2 (2006): 149. See also: Gary Miedema, "For Canada's Sake: The Centennial Celebrations of 1967, State Legitimation and the Restructuring of Canadian Public Life", *Journal of Canadian Studies*, 34 (spring 1999): 1; and Eva-Marie Kröller, "*Le Mouton de Troie:* Changes in Quebec Cultural Symbolism", *American Review of Canadian Studies*, vol. 27, no. 4 (1997): 526.
102. Catherine Hall, *Civilizing Subjects: Metropole and Colony in the English Imagination, 1830–1867* (Chicago: University of Chicago Press, 2002), 20.
103. New Canadians Allegiance Day Initiating Committee to *The New Canadians* (Toronto), May 21, 1938, file Allegeance Day Correspondence Sent, 1938, vol. 4, MG30 C72, LAC.
104. LaPierre to the Governor General of Canada, July 13, 1938, file Allegeance Day Correspondence Sent, 1938, vol. 4, MG30 C72, LAC.
105. John Murray Gibbon, *Canadian Mosaic. The Making of a Northern Nation* (London: J. M. Dent & Sons Ltd., 1939), 425.
106. Whether this would be a statutory holiday, at the provincial or at the federal level, is never specified.

Allegiances 83

107. *New Canadians' Allegiance Day. General Plan of Celebration*, 1938, pp. 5–6, file Allegeance Day Plans Publicity, Speeches, 1938, vol. 4, MG30 C72, LAC. See also: LaPierre to the Governor General of Canada, July 13, 1938, file Allegeance Day Correspondence Sent, 1938, vol. 4, MG30 C72, LAC. Although King George VI was born on December 14, 1895, he celebrated his birthday the second week of June during his reign; *New Canadians' Allegiance Day. General Plan of Celebration*, 1938, p. 3, file Allegeance Day Plans Publicity, Speeches, 1938, vol. 4, MG30 C72, LAC.
108. "Report", Bossy to Director of Studies at MCSC J. M. Manning, June 30, 1938, file MCSC Correspondence file 1936–1939, vol. 9, MG30 C72, LAC; "Notes and Instructions", *New Canadians' Allegiance Day. General Plan of Celebration*, 1938, p. 15, file Allegeance Day Plans Publicity, Speeches, 1938, vol. 4, MG30 C72, LAC. Emphasis in the original.
109. Fitzgerald to Peverne, May 27, 1938, in file Correspondence Fitzgerald, J. J., 1938–1941, vol. 3, MG30 C72, LAC. My emphasis.
110. "General Declaration of New Canadians Respecting Their Place In The National Life of Canada And Their Project Of An Annual 'New Canadians' Allegiance Day", ca. June 1938, file Allegeance Day Plans Publicity, Speeches, 1938, vol. 4, MG30 C72, LAC, supposedly signed by 'the signatures of local New Canadians, particularly those of officers of existing organizations' according to 'Notes and Instructions' in the same file.
111. "Jean-Joseph Penverne", Canadian Elections Database. Information retrieved in August 2019; LaPierre to Bossy, November 13, 1938, file Neo-Canadian Activities, New Canadian Federation Correspondence 1937–1941, vol. 4, MG30 C72, LAC.
112. *Report of the Chief Electoral Office* (1941), 674; *La Revue du barreau* (1975), vol. 35, p. 415. Bossy and Penverne had known each other at least since the 1935 federal elections, Bossy had received a letter from the Conservative Party asking him to 'expose the policies' of the party 'to the electors of Ukrainian extraction in the Outremont district'. Bossy had responded that 'as a Classocrat, I am opposed to the whole party system as being, in our complex modern societies, no longer truly representative, and therefore no longer truly democratic.' However, he added, he would be willing to 'investigate conditions and estimate possibilities' among Ukrainian electors. He admitted that after years of 'laboring for and among my people, as editor, lecturer, pamphleteer, author and organizer', he had the capacity to influence the 400,000 Ukrainian-Canadians that composed his community. 'My people know that I have never taken part in political activities in the sense of party politics; they all know me to be a convinced Classocrat', he explained. Nonetheless, he also pointed out that 'If you asked me personally [...] I would not vote Liberal'. According to Bossy, those words produced an effect among the Ukrainian community and weakened the Liberal candidate. See: Bossy to Penverne, October 2, 1935, file Political Activities Correspondence 1930–1965, vol. 8, MG30 C72, LAC.
113. "Report", Bossy to Director of Studies at MCSC J. M. Manning, June 30, 1938, file MCSC Correspondence file 1936–1939, vol. 9, MG30 C72, LAC; *Le Devoir*, May 28, 1938, p. 3. My emphasis.
114. "Report", Bossy as Auxiliary Assistant for foreign classes to Director of Studies at MSCS J. M. Manning, June 30, 1938, file MCSC Correspondence file 1936–1939, vol. 9, MG30 C72, LAC.
115. *Le Devoir*, June 10, 1938, p. 2.
116. Bossy (?), signed "Demonstration. Foreign Catholic Populations. Notre Dame Church, Montreal, Que., December 6th 1936", file Allegiance Day Plans Publicity, Speeches, 1938, file Allegeance Day Plans, Publicity, Speeches 1938, vol. 4, MG30 C72, LAC.

117. Bossy to President of the MSCS Armand Dupuis, August 18, 1939, file MCSC Correspondence 1936–1939, vol. 9, MG30 C72, LAC.
118. Letter of approval from 'His Excellency', copy to Joseph P. Archambault from Walter J. Bossy, October 1937, file Neo-Canadian Activities, New Canadian Federation Correspondence 1937–1941, vol. 4, MG30 C72, LAC.
119. Bossy to President de la Conférence de S. Vincent Paul Maurice Julien, September 25, 1937, file Neo-Canadian Activities, New Canadian Federation Correspondence 1937–1941, vol. 4, MG30 C72, LAC.
120. "Order of March of National Groups partaking in New Canadians' Allegiance Day", file Allegeance Day Plans, Publicity, Speeches 1938, vol. 4, MG30 C72, LAC.
121. File The New Canadians Allegiance Day Committee, Montreal, July 7, 1938, vol. 4, Neo-Canadian Activities, New Canadian Federation Correspondence 1937–1941, MG30 C72, LAC; "The New Canadians present First International Film Festival November 1938 to March 1939", file Allegeance Day Plans, Publicity, Speeches 1938, vol. 4, MG30 C72, LAC.
122. *Un Mouvement, Une Oeuvre*, 30–1, file New Canadians Service Bureau, vol. 5, MG30 C72, LAC.
123. Ibid.
124. Note that most Syrians who settled in Canada from the 1880s until the 1960s were of the Christian faith. See: Jean Leonard Elliott, *Two Nations, Many Cultures: Ethnic Groups in Canada* (Scarborough: Prentice-Hall of Canada, 1983), 468–72.
125. Sarah Gualtieri, "Becoming 'White': Race, Religion and the Foundations of Syrian/Lebanese Ethnicity in the United States", *Journal of American Ethnic History*, vol. 20, no. 4 (summer 2001): 41–3.
126. The use of the verb 'colonizing' and not 'migrating', for example, denotes the idea that English and French were Christian soldiers taking possession of land guided 'by an unshakable hermeneutic of Providence'. See: Jeannine Fletcher Hill, *The Sin of White Supremacy: Christianity, Racism, & Religious Diversity in America* (New York: Orbis Books, 2017). This is a view defended by Canadian J. S. Woodsworth, for example, who uses American Phillips Brooks' to justify restricted immigration: 'No nation, as no man, has a right to take possession of a choice bit of God's earth, to exclude the foreigner from its territory [...] But if to this particular nation there has been given the development of a certain part of God's earth for universal purposes; if the world, in the great march of centuries, is going to be richer for the development of a certain national character, built up by a larger type of manhood here, then for the world's sake, for the sake of every nation that would pour in upon it that which would disturb that development, we have a right to stand guard over it' (*Strangers Within Our Gates*, 1909, 277–8).
127. "Order of March of National Groups partaking in New Canadians' Allegiance Day", file Allegeance Day Plans Publicity, Speeches, 1938, vol. 4, MG30 C72, LAC; *New Canadians' Allegiance Day. General Plan of Celebration*, 1938, p. 2, vol. 4, MG30 C72, LAC. Although the Plan lists a total of 19 nationalities, future reports would point at the presence of twelve nationalities in total. See: *Un Mouvement, Une Oeuvre*, 19, file New Canadians Service Bureau, vol. 5, MG30 C72, LAC.
128. *New Canadians' Allegiance Day. General Plan of Celebration*, 1938, p. 2, vol. 4, MG30 C72, LAC.
129. Ibid., p. 3.
130. LaPierre to Adhemar Raynault, July 13, 1938, file Allegeance Day Correspondence Sent, 1938, vol. 4, MG30 C72, LAC; *Le Devoir*, June 8, 1938, p. 10; *L'Illustration Nouvelle*, June 8, 1938, p. 4.

Allegiances 85

131. Raynault to Bossy, May 6, 1938, file Allegeance Day Correspondence Sent, 1938, vol. 4, MG30 C72, LAC. See: the 'New Canadian communities in all the cities of this country are being urged to follow the example of their fellow citizens of the metropolis who this year on His Majesty's Birthday proceeded in public parade through the streets to gather around the Cenotaph dedicated to the Great War dead' in: LaPierre (Provisional Committee, New Canadians' Allegiance Day) to the Governor General of Canada, July 13, 1938, file Allegeance Day Correspondence Sent, 1938, vol. 4, MG30 C72, LAC. The event didn't take place the following summer, either in Montreal or anywhere else, due to the lack of funds and the prospect of war. See: file Neo-Canadian Activities, New Canadian Federation Correspondence 1937–1941 (1939), vol. 4, MG30 C72, LAC.
132. John Murray Gibbon, *Canadian Mosaic. The Making of a Northern Nation* (London: J. M. Dent & Sons Ltd., 1939), 425.
133. *The Toronto Daily Star,* June 25, 1938, p. 8.
134. *The Toronto Daily Star,* July 2, 1938, p. 25.
135. Ibid.
136. The local press didn't record any events taking place in 1939 that featured a similar multicultural parade celebrating cultural diversity and the New Canadians' allegiance to Canada, or that referred to the event organized the previous year as a precedent. For an elaborate collection and analysis of 'minority festivals' in Canada in the twentieth century in relation to nation-building, see: Lianbi Zhu, "National Holidays and Minority Festivals in Canadian Nation-building", dissertation (University of Sheffield, January 2012). Zhu doesn't mention Montreal's Allegiance Day in June 1938 or of Toronto's Folk Festival in July 1938.
137. R. D. Francis, Richard Jones and Donald B. Smith, *Journeys: A History of Canada* (Toronto: Nelson Education, 2009), 493–4.
138. LaPierre to Penverne, February 8, 1939, file Neo-Canadian Activities, New Canadian Federation Correspondence 1937–1941, vol. 4, MG30 C72, LAC; "General Declaration of New Canadians Respecting Their Place In The National Life of Canada And Their Project Of An Annual 'New Canadians' Allegiance Day", ca. June 1938, file Allegeance Day Plans Publicity, Speeches, 1938, p. 9, vol. 4, MG30 C72, LAC. My emphasis.
139. See copies of the Federation of New Canadians letterhead, with slogan and members of the Permanent Committee in the same folder. The organization's legal adviser was fervent anti-communist and School Commissioner G. A. Coughlin. See: LaPierre to Gerald A. Coughlin, February 8, 1939, file Neo-Canadian Activities, New Canadian Federation Correspondence 1937–1941, vol. 4, MG30 C72, LAC.
140. The Irish referred in this founding letter are the ones whose ancestors come from Protestant Northern Ireland (1921), as specified in a letter from Edward LaPierre as Secretary of the New Canadians Federation to the Secretary of State Fernand Rinfret in April 27, 1939, file Neo-Canadian Activities, New Canadian Federation Correspondence 1937–1941, vol. 4, MG30 C72, LAC. In this letter, the 'New Canadians' are described as of origins other than British or French, for which the Republic of Ireland would not be included, the Irish Catholic being thus considered 'New Canadians'.
141. Founding Letter in file Neo-Canadian Activities, New Canadians Federation, New Canadian Federation Correspondence 1937–1941, vol. 4, MG30 C72, LAC. My emphasis.
142. Ibid. See also the copy of the letter from Edward LaPierre to the Governor General of Canada signed in 13 July 1938, file Allegeance Day Correspondence Sent, 1938, vol. 4, MG30 C72, LAC, in which the same aims (integrity of the British Empire under the King-Emperor; unity of Canada; maintenance

of the national institutions of Canada: social, legal, religious; integral social justice: the good life for all) are listed, proving a direct connection between the Allegiance Movement and the soon-to-be-established New Canadians Federation.

143. March 8, 1939, file Neo-Canadian Activities, New Canadian Federation Correspondence 1937–1941, vol. 4, MG30 C72, LAC.
144. Bossy to Dupuis, August 18, 1939, file MCSC Correspondence file 1936–1939, vol. 9, MG30 C72, LAC.
145. *Le Canada*, January 10, 1940, p. 14. See also: *Le Devoir*, March 14, 1940, p. 1.
146. References to Durand's *nom de plume* in: *La Revue Légale* (1945), p. 162.
147. *Le Bien Public*, January 18, 1940, p. 1.
148. Frédéric Boily, *La pensée nationaliste de Lionel Groulx* (Quebec City: Septentrion, 2003), 46, 164.
149. "The New Canadians", June 1948, page (?), in *Un Mouvement, Une Oeuvre*, 16–7, file New Canadians Service Bureau, vol. 5, MG30 C72, LAC. Korchinsky will become the editor of *Ukrainian Toiler* in 1948, see: *Opinion: Official Publication of Ukrainian Canadian Veterans' Association*, vols. 3–5 (UCVA, 1947), p. 42.
150. *Le Devoir*, May 14, 1949, p. 1.
151. *Un Mouvement, Une Oeuvre*, 19, file New Canadians Service Bureau, vol. 5, MG30 C72, LAC. This book also specifies that Bossy will resume his position at the MCSC in summer of 1947. See also: Mead to Bossy, September 12, 1939, file Correspondence Mead, F. J. 1933–1958, vol. 2, MG30 C72, LAC.
152. The Skoropadsky family traces its origins back to the seventeenth century, when the semi-elective sovereignty or Hetmanship of Ukraine elected Ivan Skoropadsky as the new ruler. Ivan Skoropadsky was the last sovereign of an independent Ukraine until 1918, when his descendant Pavlo Skoropadsky, father of Prince Danylo, became Hetman of Ukraine. See: "Heir to the Throne of the Ukraine", file Neo-Canadian Activities Correspondence with United Hetman Organization 1924–1953, vol. 4, MG30 C72, LAC.
153. Jars Balan, *Salt and Braided Bread: Ukrainian Life in Canada* (Oxford: Oxford University Press, 1984), 35; Thomas M. Prymak, *Gathering a Heritage: Ukrainian, Slavonic, and Ethnic Canada and the USA* (Oxford: Oxford University Press, 1984), 86; Jim Mochoruk and Rhonda L. Hinther, eds., *Re-Imagining Ukrainian Canadians: History, Politics, and Identity* (Toronto: University of Toronto Press, 2011), 175; Manoly R. Lupul, *A Heritage in Transition: Essays in the History of Ukrainians in Canada* (Toronto: McClelland and Stewart, 1982), 156; "Interview", April 1972, file Bossy, Walter J. Biographical Notes, 1912–1972, vol. 1, MG30 C72, LAC. In 1939, when there were more than 300,000 Ukrainians in Canada, UHO membership stood at about 500, according to Orest T- Martynowych, as cited in: Mochoruk and Hinther, eds., *Re-Imagining Ukrainian Canadians*, 198.
154. The Hetman was also being tolerated by Hitler by his living in Berlin. On Nazi sympathies among Hetmanites, see: Mochoruk and Hinther, *Re-Imagining Ukrainian Canadians*, 180–5.
155. Mochoruk and Hinther, *Re-Imagining Ukrainian Canadians*, 181–2.
156. *L'Action Catholique*, February 4, 1938, p. 22. Apparently, the tour involved stops in New York, Chicago, Detroit, Cleveland, Philadelphia, Windsor, Toronto, Ottawa, Montreal, Sudbury, and Winnipeg. See: *Le Devoir*, November 29, 1937, p. 3.
157. Mochoruk and Hinther, *Re-Imagining Ukrainian Canadians*, 183.
158. *L'Action Catholique*, February 4, 1938, p. 22; *Le Devoir*, January 28, 1938, p. 7.

159. While in 1939 private correspondence Bossy states that Skoropadsky stayed with him 'for a couple of weeks', in later recollections he affirms he stayed 'three months'. The former seems much more coherent, given that supposedly the prince spent a total of two months touring North America. On the other hand, it seems certain that Skoropadsky was in the city at least on three occasions during the 1937–1938 winter that spanned about four months. Possibly, Skoropadsky could have stayed with Bossy intermittently. See: Bossy to Mead, June 23, 1939, file Correspondence Mead, F. J. 1933–1958, vol. 2, MG30 C72, LAC; *Un Mouvement, Une Oeuvre*, 18, file New Canadians Service Bureau, vol. 5, MG30 C72, LAC. For more news from Skoropadsky "de passage à" Montreal see: *Le Devoir*, November 29, 1937, p. 3; *La Presse*, November 30, 1937, p. 24; *Le Soleil*, December 1, 1937, p. 6; *L'Illustration Nouvelle*, December 1, 1937, p. 7; *L'Illustration Nouvelle*, December 3, 1937, p. 8; *Le Canada*, December 28, 1937, p. 10; *Le Devoir*, January 28, 1938, p. 7; *L'Illustration Nouvelle*, January 28, 1938, p. 10; *L'Illustration Nouvelle*, March 7, 1938, p. 17. To see a photo of Skoropadsky's arrival to Montreal, in which Bossy appears to have been waiting for him, see: *L'Illustration Nouvelle*, November 29, 1937, p. 1.
160. File Ukrainian, vol. 14, MG30 C72, LAC, contains some information in Ukrainian on Bossy's acquaintance with Arcand. I thank professor Orest Martynowich for having provided me with such information in April 2019. The same file also contains some information on Arcand's speech, delivered in Montreal on 29 November 1937, at a Hetmanite reception for Danylo Skoropadsky, the Hetman's son, who was touring North America. See: Ivan Isaiv [John Esaiw], ed., *Za Ukrainu: Podorozh Velmozhnoho Pana Hetmanycha Danyla Skoropadskoho do Zluchenykh Derzhav Ameryky I Kanady, osin 1937– vesna 1938* (Chicago: United Hetman Organizations, 1938). This Ukrainian-language commemorative publication chronicles the tour in detail (from the Hetmanite perspective).
161. "Strictly Confidential. Memo. Re: Chief Postal Censor's Office", January 14, 1940, file Correspondence Mead, F. J. 1933–1958, vol. 2, MG30 C72, LAC. Bossy argues here that the 'Jewish race is strongly in favour of Communism in general and of the Soviet Union in particular.'
162. Paul Hanebrink, *A Specter Haunting Europe: The Myth of Judeo-Bolshevism* (Cambridge: Harvard University Press, 2018), 14.
163. James Chappel, *Catholic Modern: The Challenge of Totalitarianism and the Remaking of the Catholic Church* (Cambridge: Harvard University Press, 2018), 14.
164. Mead to Bossy, November 27, 1939, file Correspondence Mead, F. J. 1933– 1958, vol. 2, MG30 C72, LAC; "Strictly Confidential. Memo. Re: Chief Postal Censor's Office", January 14, 1940, file Correspondence Mead, F. J. 1933–1958, vol. 2, MG30 C72, LAC. In these documents Bossy argues particularly against the recruitment of 'employees of Jewish extraction in the censorial work', stating that the Jewish community lacks any 'natural' ability to properly perform duties related to linguistics, and linking the appointment of Jewish employees to political favours by 'local Liberal committees'. See also: Mead to Bossy, August 19, 1943, file Correspondence Mead 1930–1958, vol. 2, MG30 C72, LAC. In this letter, Mead refers to Bossy's belief that Communist Party member (and communist spy) Fred Rose was elected member of the Canadian Parliament thanks to 'the Jewish vote'.
165. Bossy to Mead, June 23, 1939, file Correspondence Mead, F. J. 1933–1958, vol. 2, MG30 C72, LAC.
166. Norman Rich, *Hitler's War Aims: Ideology, the Nazi State, and the Course of Expansion* (New York: Norton & Company, 1992), 111–2.

88   *Allegiances*

167. Apparently, the Führer 'thought the Habsburgs had erred in insisting on Ukrainian independence in WWI and [besides] he could never forgive Ukrainians themselves for the killing of the German military governor there in 1918'. See: Mark Mazower, *Hitler's Empire: Nazi Rule in Occupied Europe* (New York: The Penguin Press, 2008), 458.
168. E. M. Robertson, *Hitler's Pre-War Policy and Military Plans 1933–1939* (New York: Citadel Press, 1967), 152–5; Bohdan S. Kordan, *Canada and the Ukrainian Question, 1939–1945: a study in statecraft* (Montreal: McGill-Queen's University Press, 2001), 11–4; Rich, *Hitler's War Aims*, 115–6; Mazower, *Hitler's Empire*, 458.
169. Bossy to Mead, June 23, 1939, file Correspondence Mead, F. J. 1933–1958, vol. 2, MG30 C72, LAC. See Mead's answer expressing his disappointment 'over the turn of events in regard to the Ukrainian independence' in Mead to Bossy, July 21, 1939, file Correspondence Mead, F. J. 1933–1958, vol. 2, MG30 C72, LAC.
170. Mead to Bossy, September 12, 1939, file Correspondence Mead, F. J. 1933–1958, vol. 2, MG30 C72, LAC.
171. Bossy to A. R. Gagnon, officer Commanding Division C, RCMP, September 25, 1939, file Correspondence Jenkins, J. H. 1939, vol. 2, MG30 C72, LAC. See applications for commission as Lieutenant on September 3, 1940, file Loyola COTC Applications For Commission 1939–1941, vol. 1, MG30 C72, LAC; October 10, 1941, file Bossy, Walter J. Employment 1936–1953, vol. 1, MG30 C72, LAC; November 21, 1940, file Loyola COTC Applications For Commission 1939–1941, vol. 1, MG30 C72, LAC. All these applications were rejected.
172. J. H. Jenkins to Bossy, November 29, 1939, file Correspondence Jenkins, J. H. 1939, vol. 2, MG30 C72, LAC.
173. December 20, 1940, file People's Gazette Correspondence PT. III 1940–1941, vol. 5, MG30 C72, LAC.
174. Victor Howard, *MacKenzie-Papineau Battalion: The Canadian Contingent in the Spanish Civil War* (Carleton: Carleton University Press, 1986), 33; Bossy to Mead, December 28, 1940, file People's Gazette Correspondence PT. III 1940–1941, vol. 5, MG30 C72, LAC.
175. Kordan, *Canada and the Ukrainian question*, 13; Wasyl Veryha, "The Ukrainian Canadian Committee: Its Origins and War Activity", Master's thesis (University of Ottawa, 1967), pp. 98–9.
176. Bossy to Mead, December 28, 1940, file People's Gazette Correspondence PT. III 1940–1941, vol. 5, MG30 C72, LAC.
177. Paul Yuzyk, *The Ukrainians in Manitoba: a social history* (Toronto: University of Toronto Press, 1954), 95; Kordan, *Canada and the Ukrainian Question*, 31; Thomas M. Prymak, *Gathering a Heritage: Ukrainian, Slavonic, and Ethnic Canada and the USA* (Toronto: University of Toronto Press, 2015), 320. See more on Teodor Datzkiw in: Thomas M. Prymak, *The Maple Leaf and Trident: The Ukrainian Canadians During the Second World War* (Toronto: Multicultural History Society of Ontario, 1988), especially Chapter 2.
178. Kordan, *Canada and the Ukrainian Question*, 43.
179. Bossy to Datzkiw, December 30, 1940, file People's Gazette Correspondence PT. III 1940–1941, vol. 5, MG30 C72, LAC.
180. Ibid.
181. Ibid.
182. Mead to Bossy, January 7, 1941, file People's Gazette Correspondence PT. III 1940–1941, vol. 5, MG30 C72, LAC; Mead to Bossy, January 13, 1941, file People's Gazette Correspondence PT. III 1940–1941, vol. 5, MG30 C72, LAC.
183. Bossy to Mead, January 8, 1941, file People's Gazette Correspondence PT. III 1940–1941, vol. 5, MG30 C72, LAC.

Allegiances 89

184. Mead to Bossy, January 13, 1941, file People's Gazette Correspondence PT. III 1940–1941, vol. 5, MG30 C72, LAC.
185. Bossy to Mead, January 20, 1941, file People's Gazette Correspondence PT. III 1940–1941, vol. 5, MG30 C72, LAC.
186. See letters of rejection for 'commission as Lieutenant' positions in: file Loyola COTC Applications For Commission 1939–1941, vol. 1, MG30 C72, LAC; and file Bossy, Walter J. Employment 1936–1953, vol. 1, MG30 C72, LAC. For Bossy's new position, see: October 10, 1941, file Bossy, Walter J. Employment 1936-1953, vol. 1, MG30 C72, LAC. See also: "Ex-officier de l'armée autrichienne, enrôlé dans le CEOC du Loyola", file Loyola COTC 1938–1940, vol. 1, MG30 C72, LAC.
187. *Star*, April 17, 1941, file Correspondence On Speeches And Speaking Invitations 1938–1949, vol. 5, MG30 C72, LAC.
188. Bossy to Mead, January 23, 1941, file People's Gazette Correspondence PT. III 1940–1941, vol. 5, MG30 C72, LAC.
189. Mead to Bossy, January 27, 1941, file People's Gazette Correspondence PT. III 1940–1941, vol. 5, MG30 C72, LAC. See also: S. T. Wood to Bossy, January 28, 1941, file RCMP 1937–1958 file, vol. 11, MG30 C72, LAC.
190. Mead to Bossy, March 29, 1943, file Correspondence Mead 1933–1958, vol. 2, MG30 C72, LAC; Bossy to Mead, April 9, 1943, file CORRESPONDENCE MEAD 1933–1958, vol. 2, MG30 C72, LAC.
191. Fitzgerald to Bossy, April 13, 1943, file Correspondence Fitzgerald 1943, vol. 3, MG30 C72, LAC.
192. John Francis Noll, *Civilization's Builder and Protector* (Huntington: Our Sunday Visitor Press, 1940), 44, 47, 93.
193. Ibid., 68.
194. Ibid., 181–2.
195. Ibid., 185.
196. Fitzgerald to Bossy, February 24, 1942, file Correspondence Fitzgerald, 1938–1941, vol. 3, MG30 C72, LAC.

4 Networks

> For sound reasons, this project will leave out of its action certain ethnic groups that are too particular: the Jews, the Chinese, the Japanese, and the Negroes.
>
> Walter J. Bossy, in French, April 1948[1]

L'Action corporative

In 1937, l'Action Corporative (Corporative Action, AC) was created in Montreal.[2] Just like the Classocracy League of Canada (CLC) had done since 1934, AC advocated a nationwide guild system. However, it didn't draw on the European authoritarian corporatist experiments to justify its value. The difference was especially important now that Germany and Italy were getting closer, and that the Pope had just released the encyclical *Mit brennender Sorge* (With Burning Concern, 1937) condemning Germany's Nazi state.[3] In other words, supporting the fascist model could be associated with supporting the Nazi state. AC insisted that the guild system was a democratic endeavour sustained by, and protective of, democratic institutions.[4] It was liberal democracy rather than democracy *per se,* it argued, which should give cause for concern. By ensuring that the Christian principles – which 'are consistent with the national and religious traditions of Canadians' – permeate all social and political spheres, the guild system would turn aspiring democratic states into real democracies.[5]

Members of AC included Maximilien Caron, lawyer and law professor at Université de Montréal; Esdras Minville, director of l'École des Hautes Études Commerciales (the School of Higher Commercial Studies) and member of the Conseil de la Vie Française en Amérique (the Council for French Life in America) as well as president of the nationalist movement Ligue d'Action Nationale (National Action League); L. Athanase Fréchette, president of the society Saint-Jean-Baptiste and also of the Ligue; Hermas Bastien, secretary of the Ligue d'Action Nationale; and Léon Mercier Gouin, lawyer and professor at the Université de Montréal; and a number of representatives of professions and related associations.[6] But the actual architect of l'Action Corporative was Joseph-Papin Archambault, who as

DOI: 10.4324/9781003283348-4

director of *l'École Sociale Populaire* had helped to launch Bossy's CLC and its first manifesto (*A Call to All Socially Minded Christian Canadians*) in 1934 as well as its reform program (*Déclaration, thèse, statuts*) in 1935.[7]

John J. Fitzgerald, Edward LaPierre and Bossy had been planning the re-launch of the CLC since July 1937, hoping that Archambault would support them by organizing fundraising events, and by publishing Bossy's biography to encourage donations for the establishment of a New Canadians Federation – which would constitute the means to mobilize the 'third force' nationwide.[8] But, by June 1937, Archambault had decided to put his efforts into a different corporatist project. Much like the CLC, l'Action Corporative described corporations as bodies 'bringing together all the members of the same profession under a single authority, having the power to act for the common good and to impose its decisions on all those concerned.'[9] At the same time, AC aimed to promote and coordinate the establishment of corporations at the provincial level rather than at the federal level.[10] In addition, it openly rejected the state corporatism incarnated by Mussolini's Italy, which the CLC had publicly praised,[11] and promoted Catholic social corporatism instead, while also drawing from the traditionalist nationalism epitomized by the philosophy of Lionel Groulx.[12]

Unlike the CLC, whose fight for national integration was linked to the New Canadians' fight for recognition at the federal level, AC's fight against 'economic liberalism' was very much connected to its members' wish to protect the equal status of the French-Canadian community as a 'founding nation'. Its members perceived Quebec as a homogeneous entity, recognizing no minorities therein other than the English-speaking community, 'the undisputed masters of commerce, industry and finance'. Even though they used 'universality' to frame their discourse on the nationwide establishment of a guild system, theirs was a narrative designed to perpetuate a binary understanding of Canadian identity.[13] According to AC, liberal democracy and its liberal economy had jeopardized the equal status of the founding nations, as it led to the unequal success of peoples. Corporatism, on the other hand, ensured that all groups would be protected equally under the same status, thus allowing Canada to finally be a democracy. In conclusion, corporatism, 'far from being undemocratic … it's a condition for democracy', said member of AC François-Albert Angers.[14]

As a member of AC, Archambault similarly presented the guild system not as an alternative to, but as the saviour of, Canadian democracy.[15] He argued that corporatism suited democracy better than any other regime: 'Far from destroying it, it strengthens it. Far from lowering it, it elevates it. Far from harming it, it purifies it'. Corporatism was, he said, the 'lifeline'; a means by which democracy would finally be 'Christianized'.[16] Likewise, the president of AC Maximilien Caron explained that democracy in Canada as it stood did not live up to the expectations of what democracy should be. For one thing, the current system was not bringing socio-economic justice to French Canadians, thereby undermining the very principles of democracy. Allegedly, this failure was partly due to the prioritization of individual interests over the common good, which led to the empowerment of the dominant group.[17] Instead, corporatism established a common interest which benefited all groups equally. So, concluded Caron, unless Quebec wants to 'sign the death warrant of its nationality', it must defend corporatism as a way to achieve the 'sanitation' of Canadian democracy.[18]

Quebec sociologist Jean-Philippe Warren insists that, 'corporatism in French Canada represented an attempt to democratize public space by debating the issues related to the hidden struggles of the market, and by breaking the domination by moneyed powers over the French-Canadian population.' Even so, Warren does not deny its 'profound authoritarianism'.[19] Undeniably, the type of democracy that Caron had in mind when suggesting 'sanitation' was not exactly liberal. He insisted upon the need for a 'strong state, capable, when necessary to safeguard the general good, to impose its will' as well as the need for 'order' against the right to 'strikes' and 'lock-out'.[20] He also praised French absolutism as well as Oliveira Salazar's corporatist dictatorship Estado Novo in Portugal as hallmarks of political stability.[21] Léon Mercier Gouin also referred to Portugal as a source of inspiration, and to Salazar as a 'great statesman'.[22] The reason why AC believed Portugal to be a legitimate source of inspiration was its being 'dominated by Christian influence', as its being rooted in democratic procedures.[23] Precisely, Esdras Minville argued that the Portuguese dictator was not 'an omnipotent leader', as his power had been 'entrusted by the President of the Republic'.[24] Overall, Portugal appeared as a valid reference to a group of people who wished to 'master their destiny' through 'a moderate nationalism' sustained by a type of corporatism that was rooted in Christian principles.[25]

To French-Canadian working-class newspapers like *Le Monde Ouvrier* (The Working World), by speaking of '[the] good Salazar in Portugal', AC did nothing but damage the liberties that the French Revolution had achieved, namely liberty, fraternity, and equality.[26] Likewise, communist newspapers like *Daily Clairon* and *Clarté* (Clarity) described AC as a 'political committee which must propagate the corporatism of Mussolini'.[27] Indeed, even though AC chose to acclaim only Salazar from among the European corporatist experiments, Mussolini had also referred to corporatism as the means to achieve true democracy – when in fact undermining its fundamental tenets, including individualism, pluralism, and freedom of speech.[28] It was precisely the illusion that corporatism was the way towards social justice and stability that made Italian fascism an acceptable 'temporary' measure.[29] Specifically, Mussolini claimed that fascism would make the Italian democratic constitution more efficient, explaining that it would not destroy, but restore democracy.[30] Italian fascism was perceived by its supporters as the 'New Democracy, a spirit compacted of Italian patriotism and Italian piety'; a '*Civitas Dei*, vowed to the pure service of God and man'.[31] Similarly, and unlike the CLC – which had presented itself as standing against 'plutocratic democracy' – AC claimed to pursue true democracy, thus appearing to be a more viable movement even though it also attacked the basic features constituting 'robust liberal or constitutional democracies'.[32]

By 1938, the CLC had more in common with Adrien Arcand's National Unity Party (NUP) than it did with l'Action Corporative. For one thing, both groups bypassed provincial specificities to stress the pursuit of Canadian unity under a Catholic-inspired corporatist system sustained by shared Christian values – non-Christian religious faiths would be tolerated 'provided that they do not conflict with ... the common good.' Furthermore, their official economic focus was not upon specific ethnic groups, but upon 'each class or social occupation', which would incorporate all ethnic groups for the success and progress of all.[33] But by 1938, as the international press raised concerns about Hitler's aggressive imperialism, the Canadian Jewish Congress began alerting the Canadian authorities about fascist groups, and specifically about Arcand's activities. Thus, while in 1937 Bossy had been happy to share his and Arcand's common admiration for Hitler's anti-communist and anti-Jewish crusade, now not only was he disappointed in Hitler's imperialist policies, which had ended Ukraine's dreams of independence,[34] but he also understood that the CLC and its promoters needed to completely disassociate themselves from Arcand and antisemitism in order to stand a chance.

Given the circumstances, then, collaborating with AC seemed like a more sensible idea. That is why in 1940 Fitzgerald decided to write a letter to leading member of AC Léon Mercier Gouin, whom he knew from his days at Loyola College. Fitzgerald told Gouin that 'the subject' (i.e., the guild system) was 'not new to [him]', and introduced him to the idea of classocracy, which he explained 'embrace[d] an elaborate plan for the complete reconstruction of the Social Order'. Fitzgerald said that the Classocracy League of Canada had failed to appeal to the broader public because it used the unsettling term 'classocracy', which had been 'a serious obstacle'. He thought the name 'Guild System', which was the term primarily used by l'Action Corporative, was far more appropriate to describe what they had been trying to achieve. Fitzgerald suggested that they cooperate.[35] Gouin knew Fitzgerald to be 'a pioneer of Corporatism' and seemed delighted to receive his letter.[36] However, he did not show interest in collaborating, and answered Fitzgerald's letter by simply sending a pamphlet entitled 'Catéchisme de l'organisation corporative' (Catechism of corporate organization), by the Jesuit Richard Arès – who later in the 1950s would become a 'big name in the [French] nationalist movement'.[37]

Arès viewed corporatism as the means to protect the French Canadians' status as a 'founding nation', which had allegedly been jeopardized by individualism, liberalism, and the Confederation (federalism).[38] He argued that the guild system, or the reorganization of Canadian society in 'natural groups' such as professions, would allow Quebec to 'break the economic dictatorship' and allow 'its rulers a truly national policy'.[39] Clearly, Gouin was concerned with using corporatism in order to bring back the foundational rights of French Canada rather than to expand Canadian identity.[40] As Fitzgerald saw it, the guild system presented by AC was ultimately too narrow, as it promoted the restoration of a binational Canada that, in practice, did not exist.[41]

In 1940, as part of a series of courses on corporatism organized by l'Action Corporative, a leading member of the organization, André Montpetit, gave a lecture on Swiss corporatism and cultural cooperation. He praised the capacity of the Swiss federal regime to adopt corporatism in order to effectively incorporate 'disparities of cultures, languages, mentalities, necessarily different conceptions of the social order and even of the economy' – this offered more guarantees of collaboration through the idea of association based on professional life.[42] Even though Montpetit was most probably using the Swiss analogy to insist on the equal status between French- and English-speaking Canadians, as revealed in any other material produced by AC at the time, he also suggested that corporatism could be used to establish an ethnically plural state. Thus, Fitzgerald wrote to LaPierre and Bossy advising that they insist in steering AC towards classocracy.[43] At the time, LaPierre was quite busy, as he had just become the secretary of the Canadian branch of the Friends of National Spain (FNS): a transnational network which promoted Francisco Franco's view of the Spanish Civil War (1936–1939), that is as a Christian crusade against the forces of international communism, Masonry and Judaism.[44] Bossy, whose New Canadians project had been on hold since the outbreak of the war, was free to contact Gouin, and so he wrote him a letter to which he attached a copy of *A Call to Socially Minded Christian Canadians*. In his letter, Bossy suggested that they meet in person to discuss their common interests.

Gouin responded by saying that, although he was 'greatly interested in the work of all the pioneers of the "Guild System"', he was 'very busy'. Contact was never resumed, and Bossy and Gouin never met.[45] After all, as Fitzgerald reflected, even though AC similarly believed corporatism to be a tool to better conciliate economic, political, and spiritual divergence, its approach to socio-economic reconstruction was 'quite different to ours'.[46] Their model refused to be 'all-embracing', and by doing so represented a flawed proposal, neither 'logical' nor 'well developed', said Fitzgerald.[47] Unlike AC, classocracy would allow for a system where 'each can play his part with the inspiration of being an active vital unit in a cohesive whole', honouring the Christian principle that 'all men are created equal and endowed by their Creator with inalienable rights'.[48] Yet, with the possibility of cooperating with a seemingly analogous movement off the table, and the few members of the CLC being gradually disbanded (Archambault chose AC over the CLC; LaPierre went on to lead the Canadian section of the FNS; and Bossy began planning to resume his interwar New Canadians movement), by early 1940 the CLC disappeared from sight, never to return.

The Liberal Party

When the Second World War ended, Bossy was rehired by the Montreal Catholic School Commission (MCSC), resuming his role with *les classes étrangères* or foreign classes. But shortly after he came back to the MCSC, Bossy was accused of professional and sexual misconduct and fired. On the one hand, his coming and leaving the Commission at 'irregular intervals' did not go unnoticed, a behaviour Bossy justified by saying that, after learning the 'very shocking news from Europe that my whole family in Poland was practically wiped out of existence becoming victims of "Nazi" invasion of Poland', he had been depressed.[49] On the other, certain 'girls' (that's how the MCSC put it) had presumably been going into Bossy's office at the MCSC for purposes other than strictly professional. To that accusation Bossy responded that his 'morality' was intact and that such claims were 'baseless'.[50] For the next two years, Bossy begged the MCSC to hire him back without success. In the meantime, he bought a fruit and dairy farm at Grimsby Beach (Ontario), which ended up causing Bossy more stress and debts than anything else.[51] He eventually left Grimsby Beach to return to Montreal hoping that the MCSC would rehire him, which finally happened in October 1947.[52]

In September 1947, the MCSC had created a Comité des Néo-Canadiens or New Canadians Committee, whose goal was to 'seek out among the immigrants those who are Catholic, to notify the parish priest of their presence and to send their children to the schools of the Commission.'[53] Upon being rehired, Bossy's became the 'liaison officer between the Committee of New Canadians and new Canadian groups in the city'.[54] The ultimate purpose of the Comité des Néo-Canadiens echoed prewar cooperative efforts from Bossy and the MCSC to facilitate a cultural and spiritual rapprochement between 'New Canadians' and French Canadians. In spite of this, Bossy wasn't happy about the Comité, which he thought was not ambitious enough.[55] Trying to implement changes, he re-introduced his 1937 proposal for the creation of a 'pan-canadien' New Canadians Federation and a nationwide network of New Canadian Friendship Houses.[56] But that seemed too much to the MCSC. To Bossy, the 'scope of the project frightens the committee and the Commissioners'.[57] Frustrated, in April 1948, he quit his position as 'liaison officer' – although he kept his role as instructor.[58] There are several elements that could have contributed to him abandoning such a position. One could have been related to French-Canadian nationalism. As Robert Gagnon argues, in the late 1940s and 1950s the MCSC commissaries were mainly preoccupied with 'the integration of Catholic immigrants' into 'French-Canadian society' against 'their anglicization'.[59] Their focus was local rather than national, as it was French Canadian rather than Canadian. On the other hand, when working for the MCSC during the interwar period, Bossy had no problem supporting the idea of integrating ethnic minorities into the French-Canadian Catholic milieu against Protestantism. Besides, in his revised plan for the 'New Canadians' of 1948 (just as he did in 1937) Bossy highlighted the importance of instilling a 'Catholic mentality' upon the 'New Canadians' 'after the perspectives of Catholics and French Canadians … to strengthen Catholic influence in Canada' and eventually 'to achieve a Christian Canada'.[60] In addition, despite his nationwide aspirations, Bossy himself had pointed at the need to begin acting at the local level, and only gradually expand.[61] Thus, it would look like an organization such as the MCSC's Comité des Néo-Canadiens or New Canadians Committee would have been a good place to start. Given this, it is likely that Bossy's decision to quit was more related to the fact that the MCSC didn't give him the position of leadership of the 'New Canadians' that he desired. As a consequence, on April 22, 1948, he inaugurated his own New Canadians Bureau (henceforth NCB).[62]

'Today I am starting my campaign in my own new venture', said Bossy to Fitzgerald.[63] The NCB was re-defined as 'an agency for promoting social, cultural and political Christian action in Unison among all those people in Canada who do not speak yet at their Canadian Homes neither English, [nor] French languages'.[64] Bossy was certain that he would be able to obtain the resources he needed to maintain his endeavour through memberships, donations, and 'aid' from the 'city of Montreal' and the provincial or federal government.[65] Fitzgerald, on the other hand, was not as optimistic. Even though he thought Bossy's 'proposal for New Canadians is very … well presented', chances were, he said, that cheques would be few.[66] But Bossy was confident, and he sent to the local press his 'program of action', which was framed by a reflection upon the relationship between the French Canadians and the 'New Canadians'.[67]

In essence, in his program Bossy claimed that if French Canadians took the lead in instituting a federal New Canadians Federation and Friendship Houses, they would be able to counteract the widespread anglicization of newcomers.[68] If French Canadians decided to do nothing about the 'New Canadians', they risked being outnumbered by the Anglophones. Specifically, Bossy explained that 'French Canadians, in their own interest, should take all necessary means to gain the support of New Canadians and that by doing so the French-Canadian influence could become very great.' He also argued that immigrants chose English over French simply because 'few French Canadians are interested in them'.[69] The solution: taking advantage of the growing number of immigrants by helping them integrate into the Catholic French-speaking milieu. Assisting these 'New Canadians' spiritually and linguistically would not only strengthen the French-Canadian society, he argued, but would also protect it from communism – as with integration there would be no isolation, and therefore no radicalization.[70] Overall, Bossy insisted that, while helping the 'New Canadians', the project intended to also benefit French Canadians, the French language, and the Catholic Church.[71] Ultimately, then, as historian Mélanie Lanouette describes it, Bossy's seemed to be 'a movement that … integrates immigrants into French-Canadian society.'[72]

Upon receiving Bossy's programme and reflection, the local press 'gives him its support, at least on the French side'.[73] Indeed, numerous French-Canadian newspapers promoted Bossy's endeavour and asked their readers to financially contribute to its successful realization. These included the conservative *Le Montréal-Matin* (Roger Duhamel); *Le Soleil* (Editorial, Henri Gagnon); *Le Canada* (Roger Nadeau); *Le Devoir* (René Guénette); *Le Clairon* (Conrad Langlois); *La Patrie* (René Bonin)[74]; *l'Action Catholique* (Editorial, Georges-Henri Dagneau); and even the Franco-Albertan *Une Voix de l'Ouest* (Joseph Boulanger).[75] In all their articles, these journalists promoted Bossy's idea because they trusted Bossy's belief that a close collaboration between French Canadians and 'New Canadians' would assist the former in fighting Canada's anglicization.[76] René Bonin (*La Patrie*) gathered that by mobilizing 'in their favor the great resources of New Canadians (at least those Catholics)', French Canadians 'will grow in number and gain ground in the conflict of languages, religious denominations, points of view and influences in Canada.'[77] After reading Bossy's report, described as 'very intelligent, very detailed, and very understanding', Henri Gagnon (*Le Soleil*) insisted that Catholicism was the 'middle ground' from which an alliance between the French Canadians and the 'New Canadians' could flourish to the advantage of both.[78] Roger Duhamel (*Montréal-Matin*), who was the former president of the Société Saint-Jean-Baptiste de Montréal (1943-1945),[79] stated that 'it seems timely, not to say urgent' to establish a Federation of New Canadians. Quebec, he said, must make the effort to attract 'to us those who have religious and cultural affinities with us' so that 'we strengthen the prestige and influence of our ethnic group throughout the country, [and] we obtain certain valuable assistance in support of our fair claims.'[80] Duhamel insisted that the New Canadians Bureau was 'particularly relevant in our time. Perhaps it will contribute to increasing French and Catholic influence in Canada.'[81] Langlois (*Le Clairon*) accused 'the isolationist, separatist, racist mentality of too many representatives of French-Canadian nationalism' of causing the 'New Canadians' to become anglicized. In order for 'New Canadians' to assimilate, he said, barriers had to be broken down rather than built up – support for Bossy's New Canadians Bureau was crucial.[82] Franco-Albertan Joseph Boulanger, who was the president of the Société Saint-Jean-Baptiste d'Edmonton, celebrated Bossy's proposal and described Bossy as 'so proud, so patriotic'.[83] Georges-Henri Dagneau (*L'Action Catholique*) concluded that 'there is no surer way to serve the cause of French influence in Canada than to disdainfully reject them [i.e., New Canadians]. On the contrary, it is important to seek the friendship of new Canadians.'[84]

In addition, Bossy received letters of support from François-Albert Angers, former editor in chief of *l'Action Nationale* and a member of l'Action Corporative, and Dominique Beaudin, who also worked at l'*Action Nationale*. Angers celebrated Bossy's launching a movement that will foster 'closer collaboration between French Canadians and new Canadians'.

His hope was that 'your appeal will be heard by many French Canadians and that you will obtain all the cooperation you need to carry out your task.' In the meantime, he attached 'a check to that effect.'[85] Beaudin explained that the French Canadians, 'as a national group, we left the immigrants to fend for themselves and very generally to assimilate with Anglo-Canadians.' Assisting Bossy in protecting the 'New Canadians' would help to combat 'Canada's immigration policy ... directed against the growth of the French-Canadian group.' Accordingly, he offered 'my sincere collaboration', for example by saying that he would publish on Bossy's project with the hope that more people would support him – which he did only once, in November 1948.[86]

Despite the general good reception that Bossy's proposal received among the French-Canadian press, the MCSC insisted that Bossy's work was utterly independent from the Commission. In fact, the 'commissioners request the president of the school board to inform whom it may concern that the memorandum published in the newspapers is the personal initiative of Mr. Bossy and that it was published without the knowledge and without the authorization of the members of the committee.'[87] *Montréal-Matin* accused the MCSC of not supporting Bossy's plans – and 'to fire such a man' – because the institution was under the 'harmful influence of Mr. Paul Massé, outrageous nationalist and friend of separatist leader Paul Bouchard'.[88] Possibly, these suspicions were sparked by Bossy's recent public declarations: 'I don't like nationalism... which is one of the main causes of our ills'.[89] The contradictions implied in wishing to help increase the numbers of Catholic and French-speaking Canadians while also rejecting the strengthening of French-Canadian identity weren't addressed. This simply shows Bossy's disregard for French-Canadian historical role in the formation of Canada, in particular the fact that since 1837–1838 religion had become the main vehicle of French-Canadian distinctiveness, and the Catholic Church the increasingly complex institutional network that protected it.[90] But perhaps this explains why support from French-Canadian religious figures was very negligible, especially given the high number of letters that Bossy sent to ecclesiastical figures asking for help. The few who supported Bossy included Jean Bobinas, pastor of the Lithuanian parish of Saint-Casimir in Montreal,[91] who on paper became the representative for 'parishes of new Canadians' in Bossy's project; Jesuit Thomas Mignault, a professor of philosophy at the Collège de Sainte-Anne-de-la-Pocatière in Montreal, who inaugurated a column in *Relations* (a monthly magazine issued by l'École Sociale Populaire with '15,000 subscribers in 1950'[92]) whose main purpose was to promote Bossy's New Canadians Bureau;[93] *monsignor* Olivier Maurault, rector of the University of Montreal, who wrote to Bossy offering support; and Bishop of Naissus (Alberta) Henri Routhier, who volunteered to help as much as he could.[94] But these were few and rather inconsequential enthusiasts.

The most helpful was probably Jesuit Thomas Mignault. Mignault's column, entitled "Sur le Front Néo-Canadien" (On the New Canadian Front), was in the hands of himself and of Franco-Ontarian Jesuit Guy Courteau, co-founder of la Société historique du Nouvel-Ontario or the 'New Ontario' (i.e., French Ontario) Historical Society.[95] Even though it seemingly addressed issues relating to *'new'* Canadians in general, "Sur le Front Néo-Canadien" mostly talked about Bossy's New Canadians Bureau, consistently using this initiative to frame the rest of existing projects regarding the New Canadians in Quebec.[96] The column defined Bossy's movement as aiming to 'bring Catholic New Canadians more closely to the Holy Church.'[97] Specifically, Mignault explained that the project joined an already developing Quebecois movement dedicated to the 'New Canadians', which included the initiatives of the Montreal Catholic School Commission with the Comité des Néo-Canadiens (New Canadians Committee); the Comité catholique du Conseil de l'Instruction publique (Catholic Committee of the Council of Public Instruction), which aided 'the new immigrants'; and the missionary works of Charbonneau and Casgrain towards the spiritual and material assistance of victims of the Second World War.[98]

By the fall of 1948, Bossy was responding to the numerous letters of encouragement with an urgent plea for material support.[99] On October 6, Bossy even wrote to Mayor of Montreal Camillien Houde asking for money on behalf of the 'New Canadians' to 'survive as a group'. Houde responded by saying that he had never heard of Bossy or his efforts or his group, and that his concerns were surely not as pressing as Bossy thought.[100] Between December and January 1949, the local newspapers helped spread Bossy's call for 'material assistance to continue the task' of the New Canadians Bureau 'as soon as possible'.[101] But no help came. That is until spring 1949, when the Liberal Party of Louis St. Laurent 'donated a sum' to Bossy's New Canadians Bureau under the condition that he help the prime minister during his political campaign, specifically his tour of western Canada.[102] If his assistance provided an increase in the 'ethnic' vote for the Liberals in the June 1949 elections, Bossy would allegedly receive a Senate seat.[103] The man in charge of facilitating the agreement was Joseph Saine, an Armenian new Canadian of French-Canadian mother from Montreal who by 1947 had become another 'spokesperson for New Canadians', preaching the unity between those and the French Canadian against 'the centralizing policy ... starting with the oppression of minorities'.[104] By 1949, Saine was rallying alongside St. Laurent, promoting the liberal vote against communism and against the oppression of Canadian minorities.[105]

St. Laurent's tour was planned for April 1949, and it included numerous stops in the four western provinces of Canada (Manitoba, Saskatchewan, Alberta, British Columbia) and the northwestern part of the Canadian province of Ontario. The tour was 'designed to show that St-Laurent understood regional needs and to showcase how his conception of national unity responded to the supposed threat of international communism.'[106] The two-week trip included stops in Edmonton, Vancouver, Victoria, Calgary, Regina, Saskatoon, Brandon, Winnipeg, and Fort William.[107]

During his tour, St. Laurent met 'several thousand Canadians', including representatives of the 'New Canadian' communities.[108] Bossy's role in this tour was to enable the meetings that took place between the prime minister and 'New Canadian' leaders in Manitoba.[109] In particular, what Bossy did was introduce '61 directors of new Canadian organisations ... to Mr. Saint-Laurent' at the Auditorium of Winnipeg, 'the metropolis of the New Canadians'.[110] 'Bishops, clergy, journalists, and officers from almost every national, religious or other society to which western New Canadians belong' attended the meeting.[111] The meeting was characterized by St. Laurent's calls for unity and liberty, 'freedom not only personal and political, but also cultural, understood in respect of the historical rights of minorities'.[112] He insisted in 'the important role that the New Canadians can play in helping their older compatriots become the more united and stronger nation that remains their primary goal.'[113] Even though the event lasted for no more than 30 minutes,[114] it gave 'the impression that we are in the presence of a "third force" taking shape for a better destiny of the country', as described in the later book *Un Mouvement, Une Oeuvre, Walter J. Bossy* (A Movement, A Work, Walter J. Bossy), published in 1950 by the New Canadians Bureau.[115]

The Liberal Party's plans for Bossy's cooperation didn't end in Winnipeg. In May, the party decided to sponsor a *Fête des Nouveaux Canadiens* or New Canadians Day, which would be organized by Bossy together with Joseph Saine, now 'Président Provisoire du Conseil des Néo-Canadiens' (temporary or *ad hoc* chair of the New Canadians Bureau).[116] The *fête* would be based on the prewar Notre Dame demonstration (1936) and Allegiance Day (1938).[117] It would be 'a manifestation of Non-English and Non-French speaking Canadian citizens in Montreal, in order to strengthen the unity of all Canadian people'.[118] The NCB explained that the 'first New Canadians' day' celebrated more than ten years earlier had been spurred by the 'influx of refugees from Hitler's Europe'. Unfortunately, 'during the war the project was dropped, but it was felt that with the present government immigration program it was time to revive the idea.'[119] Indeed, under the leadership of Mackenzie King, in 1947 the Liberal government had embarked upon an immigration program that aimed to 'foster the growth of the population of Canada by the encouragement of immigration'.[120] It did so primarily through 'the admission of the relatives of persons who are already in Canada, and [through] assisting in the resettlement of [European] displaced persons and refugees'.[121] The program contributed to the greatest increase in Canada's population in any decade in its history.[122] In addition, it began a process (culminated in the 1960s) 'which removed preferences and reduced or eliminated exclusionary, race-based criteria' from immigration policy.[123] It was a time when the Liberal Party was clearly investing in promoting its concern about the 'New Canadians' – as its funding of Bossy's NCB demonstrates.

The *Fête des Nouveaux Canadiens* was supposed to be celebrated on the anniversary of the foundation of Ville-Marie (Montreal) that is on May 18, 1949. However, 'the Montreal Historical Society, at the suggestion of the parish priest of Notre Dame, Mr. Jean-Baptiste Vinet' suggested that the event take place on 'May 15, due to the presence of the relics of the Canadian Martyrs at Notre Dame Church.'[124] At the event would participate Mayor of Montreal Camillien Houde; Senator (and former leader of L'Action Corporative) León Mercier-Gouin; Archbishop of Montreal Joseph Charbonneau; the rector of the University of Montreal, Olivier Maurault; representatives of the Société St. Jean Baptiste; and representatives of Montreal Catholic School Commission.[125] As in the past, the event would include a parade of 'New Canadians' carrying their respective flags and wearing traditional clothing. On the one hand, the purpose of the event was 'to expose the new Canadian problem to the public of Montreal at the same time as providing all the elements that compose our population with the opportunity to get to know each other better, to fraternize and, therefore, to help each other.'[126] On the other, it suggested that, while respecting the 'two founding nations', the existence of a 'third group' could invite a closer cooperation between different national groups: 'The constitution of this third group ... certainly respects perfectly the two historical groups that already exist, even invites them to better collaborate with each other and openly offers all Canadians the opportunity to compose a rich mosaic'.[127] Specifically, the 'New Canadians' could 'serve as a link between the two great races that inhabit Canada'.[128]

As planned, on Sunday, May 15, there was 'a High Mass ... in honor of the Canadian martyrs' at Notre Dame Basilica, where various representatives of ethnic Catholic parishes attended. In the afternoon, a parade showed the 'New Canadians Folklore' with 'thousands of Europeans of every nationality' in the 'the costumes of their native countries'; and other 'educational and artistic events'.[129] The New Canadians were presented as the 'Children of the Great Migration of all origins! Armenian, Bulgarian, Belgian, Danish, Dutch, Finnish, German, Greek, Hungarian, Italian, Lithuanian, Polish, Rumanian, Russian, Swedish, Syrian, and Libanese [sic], Slovak, Ukrainian, Yugo-Slav, etc.' These groups demonstrated 'Canadian Unity in Diversity. Let us strengthen in myriad tongues our co-operation with all Canadian People regardless [of their] national origin.'[130] Having asked the 'New Canadians' to 'contribute to the unity of Canada' and encouraged them to be 'proud of their citizenship', Bossy 'made an appeal to the Federal Government to support the New Canadian Council in making New Canadians' Day a nation-wide and annual event.'[131]

Joseph Saine explained in French the motto of the event, 'Unity in Diversity', as follows: 'In Canada, three brothers came at the hour marked by Divine Providence [to] build a great country: the French first; then the English; then the New Canadian.'[132] He demanded that the 'New Canadians' receive 'a fair share in the administration of the country'.[133] Following suit, Bossy referred to the historical sacrifices – war sacrifices in particular – the 'New Canadians' had endured in the name of the Canadian nation. 'This is,' he said, 'one of the reasons why New Canadians should not feel inferior to others, but consider that they too have acquired rights in Canada and should be treated as equals by Canadians of English and French origin.'[134] Bossy demanded that the New Canadians be 'recognized by the law of the land as one hundred percent Canadian citizens [...] since they have sacrificed for Canada, their adopted country, more than 100,000 of their children who died in service and in defense of a better Christian order.' Until that occurs, he argued, the 'famous Christian democracy that our heads of state invoke' would remain a democracy only in theory, promoted 'for the sole purpose of conscription'.[135]

The New Canadians Day mobilized 'foreign groups into a third element', thereby creating 'a third ethnic power', explained *La Presse*: the 'third force'.[136] Believing the event to be a turning point, the *The Montreal Daily Star* insisted that 'there should be greater effort made to bring them [the New Canadians] into the national family ... There should be many more councils at work on the problems of new and potential Canadians.'[137] Representative of Mayor Houde and city counsellor of Irish origin, Frank Hanley, considered the *fête* 'a splendid contribution to Canadian citizenship', and celebrated the idea that the 'New Canadians' serve 'as a link in the unity between two great races.'[138] Similarly, Senator Mercier-Gouin thanked Bossy in French for having done so much 'in favor of national unity'.[139] He declared that the idea of 'New Canadians' becoming 'a link in the unity between two great races is splendid', and added: 'If we want our Canadian nation to be one and indivisible, we must remember that we are all brothers and sisters together, whatever our racial origin'. Mercier-Gouin concluded that, with the help of the 'New Canadians', Canada would 'set a good example of religious and racial harmony for the whole world'.[140]

Bossy finally appeared to be making a breakthrough. He had attracted the attention of the governing Liberal Party and had campaigned with the Prime Minister in western Canada. Then, his New Canadians Day had been widely praised. But suddenly, things went downhill. The promised seat in the Senate never came and Bossy was hospitalized due to stress.[141]

Fellow crusaders

In the postwar years, growing antifascism and antiracism among Catholic circles (whom historian James Chappel has called 'fraternal Catholics'), together with widespread calls for an 'interfaith, pluralist renaissance', pushed Bossy to look for more tolerant approaches to pluralism, especially in regard to Jewish communities.[142] One such approach had been formulated in 1942 under the title 'Directive Principles for the Institutions of the Future'. The article, issued in the American Catholic magazine *Commonweal* [sic], explained that '[a]nti-Semitism is not Christian' because it is a form of discrimination. Moreover, attacking Jews would be 'attacking that people from whom Christ came forth'. The causes for antisemitism were 'error' and 'hatred', reasons which contrary to Christianity impeded 'men's exercise of their natural rights by reason of their ethnic or religious affiliations.'[143] To Bossy, this was enlightening. After all, Christianity had historically tended to demonize Jews by accusing them of killing Christ, hence the association between Judaism and atheist communism; and reducing them to cunning 'wandering' parasites, which fuelled the idea of Jews being a threat to the stability of nations.[144] Perhaps this is why he wasn't convinced right away, and why he kept accumulating a large volume of antisemitic material together with new Christian calls for ethnic tolerance.

Bossy's antisemitic memorabilia included pamphlets revealing an international Jewish plot to rule the world; control 'the money system as well as the economic system'; and to overall end Christianity.[145] There was also material narrating the Soviet exploitation of women, forced to become public property when having less than five children.[146] In such documents, Judaism and communism were said to conspire together for the establishment of an anti-Christ global government, a pursuit that had begun with the Bolshevik revolution of 1917 in Russia. Statements like 'For My Country – Against the Jews!' and 'The Jew Created Communism' are common among Bossy's papers, as well as suggestions like 'Do not trust a Jew, no matter how great the friendship that he demonstrates may be'.[147]

Much of this material had been printed and distributed by American white supremacist and neo-Nazi William Luther Pierce. A fierce antisemitic ideologue, Pierce was a prominent figure in the American Nazi Party, and would soon become co-leader of the National Youth Alliance, an anti-communist American political organization dedicated to countering liberal and Marxist groups on college and university campuses.[148] Other works had been written by Gerald L. K. Smith, like the antisemitic *Is Communism Jewish?* (1947) and *My Fight for the Right!* (ca. 1950). Founder of the American supremacist group Christian Nationalists, Smith talked about 'the plot of the international Jew for [the] control of the world', particularly through the media.[149] Likewise, he publicised the idea that the Bolshevik revolution in Russia was financed by Jews, specifically by an alleged 'Jewish millionaire of New York City', and argued that, when it came to Jews, class did not play a role as much as race did. The book also included a series of sketches of communist leaders like Hungarian Communist dictator Béla Kun or Bolshevik revolutionary leader Moisei Uritsky, which showed stereotypical features associated with Jews such as long hooked noses, thick lips, dark curly hair, and narrow eyes – which are supposed to express suspicion and concealment.[150] Smith's predictable conclusion was that communism and Judaism were one and the same.[151]

Bossy's file on Judaism also included a short 'tract' entitled 'Out of the Mouth of the Jew', which had been issued by the Patriotic Tract Society of St. Louis (US), a group affiliated with Smith's Christian Nationalists.[152] The tract discredited Zionism and accused contemporary Jews of praising the crucifixion of Christ.[153] Attached to 'Out of the Mouth of the Jew', Bossy had stapled material which promoted Holocaust denial narratives and condemned the creation of the State of Israel.[154] Such material was written by the 'Canadian Gentile Congress', which collaborated with former 'lieutenant' of Adrien Arcand's Christian Party, Paul-Émile Lalanne, to spread antisemitic propaganda in the postwar period.[155] Alongside this, there are pamphlets advertising the book *The Whole World is Crying: To Madagascar with the Jews in order that we finally may get peace on Earth* (1947), by Swedish antisemite Einar Aberg.[156] Founder of the Anti-Jewish Action League of Sweden and author of works such as *Behind Communism Stands the Jew* or *The Jews Are Also Human Beings Some People Say*, Aberg had been writing against the 'Jewish menace' since 1933, first nationally and, since 1946, internationally. Regarding the Jews as one of the 'greatest enemies in the world today', Aberg had been 'in close touch' with the Nazis in Germany even before Hitler came to power, and after the Second World War he became 'the Swedish father of Holocaust denial'.[157]

But while studying conspiracy theories on Judeo-Communism, Bossy seemed also interested in reading about the reassessment of Judaism by Christian communities and, especially, about the new kinds of missionary work aimed to convert Jews to Christianity. In particular, he began learning about the Archconfraternity of Prayer for Israel of the apostolate of Notre Dame de Sion.[158] The congregation of Notre Dame de Sion was established in 1843 by French-Jewish convert Marie Théodore Ratisbonne with the goal being 'the conversion of the Jews'.[159] The organization received the approval of the Pope in 1874 and was raised to the rank of Archconfraternity by Pius X in 1909.[160] Despite seemingly trying to reduce the gap between Jews and Catholics, the philosophy of the archconfraternity was never to see Jews and Catholics as equal partners and 'no effort was made to invite an "adult" dialogue with Jews on the matter of religion' – what they hoped was for Jews to simply renounce to their religious identity. This in part explains the more 'indirect path of prayer' followed by the group.[161]

Bossy became so enthusiastic about the missionary work of the apostolate of Notre Dame de Sion that, when the Second World War ended, he joined the Centre Ratisbonne in Montreal, established by the local Archconfraternity of Notre Dame de Sion after Marie Théodore Ratisbonne.[162] In theory, the Centre aimed at teaching Catholics about Judaism and Jews about Catholicism in order 'to eliminate reciprocal prejudices and in particular to combat anti-Semitism.'[163] In practice, however, 'this moderate center remained in the grip of centuries' old prejudices' in the same way that 'during the era of the Enlightenment, several judeophilic [sic] philosophies foresaw a solution of the "Jewish problem" through the Jews abandoning their Jewish national identity'.[164] Illustratively, according to the Archconfraternity the 'preservation' of Jews 'through so many centuries of dispersion and persecution' was a 'sign of the fidelity of God' and of the fact that Jews 'still have a role to play in carrying out God's purposes for humanity'. At the same time, it seemed that no role was to be played until conversion occurred, for only 'their encounter with Christ in the Church' would bring 'a reintegration and a reconciliation, the outcome of a true rapprochement'. Such a rapprochement would lead to 'regain consciousness of the historical, ecumenical and eschatological dimensions of Christian life' and to 'rejuvenating our Christian attitudes towards Israel'. In other words, it would lead to social and spiritual progress.[165]

Besides joining the Centre Ratisbonne in Montreal, Bossy also became a leading 'crusader' for Montreal's English-speaking section of Our Lady's Blue Army of Fatima.[166] Founded in 1946 in the US by Harold V. Colgan, parish priest in New Jersey, the Blue Army became an international Catholic organization aiming to Christianize the Soviet Union (or, more generally, communists), with millions of members in a total of 34 countries.[167] On December 11, 1959, Bossy received Colgan's blessing to lead a section in Canada.[168] His section was in addition to existing French-speaking Blue Army sections in Montreal and in Ottawa.[169]

In addition to becoming a new leading figure of the Blue Army in Canada, Bossy registered with the Convert Makers of America, based in Glendale (California), through which he started to receive weekly bulletins 'which carry ... tips on convert making projects ...'. Bulletins included articles like "Nine-year Old Becomes Convert Maker" or "Ingenious Laymen Develop Own Conversion Techniques", and pamphlets like "So... You Want to Make Converts", which explained how to bring 'the truth' to non-Catholics.[170] Furthermore, he began learning about Jewish converts, in particular about Arthur B. Klyber, a Jewish New Yorker who became a Catholic at the age of twenty, was ordained a priest in 1932, and 'dreamed of bringing Christ to his people.' Klyber believed that 'Catholics are the true Jews grown up'. Therefore, he explained, to become a convert meant to become 'a true Jew', a Jew who has 'come to the Fulfillment of their Religion in the Catholic Church'. In fact, he said, 'The Jew is as near to the Catholic Church as a blossom is to its fruit'.[171] Klyber talked of 'common inheritance', exemplifying the new discourse on Judeo-Christian tradition, which stated that 'every spiritual gift of our [Christian] religion has been willed to us through the hands and martyrdoms of Jews'.[172]

A very similar argument was put forward in *Ransoming the Time* (1941), by Jacques Maritain, which Bossy read. A liberal Catholic humanist, Maritain was a very different kind of figure from the others Bossy was seeking inspiration from. However, in *Ransoming the Time,* Maritain echoed some of Bossy's concerns regarding Jews and their cultural integration. Even though in his book Maritain never once explicitly referred to conversion as a way to foster cooperation between different peoples – in fact, he spoke against proselytism –[173], he often suggested that Christianity was the fulfilment of Judaism, and thus a higher form of religious expression. Specifically, Maritain wrote about 'the struggle of the Church for the salvation of the world and the salvation of Israel', implying that the Jews must somehow be assisted by Christians in order for global progress to occur.[174] Moreover, Maritain described the 'mystic[al] body of Israel' as a 'Church fallen from a high place', again insinuating that Christianity is higher on a spiritual scale.[175] Judaism, explained Maritain, is by essence 'Christianity's first outline and imperfect beginning'.[176] 'Gentiles', he said, are in 'fullness', a fullness come about 'through the breach offered by [Israel's] fall' and 'failure'.[177] Finally, he insisted that 'for a Jew to become a Christian is a double victory: his people triumphs [sic] in him'.[178] In *Ransoming the Time*, then, Maritain implicitly stated that Jews were at least spiritually inferior, thereby suggesting that some sort of civilizing mission could only bring them, and societies as a whole, closer to God.[179]

While flirting with the idea of conversion with a view to ultimately accepting Jews into his vision of Canada, Bossy's new form of antisemitism was the result of strategy rather than of change. This is made clear by his correspondence with John J. Fitzgerald between 1945 and 1947. At that time, Fitzgerald became the president of the Social Credit League of Ontario after publishing *Help!*, a pamphlet that suggested the existence of a world plot aiming to corrupt western civilisation with communism and atheism.[180] Upon the release of *Help!*, Fitzgerald received a letter from Norman Jaques, a leading member of the Social Credit Party of Alberta, who enthusiastically proposed that Fitzgerald send copies of his pamphlet to the Chairman of the Social Credit Board in Alberta so that the information therein disclosed could be distributed among party members.[181]

The Social Credit Party of Canada was a reform-oriented group originally established in England in 1932 by engineer Clifford Hugh 'C. H.' Douglas.[182] The Party argued that 'economic hardships resulted from an inefficient capitalist economy that failed to provide people with enough purchasing power for them to enjoy the fruits of a society's economic production.'[183] The solution offered by Douglas was a credit distribution system which would ensure the adequate distribution of money. Economics aside, C.H. Douglas and his social crediters had also promoted the conspiracy theory that Judaism was the foundation upon which 'monopoly capitalism' but also socialist and communist 'collectivism' was based, a theory relying on the falsehoods promoted by the antisemitic *Protocols of the Elders of Zion*.[184]

Even though antisemitism was not central to the propaganda of the Social Credit Party of Canada, *The Canadian Social Crediter*, the official party newspaper, was a great disseminator of antisemitic conspiracies.[185] This type of narrative was also encouraged by party leader and member of parliament (MP) like Norman Jaques, who claimed that any attempts to accuse the Social Credit Party of antisemitism resulted from Jews raising the 'bogey' of antisemitism as a 'communist smokescreen'.[186] A proper 'Douglasist', Jaques believed in an international financial Jewish conspiracy based on the *Protocols*, whose content he had occasionally referred to in the House of Commons.[187] He promoted the principle of 'Canada for Canadians', which was the motto of Adrien Arcand's new National Unity Party, while emphasizing that 'I am totally free of bias on all questions involving race, creed and/or religion'.[188] His discourse evolved around the idea of establishing a

Christian and 'properly functioning democracy' against the 'powerful forces [that] consistently have barred the way to that goal ... forces that seek to establish a ruthless and pagan dictatorship over the lives of men.'[189] By publishing *Help!*, Fitzgerald legitimized Jaques' ideas. In his letter, Jaques thanked him for his insights, and shared his agreement with the existence of an international conspiracy: 'Communism is a Jewish ... policy', and behind the 'leftist' rhetoric of western democracies there were 'Zionists'.[190]

Only days after Fitzgerald's *Help!* was distributed among Social Credit Party members, evangelical preacher and MP for the Social Credit Party (1935–1958) Ernest George Hansell was presenting it at the House of Commons as evidence against the Canadian Broadcasting Corporation and its alleged pro-Soviet content.[191] Once described as a 'Bible thumper from the prairies, a funnymoney [sic] man, a fanatic, a flaming evangelist, an anti-Semitic and a Fascist', Hansell believed the anti-communist struggle of the Social Credit Party to be almost part of a crusade, the result of 'missionary work, a skirmish'.[192] Over a year after Hansell's intervention at the House of Commons, Fitzgerald was invited to become the president of the Social Credit League of Ontario – he accepted.[193]

To Bossy, Fitzgerald's 'political elevation' meant that 'Providence [had] accepted our tacit prayers'. At last, Fitzgerald would be in a position to carry on the work they began pursuing 12 years before, when Bossy 'happily met [Fitzgerald] at the Beacon'. Now, he said, 'big days lay ahead'.[194] The Social Credit was the only political party in Canada 'capable to safeguard this democracy because it is explicitly and implicitly Christian', he said, and therefore can fight the 'secular spirit' in 'this period of materialistic supremacy'.[195] Unfortunately, Bossy lamented, their 'well[-]reasoned and truly Christian appeals' had been 'obstinately, unreasonably and repeatedly ignored', which proved that the federal government was 'not to be concerned with Christian ideas nor principles of true Democracy'.[196] In spite of celebrating Fitzgerald's association with the Social Credit movement, in 1947 Bossy sent a warning about the disadvantages of the party's fervent antisemitism:

> I saw before my eyes 3 great organized antisemitic movements: Hitler's in Europe, Father Coughlin's in USA and Arcand in Canada... Hitler succeeded in organizing the whole Europe and still... see Germany and Europe now... Father Coughlin succeeded in having 5 millions of followers of his "Social Justice" movement... Where are these followers today? Where is Arcand today? I predict that no matter how many thousands of followers we may succeed in organizing behind "Socred" [i.e., Social Credit] once we will associate ourselves with this Antisemitic attacks and theories of "Jewish world conspiracy" we will consequently find ourselves where are Coughlin and Arcand today.[197]

Especially problematic, said Bossy, was the close relationship between Norman Jaques and founder of the American Christian Nationalists Gerald

L. K. Smith. A white and Christian supremacist, Smith had been discredited in the United States and accused of steering religious and race hatred, especially with his fervent antisemitism.[198] Due to his being friends with Smith, Jaques was now accused in Canada of being a 'quisling', or a traitor, by CCF leader James William Coldwell.[199] Bossy was particularly worried about Jaques' recent public statements regarding the *Protocols* being a 'true document'.[200] If the Social Credit Party's 'strategy and tactic' was not 'explicitly limited by the discipline of the Church', it would fail.[201] Conversion, he concluded, was the only 'constructive answer' to the Jewish 'problem'; and a 'Christian State [was the only] noble and only true conception' of Canada.[202] In other words, Bossy never renounced his antisemitic beliefs and yet, by the early postwar period, he realized that overt antisemitism would do nothing to help him or his allies succeed in politics. The solution was to change the words, although not necessarily the message. Jews could stay – so long as they no longer existed.

A white 'third force'

Upon inaugurating his New Canadians Bureau (NCB) in 1948, Bossy explained that 'for sound reasons, this project will leave out of its action certain ethnic groups that are too particular: the Jews, the Chinese, the Japanese, and the Negroes.'[203] Bossy spoke of the 'New Canadians' as Europeans, and discussed the problem of their ghettoization based on 'long-rooted from European history animosities' and on the political differences 'that Europe transmitted'.[204] According to Bossy, the role of the NCB would be to 'dissolve all animosities among various European racial groups in Canada'.[205] The European character of the 'New Canadians' was similarly highlighted in the 1950 commemorative book on Bossy's movement, *Un Mouvement, Une Oeuvre, Walter J. Bossy*, which defined the New Canadians as 'of European descent other than British, French and Jewish', excluding too 'Japanese, Chinese, and Negroes'. Using a presumed identity to highlight the possibility of the 'New Canadians' cooperating with the 'two official races' to foster 'national unity', the book specified that Europeans were 'very competent, very strong ... by their spiritual affinities, they are sympathetic to us and will be able to cooperate with us in the anti-communist crusade' and added that, after all, 'Culture is not static, but dynamic'.[206] It even claimed that a new Canadian unification might inspire the establishment of 'a European Federation', implying that an integrated Canada would be a reflection of *European* ethnic integration.[207]

Bossy's claim that 'European racial groups in Canada' should be united in 'tolerance and in a good spirit of common Canadian citizenship' stood together with his idea that the 'Christian character of Canada ... should be upheld and be remembered when selecting prospective immigrants'.[208] Thus, *European* and *Christian* are presented as fundamental to Canada's character and, consequently, as legitimizing factors for the inclusion of what Bossy understood as 'New Canadians'.[209] Yet, before Bossy adopted the term 'New Canadians' or 'Nouveaux Canadiens', previous understandings of it didn't reflect these ideas. From definitions provided by the Canadian Government to those conceptualized by intellectuals or spread by the press, it is possible to infer that almost any inhabitant of Canada (except Indigenous communities) could fall under the category of 'New Canadian' before Bossy began using it for his own purposes.

In the early twentieth century, 'Nouveaux Canadiens' was generally employed to describe those that couldn't relate to the terms 'old Canadians', 'first Canadians', or 'Canadiens', which originally referred to the French Canadians.[210] In January 1912, *Le Devoir* defined 'the New Canadians' as those whose ethnic groups ('leurs nationaux') were different from the French and the English.[211] In Alberta, the liberal and upper-class *Mirror Journal* referred to the 'New Canadians' or 'foreign-born' as those who were not settlers of 'British-born and English-speaking' descent.[212] By contrast, the progressive *Lomond Press* included English-born immigrants into the category of 'New Canadians', just as *The Bulletin de la Société de géographie de Québec* did.[213] In the interwar period, *Le Soleil* defined 'New Canadian' as neither French nor English, while the conservative *L'Ordre* classified 'the New Canadians' as neither 'Americans' nor 'Anglophones' and made no reference to the French Canadians, thus protecting British immigrants only from that categorization.[214] In spite of the lack of a standard or common definition, the Canadian press seemed to feel comfortable equating 'New Canadians' to adjectives like 'foreigner' or 'immigrant' – even if they were 'naturalised' – and more often than not did not bother making references to any specific ethnic group, assuming that readers would understand the meaning implied behind those signifiers.[215]

In other early-twentieth-century French-Canadian texts addressing immigration to Canada or the existence of communities other than British and French Canadians, the term 'nouveaux venus' (newly arrived or newcomers) appears to replace that of 'nouveaux canadiens' (new Canadian). For example, French-Canadian political leader Henri Bourassa referred to the 'nouveaux venus' in *Les Canadiens-Français et l'Empire Britannique* (The French Canadian and the British Empire, 1903), and later in 1915, when talking about European immigrants to Quebec such as the 'Portuguese, Slavic or Hungarian'.[216] In *Notre Avenir Politique* (Our Political Future, 1923), L'Action française (later Action Nationale or National Action) defined 'nouveaux venus' (newcomers) as including 'the yankees and the Europeans'.[217] In such cases, Canadians of British and French descent would be excluded from this terminology, as would Indigenous groups, and immigrants of descent other than European.

In English-written texts, the concept of 'New Canadians' seemed to be widely used during the first half of the twentieth century as an 'umbrella term' to define the foreign-born who had immigrated to Canada. Alfred Fitzpatrick's *Handbook for New Canadians* (1919), for instance, used 'New

Canadians' to describe 'immigrants', 'foreigners' or 'foreign-born', and 'new-comers', but above all 'non-English-speaking races'.[218] While this definition included Canadians of Chinese and Japanese descent, it did not acknowledge Canadians of African or Indigenous descent. Regarding Jewish communities, the book highlighted that even though they have 'no nation of his own', they have proven to historically be loyal to Canada and therefore are to be considered 'a part of the Canadian people'.[219] Similarly, in *Education Among New Canadians* (1920), educator Rose A. Hambly defined 'New Canadians' as all those whose first language is different than English, thus portraying the English as the founders of Canada or the first and true Canadians. This definition was illustrated by a song that the author's students would arguably sing: 'Who are? Who are? Who are we? We're the NEW CANADIANS, don't you see? Can we speak English? Well! I guess!! Do we love Canada. Yes! Yes!! Yes!'.[220]

In the textbook *The Book of New Canadians* (1930), a schoolteacher named D. J. Dickie wanted Canadian children to be able to learn about their immigrant classmates. Questions like where Scotland or the Great Wall of China are, or what a Japanese Tea Party consist of were among those the children would address in class based on the material provided by the book. The book consisted of stories seemingly explained by immigrant children (and interpreted by Dickie) and included memories (sometimes with images) as well as insights into their ways of adapting group traditions to the Canadian setting.[221] As opposed to Fitzpatrick and Hambly, *The Book of New Canadians* defined 'New Canadians' as 'People who came from other lands to live in Canada', 'have become citizens of Canada' and are now 'the nation[']s representatives'.[222] Dickie rejected the idea that the French could be considered *new* Canadians ('since 1763 immigration from France has been very small ...'), and made no mention of Indigenous peoples. Canadians of African, Jewish, Chinese and Japanese descent (as well as Indians and Middle Easterners) were here explicitly considered 'New Canadians' and had their own sections in the book.[223]

In 1938, Scottish-Canadian writer and cultural promoter John Murray Gibbon published *Canadian Mosaic*. In it, he used a 1922 definition of 'New Canadians', which he came across in his search for early uses of the term 'mosaic'. This definition referred to the 'New Canadians' as foreign-born inhabitants of Canada 'representing [the] many lands and widely separated sections of Old Europe ...' – which included the scattered Jewish peoples.[224] Gibbon devoted all of his nineteen chapters to discussing the European 'races', ignoring groups of Asian or African descent, as well as Indigenous groups. He envisioned 'the Canadian race of the future' as resulting from 'over thirty European racial groups'.[225] Not unlike the idea of the American 'melting pot', Gibbon wanted this resulting race to perpetuate the Anglo-Saxon racial and cultural heritage.

Shortly after Murray wrote *Canadian Mosaic*, Canadian scholar and translator Watson Kirkconnell[226] published *Canadians All* (1941). The book listed 'all' Canadians by ethnicity and alphabetically, describing their geographic and cultural origins and pointing at their contributions to Canada. Unlike Gibbon's text, this included 'Asiatic Canadians' – Japanese and Chinese more specifically – as well as Jewish Canadians, who the author defined as a 'cultural group' – rather than a racial group – and, although the author mentioned 'some negroes brought in [to Canada] from Africa', he decided not to create a section for Canadians of African descent. No acknowledgment of Indigenous groups was made, eliminating them from the conceptualization of Canada altogether.[227]

The fact that all these definitions of 'New Canadians' vary reveals that the term is a social construct. This means that it conceals an idea or a mental representation of something unreal, but that it is nonetheless used to describe and organize reality. Regardless of who employed the term, 'New Canadians' had always conveyed the existence of an 'imagined community' of alleged newcomers (who might or might not be new to Canada) and it has consistently been used with the intention of creating, preserving, altering, or challenging relations of power. As others had done before, then, Bossy chose to signify the term in a way that reflected or favoured his own vision of Canada. That is, in a way that excluded certain groups and differentiated ethnic minorities of European and Christian descent from 'the other'. In doing so, he communicated a desire to alter power relations to the detriment of Canadians of Jewish, African, and East Asian descent in particular. Finally, in speaking of 'sound grounds' Bossy used what appeared to be common sense to legitimise such divergence – a technique intimately connected to traditional conservative values and what Ruth Wodak calls 'aggressive exclusionary rhetoric'.[228]

In order to justify his rhetoric, Bossy's discourse on the 'New Canadians' tapped into traditional stereotypes. For example, it referred to the 'well defined' Asian and Black ghettos in Montreal, and the dispersed nature of Jews, living 'in *our* home ... without ghetto' but also 'without limits'.[229] In the abovementioned *Un Mouvement, Une Oeuvre, Walter J. Bossy* (1950), the Jewish community was classified as belonging to 'foreign colonies', and their commercial businesses were described as a 'spiderweb'.[230] By associating Jews to spiders and describing their businesses as spiderwebs, the book was using an old trope in Christian antisemitic discourse, which even graced the cover of a 1934 French edition of the *Protocols of the Elders of Zion*.[231] Commonly, antisemitic rhetoric related Jews to subhuman forms such as spiders, octopuses or snakes, images that were meant to spark feelings of phobia and repulsion. But the spider reference had, as in this specific text, been typically used to illustrate the Jewish 'web of economic ruin and moral destruction', a metaphor which related to financial and spiritual (and political) aggression against the will, a useful imaginary to illustrate Judeo-Communist conspiracies and the idea that the Jews controlled world finances.[232]

And while forming a relatively scattered community posed a threat in the case of Jews, being scattered was precisely what according to Bossy himself made of 'the Scandinavian, Germanic and Slavic groups' valuable counterparts to be sorted into the category of 'Cosmopolitan Montreal': forming 'a richly colored mosaic' and defining 'the city of nations'.[233] Similarly, whereas religion and culture were not mentioned as contributing factors to the exclusion of Jews, Blacks and Asians (classified too as 'foreign colonies'), being Christian appeared to facilitate the incorporation of non-European groups such as the Syrian and the Armenians into his understanding of 'New Canadians'.[234] Such an incorporation occurs simultaneously with what looks like a Europeanizing or even whitening process: '[C]hristians of the Near East', Syrians and Armenians were not to be defined as of 'Asian race' but 'of *Indo-European* culture, race, language and civilization'.[235] Supposedly, these groups were included because of 'their unfailing love for France' and their 'same cultural tastes and same Catholic conception of life'.[236] Clearly, however, religion served as a means to interpret or construct race, and to further equate the 'European race' to Christianity.

After the Second World War, Bossy claimed that his views on the Jews had evolved, and that he was ready to reach a 'modus vivendi', as he put it, while protecting Christian civilization.[237] Yet, nothing in the sources reveals any dramatic change in perspective. Nothing indicates that the horrors of the Holocaust in particular had any impact on Bossy's understanding of the Jewish community and of the need for ethnic cooperation. In fact, the only information regarding the Holocaust that Bossy kept as valuable framed it as a conspiracy. On the other hand, the Second World War worsened the already delicate relationship between Jewish and Ukrainian communities, in Europe as in Canada, which might have influenced Bossy's obstinate stance as well. Even though Jews and Ukrainians shared a common geographic origin in Eastern Europe, they had a very different understanding of their history: while both Ukrainians and Jews shared a common sense of dispossession, and struggle for collective survival, they saw each other as oppressors. The Holocaust only worsened such feelings: the Jewish community insisted that the Holocaust wouldn't have happened without 'the willful participation of local populations. Nowhere, many Jews believe, was that more readily given than in the Ukraine'. Meanwhile, Ukrainians claimed that they were 'trapped between Soviet and Nazi armies ... [so] active or passive collaboration ... offered a better chance of physical and national survival ...'.[238] After 1945, Jewish-Ukrainian sensitivities in Canada increased even further due to the Government's decision to accept the immigration of former members of the Galicia Division, or the Ukrainian flank of the German S.S. (*Schutzstaffel*). In addition, the number of incoming immigrants from Eastern Europe facilitated the growth of Ukrainian organization life in Canada, which became more nationalist, anti-Soviet, and antisemitic.[239] Ultimately, after the Second World War Bossy was as fearful and suspicious of the Jews as much as he had been during the 1930s. It is possible that the transition to which Bossy referred indicated a shift from a prewar defence of Jewish persecution to a support for their conversion to Christianity. Rather than evolving, though, this was more of a strategy to remain relevant after the war (and the discredit of the right) than a product of reflection. Now he simply argued that conversion was easier than pogroms, which were useless, he said, as Jews 'know in self[-]preservation how to defend themselves: They destroy you first.'[240]

Conclusion

The nature and outcome of Bossy's political and intellectual interactions, as well as of his rhetoric, during the early postwar period demonstrate that his intention remained (as was in the 1930s) to establish a Canadian state defined by religious and racial uniformity. Neither the experience of the Second World War nor the Holocaust changed his opinion about racial minorities and the Jewish community in particular. On the contrary, while this period contains some attempts to find common ground between Bossy's endeavours and those of more progressive movements, correspondence and literature available among Bossy's papers reveal that such attempts were more a product of opportunism (a means to attain visibility and power) than a product of genuine belief.

Notes

1. "Canadiens Français et Néo-Canadiens. Mémoire et Projet de W. J. Bossy, ancien Directeur des classes étrangères de la Commission des Écoles Catholiques de Montréal presentés Au Gouvernement, à l'Église et à la population canadienne-française de la Province de Québec", April 1948, file "New Canadians Service Bureau Miscellaneous 1948–1962", vol. 5, MG30 C72, LAC.
2. Although André J. Bélanger affirms that l'Action Corporative was created in 1938 by *L'Ordre Nouveau* and l'École Sociale Populaire [see: André-J. Bélanger, *L'Apolitisme des Idéologies Québécoises 1934–1936* (Quebec: Les Presses de l'Université Laval, 1974), 322], there are primary sources that demonstrate the earlier existence of this group. See: Eugene Forsey, "Clerical Fascism in Quebec", *Canadian Forum,* Vol. XVII, no. 197 (June 1937): 90–2; *L'Ordre Nouveau*, December 5, 1938, p. 1; *L'Ordre Nouveau*, June 5, 1939, pp. 1–2; *L'Ordre Nouveau*, January 5, 1940, p. 1. It seems that the group might have been active until 1950, see: *Progrès du Saguenay,* August 24, 1950, p. 5.
3. Christian Goeschel, "Staging Friendship: Mussolini and Hitler in Germany in 1937", *The Historical Journal*, vol. 60, no. 1 (March 2017).
4. L. M. Gouin, "New Guild System to Rebuild Society. Corporatism Offers Constructive Plan For Reorganization of the Social Order in Accordance With the Spirit of the Papal Encyclicals", *The Social Forum*, October 1940, page (?), file Fitzgerald Correspondence 1938–1941, vol. 3, MG30 C72, LAC.
5. *Le Devoir,* September 21, 1940, pp. 2, 6. Here 'Canadiens' is described as formed solely by British and French Canadians.
6. *L'Ordre Nouveau*, December 5, 1938, p. 1; *L'Illustration Nouvelle*, Septembre 21, 1938, p. 7; Marcel Martel, *Deuil d'un Pays Imaginé: Rêves, Luttes et Déroute du Canada Français* (Ottawa: University of Ottawa Press, 1997), 181.

7. Jean-Marie Mayeur, Luce Pietri, André Vauchez, *Guerres mondiales et totalitarismes (1914–1958): Histoire du christianisme* (Paris: Desclée-Fayard, 1990), 937. This book describes Archambault as 'social' and 'modern', implying that l'Action Corporative was a social initiative that rejected totalitarian experiments – however, it does not give any specific information on this movement.
8. Fitzgerald to LaPierre and Bossy, July 24, 1937, file Correspondence Fitzgerald, J. J., 1935–1937, vol. 3, MG30 C72, LAC; Bossy to Fitzgerald, July 30, 1937, file Correspondence Fitzgerald, J. J., 1935–1937, vol. 3, MG30 C72, LAC.
9. *L'Ordre Nouveau*, December 5, 1938, p. 1.
10. *L'Action Nationale*, vol. VIII, no. 1, September 1936, pp. 24–34.
11. *La Presse*, March 9, 1936, p. 9; *Le Devoir*, March 21, 1936, p. 7.
12. E.-Martin Meunier and Michel Bock, "Essor et déclin du corporatisme au Canada français (1930–1960)", in Olivier Dard, ed., *Le Corporatisme dans l'aire francophone au XXe siècle* (Bern: Peter Lang AG, 2011), 170–200.
13. Esdras Minville, "Comment établir l'Organisation corporative au Canada", *École Sociale Populaire*, no. 272 (1936).
14. *Le Canada*, November 25, 1940, p. 6.
15. Maximilien Caron, "L'organisation corporative au service de la démocratie", *École Sociale Populaire*, no. 347 (1942): 16.
16. *Le Devoir*, "Puisse le Canada être l'un des premiers pays à donner l'exemple de la vraie, de la saine démocratie?", Joseph-Papin Archambault, Septembre 25, 1942, p. 7.
17. *L'Ordre Nouveau*, "Corporatisme et démocratie, président de l'Action corporative, au dîner-causerie de la section Duvernay de la Société Saint-Jean-Baptiste le 21 novembre 1938", Maximilen Caron, December 5, 1938, p. 2.
18. *La Presse*, "Les bons citoyens font les bonnes républiques", Maximilen Caron, September 28, 1942, p. 14; Maximilien Caron, "L'organisation corporative au service de la démocratie", *École Sociale Populaire*, no. 347 (1942): 4; *Le Devoir*, October 1, 1942, p. 4. On the problem of majorities undermining minorities in democratic systems, see: Michael Mann, *The Dark Side of Democracy: Explaining Ethnic Cleansing* (Cambridge: Cambridge University Press, 2005).
19. Jean-Philippe Warren, "Le corporatisme canadien-français comme 'système total'. Quatre concepts pour comprendre la popularité d'une doctrine", *Recherches sociographiques*, vol. 45, no. 2 (May–August 2004): 219–38, 230.
20. *L'Ordre Nouveau*, "Corporatisme et démocratie", Maximilen Caron, December 5, 1938, pp. 1–2; Peter Neville, *Mussolini* (London: Routledge, 2004), 258. In Fascist Italy, strikes were interpreted as a sign of 'class war' and 'social revolution', which is why it sought to suppress it – as Caron was hoping for. See: Philip Morgan, *The Fall of Mussolini: Italy, the Italians, and the Second World War* (Oxford: Oxford University Press, 2007), 72–84; David I. Kertzer, *The Pope and Mussolini: The Secret History of Pius XI and the Rise of Fascism in Europe* (Oxford: Oxford University Press, 2014), 87, 193.
21. Maximilien Caron, "L'organisation corporative au service de la démocratie", *l'École Sociale Populaire*, no. 320 (September 1942), pp. 4, 15.
22. Maximilien Caron, et al., "Vers un ordre nouveau par l'organisation corporative", *École Sociale Populaire*, no. 312 (January 1940): 10–1.
23. Maximilien Caron, "L'organisation corporative au service de la démocratie", *l'École Sociale Populaire*, no. 320 (September 1942): 3.
24. *Le Canada*, "Salazar et le corporatisme au Portugal", Esdras Minville, January 11, 1939, p. 4.
25. *L'Ordre Nouveau*, "L'œuvre de Salazar", Hermas Bastien, March 20, 1937, pp. 1–2.
26. *Le Monde Ouvrier*, May 21, 1938, p. 1.

27. *L'Ordre Nouveau*, November 5, 1938, p. 3.
28. Lars Rensmann, "The Persistence of the Authoritarian Appeal: On Critical Theory as a Framework for Studying Populist Actors in European Democracies", in Jeremiah Morelock, ed., *Critical theory and authoritarian populism* (London: University of Westminster Press, 2018), 29–30.
29. Neville, *Mussolini,* 347; Gaetano Salvemini, *Under the Axe of Fascism: The definitive study of the creation of the Italian Fascist State* (New York: Citadel Press, 1971, originally published in 1936), 124–6.
30. Gertrude M. Godden, *Mussolini. The Birth of the New Democracy* (New York: PJ Kennedy, 1923), 22, 29.
31. Ibid., 4, 106–7, 168.
32. Lars Rensmann, "The Persistence of the Authoritarian Appeal", 29–30.
33. Hughes Théoret, *The Blue Shirts: Adrien Arcand and Fascism Anti-Semitism in Canada* (Ottawa: University of Ottawa Press, 2017).
34. "Interview", April 1972, pp. 8–9, file Bossy, Walter J. Biographical Notes, 1912–1972, vol. 1, MG30 C72, LAC. According to Bossy, he received "letters and letters" from Arcand with death threats, but I have found no such letters.
35. Fitzgerald to Gouin, October 23, 1940, file Fitzgerald Correspondence 1938–1941, vol. 3, MG30 C72, LAC.
36. Gouin to Fitzgerald, October 26, 1940, file Fitzgerald Correspondence 1938–1941, vol. 3, MG30 C72, LAC.
37. Fitzgerald to Bossy, October 28, 1940, file Correspondence Fitzgerald 1938–1941, vol. 3, MG30 C72, LAC; Michel Bock, *A Nation Beyond Borders: Lionel Groulx on French-Canadian Minorities* (Ottawa: University of Ottawa Press, 2014), 247.
38. Bock, *A Nation Beyond Borders*, 247. Arès was especially concerned about the increasing assimilation of French-speaking Canadians throughout the country, arguing that the 'federal regime was "very costly for the French language: not only was the French-speaking community unable to retain its numbers, but it lost more than 400,000 among those who used to be French-speakers."', cited in: Marcel Martel, "Hors du Québec, point de salut!", in Michael D. Behiels, and Marcel Martel, eds., *Nation, Ideas, Identities: Essays in Honour of Ramsay Cook* (Oxford: Oxford University Press, 2000), 136.
39. Richard Arès, "Catéchisme de l'organisation corporative", *L'École Sociale Populaire*, no. 289–90 (1938, 1946).
40. Fitzgerald to Gouin, October 23, 1940, file Fitzgerald Correspondence 1938–1941, vol. 3, MG30 C72, LAC. In this letter, Fitzgerald highlights that the guild system as proposed by l'Action Corporative seems 'best adapted to the Canadian needs [but] more specially the needs of the Province of Quebec'.
41. Fitzgerald to Bossy and LaPierre, January 10, 1940, file Fitzgerald Correspondence 1938–1941, vol. 3, MG30 C72, LAC.
42. *Le Devoir*, November 12, 1940, p. 2; *L'Illustration Nouvelle*, November 19, 1940, p. 17. On Switzerlands' interwar corporatist nature, see: Peter J. Katzenstein, *Corporatism and Change: Austria, Switzerland, and the Politics of Industry* (Ithaca: Cornell University Press, 1984), 124.
43. Fitzgerald to Bossy and LaPierre, January 10, 1940, and January 20, 1940, file Fitzgerald Correspondence 1938–1941, vol. 3, MG30 C72, LAC.
44. Bàrbara Molas, "Transnational Francoism: the British and the Canadian Friends of National Spain (1930s–1950s)", vol. 35, no. 2, *Contemporary British History* (August 4, 2020): 165–86.
45. Bossy to Gouin, October 29, 1940, file Fitzgerald Correspondence 1938–1941, vol. 3, MG30 C72, LAC; Gouin to Bossy, October 31, 1940, file Fitzgerald Correspondence 1938–1941, vol. 3, MG30 C72, LAC; Bossy to Fitzgerald, November 8, 1940, file Fitzgerald Correspondence 1938–1941, vol. 3, MG30 C72, LAC.

46. Fitzgerald to Bossy, November 15, 1940, file Fitzgerald Correspondence 1938–1941, vol. 3, MG30 C72, LAC.
47. Fitzgerald to Bossy and Fitzgerald, January 10, 1940, and January 20, 1940, file Fitzgerald Correspondence 1938–1941, vol. 3, MG30 C72, LAC.
48. Fitzgerald to C. G. Power, March 21, 1944, file Correspondence Fitzgerald J. J. 1944, vol. 3, MG30 C72, LAC; John Francis Noll, *The Decline of Nations: its causes and cure* (Huntington: Our Sunday Visitor Press, 1940), 222, 224 – Fitzgerald mentioned to Bossy that Noll was the main source of inspiration for the reassessment of classocracy as part of a democratic effort for progress. See: Fitzgerald to Bossy, April 13, 1943, file Correspondence Fitzgerald 1943, vol. 3, MG30 C72, LAC. Especially important to such a reassessment was Noll's *Civilization's Builder and Protector*, in which Noll argues for the establishment of a guild system sustained by a common interest 'by which the many nations can be united in peace, and there is no conceivable bond other than a spiritual one'. Peoples of all nations, he said, 'must have some common interest which means more to them than their nationalism, and that common interest would be a common religion obligating all to love one another as children of the same Heavenly Father'. See: John Francis Noll, *Civilization's Builder and Protector* (Huntington: Our Sunday Visitor Press, 1940?), 181–2, 415–6.
49. Bossy to General Director of Studies of the MCSC Trefflé Boulanger, September 28, 1945, file MCSC Correspondence, 1942–1949, vol. 9, MG30 C72, LAC.
50. Bossy to MCSC president Alfred F. Larose, March 25, 1946, file MCSC Correspondence, Bossy's Position 1938–1949, vol. 9, MG30 C72, LAC.
51. Fitzgerald to Watson Kirkconnell, June 5, 1946, file Correspondence Fitzgerald, J. J. 1946, vol. 3, MG30 C72, LAC; Bossy to Fitzgerald, January 6, 1947, file Correspondence Fitzgerald, J. J. 1947, vol. 3, MG30 C72, LAC.
52. Bossy to Gustave Monette, October 10, 1947, file MSC Correspondence, Bossy's Position 1938–1949, vol. 9, MG30 C72, LAC.
53. Robert Gagnon, *Histoire de la Commission des Écoles Catholiques de Montréal* (Montreal: Boréal 1996), 227–8; *Le Devoir*, July 16, 1948, p. 9; Michael D. Behiels, "The Commission des écoles catholiques de Montréal and the Néo-Canadian Question: 1947–1963", *Canadian Ethnic Studies*, 18, 2 (1986): 42.
54. Gagnon, *Histoire de la Commission*, 228; *Le Devoir*, July 16, 1948, p. 9. In her dissertation, Mélanie Lanouette indicates that, specifically, Bossy was "chargé des Ukrainiens". See: CECM, *Délibérations* – Comité des Néo-Canadiens, November 21, 1947, ACSDM, cited in: Mélanie Lanouette, "Penser l'éducation, dire sa culture. Les écoles catholiques anglaises au Québec, 1928–1964", dissertation (Université Laval, 2004), 137.
55. April 30, 1948, file MCSC Correspondence, Bossy's Position, 1938–1949, vol. 9, MG30 C72, LAC; *Un Mouvement, Une Oeuvre. 25 ans au service des Néo-Canadiens (1925–1950)* (1950), 18, file New Canadians Service Bureau, vol. 5, LAC. Possibly, the idea of establishing an independent Bureau was also encouraged by a note that Bossy kept in 1946 written by priest Gustave Bellemarre. In it, Bellemarre spoke of the union and universality of the Church (ecumenism) and suggested that "...un institut ou centre néo-canadien comprenant bibliothèque, salle de lecture, salle de conférences" be established to work towards that unity. "Les Canadiens", it reads, "pourraient y connaître des Néo-Canadiens, leur langue etc, et [in due course], les Néo-Canadiens pourraient y apprendre le français ou l'anglais et étudier le Canada". See: Père Gustave Bellemarre, "Rapport Préliminaire et Privé", March 27, 1946, file New Canadians Service Bureau Plans of Action 1948–1949, vol. 5, MG30 C72, LAC.

56. April 30, 1948, file MCSC Correspondence, Bossy's Position, 1938–1949, vol. 9, MG30 C72, LAC; *Un Mouvement, Une Oeuvre*, 18, file New Canadians Service Bureau, vol. 5, LAC. See also: Lanouette, "Pense l'Éducation, Dire Sa Culture", 131.
57. *Un Mouvement, Une Oeuvre*, 19, file New Canadians Service Bureau, vol. 5, LAC.
58. April 30, 1948, file MCSC Correspondence, Bossy's Position, 1938–1949, vol. 9, MG30 C72, LAC; *Un Mouvement, Une Oeuvre*, 18, file New Canadians Service Bureau, vol. 5, LAC.
59. Gagnon, *Histoire de la Commission*, 227–8, 231.
60. Bossy, "Canadiens Français et Néo-Canadiens. Mémoire et Projet de W. J. Bossy, ancien Directeur des classes étrangères de la Commission des Écoles Catholiques de Montréal présentés Au Gouvernement, à l'Église et à la population canadienne-française de la Province de Québec", April 1948, p. 4, file New Canadians Service Bureau Miscellaneous 1948–1962, vol. 5, MG30 C72, LAC.
61. Ibid.
62. Robert Gagnon indicates that Bossy quit the MCSC to inaugurate his own "Service des Néo-Canadiens" in 1949, but Bossy's records and the local press from 1948 show that he did so a year earlier. See: Gagnon, *Histoire de la Commission...*, 229. Lee Blanding states the Bossy inaugurated the Bureau in 1949 "at the urging of the School Board", but based on the primary sources I studied, this would be incorrect. See: Lee Blanding, "Re-branding Canada: The Origins of Canadian Multiculturalism Policy, 1945–1974", dissertation (University of Victoria, 2013), 111, 185.
63. Bossy to Fitzgerald, April 22, 1948, file Correspondence Fitzgerald, J. J. 1948, vol. 3, MG30 C72, LAC.
64. "Le Bureau du Service des Néo-Canadiens. General Plan of Envisaged Action", p. 1, file New Canadians Service Bureau Plans of Action 1948–1949, vol. 5, MG30 C72, LAC.
65. Bossy, "Canadiens Français et Néo-Canadiens. Mémoire et Projet de W. J. Bossy, ancien Directeur des classes étrangères de la Commission des Écoles Catholiques de Montréal présentés Au Gouvernement, à l'Église et à la population canadienne-française de la Province de Québec", p. 16, April 1948, file New Canadians Service Bureau Miscellaneous 1948–1962, vol. 5, MG30 C72, LAC.
66. Fitzgerald to Bossy, April 24, 1948, file Correspondence Fitzgerald, J. J. 1948, vol. 3, MG30 C72, LAC.
67. Bossy, "Canadiens Français et Néo-Canadiens. Mémoire et Projet de W. J. Bossy, ancien Directeur des classes étrangères de la Commission des Écoles Catholiques de Montréal présentés Au Gouvernement, à l'Église et à la population canadienne-française de la Province de Québec", April 1948, file New Canadians Service Bureau Miscellaneous 1948–1962, vol. 5, MG30 C72, LAC.
68. Bossy, "Canadiens Français et Néo-Canadiens. Mémoire et Projet de W. J. Bossy, ancien Directeur des classes étrangères de la Commission des Écoles Catholiques de Montréal présentés Au Gouvernement, à l'Église et à la population canadienne-française de la Province de Québec", p. 4, April 1948, file New Canadians Service Bureau Miscellaneous 1948–1962, vol. 5, MG30 C72, LAC.
69. *Le Canada*, April 27, 1948, p. 3.
70. Bossy, "Canadiens Français et Néo-Canadiens. Mémoire et Projet de W. J. Bossy, ancien Directeur des classes étrangères de la Commission des Écoles Catholiques de Montréal présentés Au Gouvernement, à l'Église et à la population canadienne-française de la Province de Québec", pp. 5–6, April 1948, file New Canadians Service Bureau Miscellaneous 1948–1962, vol. 5, MG30 C72, LAC.

118   *Networks*

71. *Le Canada,* April 27, 1948, p. 3.
72. Lanouette, "Pense l'Éducation, Dire Sa Culture", 132–3.
73. Ibid., 132.
74. It is worth noting that René Guénette was the director of *l'École Canadienne*, the monthly review issued by the Montreal Catholic School Commission intended for its teachers. See: André Beaulieu, Jean Hamelin, *La Presse Québécoise des Origines à Nos Jours.* Tome sixième, 1920–1934 (Sainte-Foy: Presses de l'Université Laval, 1984), 96–7.
75. *Relations*, no. 9 (June 1948): 17; *Un Mouvement, Une Oeuvre*, 31, file New Canadians Service Bureau 'Un Mouvement, Une Oeuvre, Walter J. Bossy', 1948–1971, vol. 5, MG30 C72, LAC, 68.
76. *Le Montréal-Matin*, April 28, 1948, page (?), cited in: Lanouette, "Penser l'Éducation, Dire Sa Culture", 132; also mentioned in Fitzgerald to Bossy, 12 May 1948, vol. 3, file Correspondence Fitzgerald, J. J. 1948, MG30 C72, LAC. You can find a copy of *Le Montréal-Matin*'s piece on Bossy's New Canadians Bureau and project in 27 April, 1948, in vol. 17, MG30 C72, LAC); *Le Soleil*, April 27, 1948, p. 4; *Le Canada*, May 10, 1948, p. 4; *Le Canada*, April 27, 1948, p. 3, April 30, 1948, p. 4, and May 4, 1948, p. 4; *L'Action Catholique,* 15 June, 1948, p. 4; *La Patrie*, April 27, 1948, page (?), vol. 17, MG30 C72, LAC. Bossy's notes on "Canadiens Français et Néo-Canadiens. Mémoire et projet" mention that *L'Étoile du Lac, La Feuille d'Érable, L'Ami du Peuple*, and *La Tribune* as expressing similar enthusiasm, although I haven't seen copies of the newspapers that can confirm this. See: file New Canadians Service Bureau Plans of Action 1948–1949, vol. 5, August 1948, MG30 C72, LAC. The reference to Bossy's New Canadians Bureau published by *Une Voix de l'Ouest* is cited in: *Relations*, no. 92, August 1948, p. 241.
77. *La Patrie*, April 27, 1948, page (?), vol. 17, MG30 C72, LAC.
78. *Le Soleil*, April 27, 1948, p. 4.
79. See: http://academiedeslettresduquebec.ca/membres/decedes/roger-duhamel/. Accessed on February 8, 2021. The Société Saint-Jean-Baptiste is an institution dedicated to the protection of francophone interests in Canada.
80. *Montréal – Matin*, April 28, 1948, page (?), vol. 17, MG30 C72, LAC.
81. Ibid.
82. *Clairon-Montreal*, June 25, 1948, p. 1.
83. ACFA, *L'Almanach Français de l'Alberta* (1948), p. 30; Guy Courteau, *Relations,* no. 92, August 1948, p. 241.
84. *L'Action Catholique*, January 15, 1949, p. 4.
85. Angers to Bossy, June 3, 1948, file New Canadians Service Bureau Correspondence Received On Bureau 1948–1949, vol. 5, MG30 C72, LAC.
86. Beaudin to Bossy, June 7, 1948, file New Canadians Service Bureau Correspondence Received On Bureau 1948–1949, vol. 5, MG30 C72, LAC; *L'Action Nationale,* vol. XXXIII, no. 3, November 1948, pp. 243–4.
87. CECM, Délibérations — Comité des Néo-Canadiens, 27 avril 1948, ACSDM, cited in Laouette, "Penser l'Éducation, Dire Sa Culture", p. 133.
88. *Montréal – Matin*, May 4, 1948, page (?), vol. 17, MG30 C72, LAC. Paul Massé was also a 'fervent promoteur du rapprochement entre les groupes néo-canadiens et les francophones'. See: Robert Gagnon, *Histoire de la Commission des écoles catholiques de Montréal* (Montreal: Boréal 1996), 228.
89. *Le Canada*, Abril 27, 1948, p. 2.
90. Roberto Perin, "French-Speaking Canada from 1840", in Terrence Murphy and Roberto Perin, eds., *A Concise History of Christianity in Canada* (Oxford: Oxford University Press, 1996), 203, 257.
91. *Le Devoir*, November 21, 1932, p. 4.

92. Jean-Claude St-Amant, "L'École Sociale Populaire et Le Syndicalisme Catholique 1911–1949", Master's thesis (l'École des Gradués de l'Université Laval, Décembre 1976), 89.
93. *Le Petit Canadien*, vol. 12, no. 6 (June 1915): 16. Mignault was also, according to Xavier Gélinas, the founder of the Jeunes Lauretiens, a French-Canadian nationalist youth movement established in 1936. See: Xavier Gélinas, *La droite intellectuelle québécoise et la révolution tranquille (1956–1966)*, dissertation (York University, 2001), 23.
94. Bossy to J.P. Labarre (*surintendant de l'Instruction publique* or Superintendent of Public Instruction), April 22, 1948, file New Canadians Service Bureau Correspondence Sent On Bureau 1948–1949, vol. 5, MG30 C72, LAC; *Relations*, no. 90 (June 1948): 17; Olivier Maurault, "Canadiens Français et Néo-Canadiens", file New Canadians Service Bureau Un Mouvement, Une Ouvre, Walter J. Bossy (1948–1971), vol. 5, MG30 C72, LAC; Routhier to Bossy, 5 June, 1948, file New Canadians Service Bureau Correspondence Received On Bureau 1948–1949, vol. 5, MG30 C72, LAC.
95. See: Daniel Bouchard, *La Société historique du Nouvel-Ontario de 1942 à 1976*, Sudbury, La Société historique du Nouvel-Ontario de 1942 à 1976, collection 'Documents historiques', no. 94, 1996, cited in Lucien Pelletier, "Les Jésuites de Sudbury vers 1960: une mutation difficile", *Revue du Nouvel-Ontario*, no. 37 (2012): 20.
96. See: *Relations*, no. 90 (June 1948): 175; *Relations*, no. 91 (July 1948): 205; *Relations*, no. 92 (August 1948): 241; *Relations*, no. 96 (December 1948): 368.
97. *Relations*, no. 90 (June 1948): 175.
98. Ibid.
99. November 8, 1948, vol. 17, MG30 C72, LAC. Even though by 1951 at least 300 individuals (including priests and nuns) and institutions (including convents, residential schools or *pensionnats*, academies, hospitals, *écoles* and *collèges*) had financially contributed to the New Canadians movement, their donations generally ranged between 2$ and 10$. In fact, they mostly amounted to 2$, which was suggested as the price for the commemorative book *Un Mouvement, Une Oeuvre*, published in 1950, sent to all members or supporters. It is worth mentioning that members between 1948 and 1951 included J. A. Laprès (5$) and Taggart Smyth (10$). See: Liste de souscripteurs du Bureau des Néo-Canadiens 1951, file New Canadians Service Bureau Lists of Contributors 1948–1952, vol. 6, MG30 C72, LAC; Liste de souscripteurs du Bureau des Néo-Canadiens 1948, 1949–1950, 1951, file New Canadians Service Bureau Lists of Contributors 1948–1952, vol. 6, MG30 C72, LAC.
100. Houde to Bossy, October 9, 1948, file New Canadians Service Bureau Correspondence Received On Bureau 1948–1949, vol. 5, MG30 C72, LAC.
101. *Le Canada*, December 20, 1948, p. 4; *L'Avenir du Nord*, December 31, 1948, p. 5; *L'Étoile du Lac St. Jean*, January 20, 1949, p. 1.
102. Bossy to St. Laurent, Stuart Sinclair, Walter Harris, and Howard Prentice, March 27, 1953, cited in Kevin P. Anderson, *Not Quite Us: Anti-Catholic Thought in English Canada Since 1900* (Montreal: McGill-Queen's University Press, 2019), 189.
103. Anderson, *Not Quite Us: Anti-Catholic Thought in English Canada Since*, 189.
104. *Le Devoir,* March 25, 1947, p. 3; *La Patrie*, July 25, 1948, p. (?), vol. 17, MG30 C72, LAC. It appears that John J. Fitzgerald also played a part in facilitating this agreement, although what part exactly is not clear in the sources. See: Fitzgerald to Pearson, 11 June 1951, file Correspondence Fitzgerald, J. J. 1951, vol. 3, MG30 C72, LAC.
105. *Le Devoir*, June 18, 1949, p. 1.
106. Speeches were given in Vancouver, Victoria, Calgary, Saskatoon, Brandon, Winnipeg, Fort William, and Port Arthur, vols. 258–9, MG 26 L, LAC.

120   *Networks*

107. Michel S. Beaulieu, "Political Mapping: Louis St-Laurent's 1949 Tour of Western Canada", *The Champlain Society*, November 10, 2020. Accessed on February 10, 2021; *La Liberté et le Patriote*, April 15, 1949, p. 1.
108. *Louis St-Laurent au peuple canadien: discours du très honorable Louis S. St-Laurent, Premier ministre du Canada à l'ouverture de la campagne en vue de l'élection générale: radiodiffusé sur le réseau national de la Société Radio-Canada* (Ottawa: Cabinet du Premier ministre, 1949), 16. See: http://bilan.usherbrooke.ca/voutes/callisto/dhsp37/lois/discours/st-laurent_elections.htm.
109. *La Presse*, May 10, 1949, p. 21.
110. *Le Canada*, April 23, 1949, p. 3; *Le Devoir*, May 17, 1949, p. 10.
111. *Le Devoir*, May 17, 1949, p. 10.
112. *La Liberté et le Patriote*, April 22, 1949, p. 5.
113. *Le Canada*, April 23, 1949, p. 3.
114. *La Liberté et le Patriote*, April 22, 1949, p. 5.
115. *Un Mouvement, Une Oeuvre*, 57–8, file New Canadians Service Bureau 'Un Mouvement, Une Oeuvre, Walter J. Bossy', 1948–1971, vol. 5, MG30 C72, LAC. I have found no information about Louis St. Laurent's tour of western Canada among the digitally available English-speaking newspapers. Because the archives are currently unavailable due to COVID-19, the question of why English-speaking newspapers seemed to care less about the tour remains, for now, unanswered.
116. Joseph Saine to clergy, May 7, 1949, file New Canadians Service Bureau Correspondence on New Canadian Day 1949, vol. 5, MG30 C72, LAC; New Canadians General Information and Program, file New Canadians Service Bureau Correspondence on New Canadian Day 1949, May 9, 1949, vol. 5, MG30 C72, LAC; *The Gazette,* 16 May 1949, page (?), vol. 17, MG30 C72, LAC; Annual Report, City of Montreal, December 31, 1948, file New Canadians Service Bureau Correspondence Received on Bureau 1948–1949, vol. 5, MG30 C72, LAC.
117. New Canadians General Information and Program, file New Canadians Service Bureau Correspondence on New Canadian Day 1949, May 9, 1949, vol. 5, MG30 C72, LAC.
118. Ibid.
119. *The Standard,* Montreal, 14 May 1949, page (?), vol. 17, MG30 C72, LAC.
120. House of Commons Debates, 1 May 1947, pp. 2644–6. See: http://www.abheritage.ca/albertans/speeches/king_1.html.
121. Ibid.
122. G. A. Rawlyk, "Canada's Immigration Policy, 1945–1962", *Dalhousie Review*, vol. 42, no. 3, (Autumn, 1962): 290. The wave of immigration, combined with the higher postwar birth rate, dramatically increased Canada's population from some 12 million in 1945 to nearly 16 million by the mid-1950s. See: *The New Encyclopedia Britannica* (Edinburgh: Encyclopaedia Britannica Inc. 1997), vol. 15, p. 470.
123. Paul Andrew Evans, "The Least Possible Fuss and Publicity: The Policies of Immigration in Postwar Canada, 1945–1963", dissertation (University of Waterloo, 2018), 178. In 1948, more than 125,000 immigrants were admitted and, although the flow of arrivals dropped in 1949–1950, it subsequently increased to reach a peak of some 282,000 in 1957.
124. *La Presse,* May 10, 1949, p. 21.
125. *The Herald*, May 7, 1949, page (?), vol. 17, MG30 C72, LAC; *Le Devoir*, May 13, 1949, p. 7; *Le Canada*, May 14, 1949, p. 3; and *La Presse*, May 10, 1949, p. 1.
126. *La Presse*, May 10, 1949, p. 21.
127. *Le Canada*, May 12, 1949, p. 4.
128. *Le Devoir*, May 17, 1949, p. 10.

129. *The Gazette*, May 16, 1949, and *La Patrie,* May 16, 1949, pages (?), vol. 17, MG30 C72, LAC; New Canadians General Information and Program, file New Canadians Service Bureau Correspondence on New Canadian Day 1949, 9 May 1949, vol. 5, MG30 C72, LAC.
130. Advertisement, file New Canadians Service Bureau Correspondence on New Canadian Day 1949, vol. 5, MG30 C72, LAC. Emphasis in the original. See also: "Allegiance Day Program Set. New Canadians Plan. Mass, Parade, Concert", vol. 17, MG30 C72, LAC.
131. *The Gazette*, May 16, 1949, pages (?), vol. 17, MG30 C72, LAC.
132. *Un Mouvement, Une Oeuvre*, 31, file New Canadians Service Bureau 'Un Mouvement, Une Oeuvre, Walter J. Bossy', 1948–1971, vol. 5, MG30 C72, LAC, 67.
133. *Un Mouvement, Une Oeuvre*, 31, file New Canadians Service Bureau 'Un Mouvement, Une Oeuvre, Walter J. Bossy', 1948–1971, vol. 5, MG30 C72, LAC, 21.
134. *Le Devoir*, May 17, 1949, p. 1.
135. "Les Néo-Canadiens et les Canadiens français. Résumé d'un plan d'action", file New Canadians Service Bureau Plans of Action 1948–1949, August 1948, vol. 5, MG30 C72, LAC.
136. *Un Mouvement, Une Oeuvre*, 31, file New Canadians Service Bureau 'Un Mouvement, Une Oeuvre, Walter J. Bossy', 1948–1971, vol. 5, MG30 C72, LAC, 20, 67; *La Presse*, January 31, 1950.
137. *The Montreal Daily Star,* May 16, 1949, pages (?), in vol. 17, MG30 C72, LAC.
138. *The Gazette,* May 16, 1949, pages (?), vol. 17, MG30 C72, LAC.
139. Ibid.
140. *The Gazette,* May 16, 1949, and *La Patrie,* May 16, 1949, pages (?), in vol. 17, MG30 C72, LAC.
141. Bossy to St Laurent, Stuart Sinclair, Walter Harris, and Howard Prentice, March 27, 1953, cited in Kevin P. Anderson, *Not Quite Us: Anti-Catholic Thought in English Canada Since 1900*, p. 189.
142. Saul Friedländer, *Nazi Germany and the Jews: The years of persecution* (London: Weidenfeld & Nicolson, 1997), 251; *Jewish Telegraphic Agency*, September 18, 1938, vol. IV, no. 142, p. 1. Accessed on November 5, 2020, here: http://pdfs.jta.org/1938/1938-09-18_142.pdf?_ga=2.162112116.950082366.1604585015-1507896659.1604585015. See also: James Chappel, *Catholic Modern: The Challenge of Totalitarianism and the Remaking of the Catholic Church* (Cambridge: Harvard University Press, 2018), 110–1, 113, 135.
143. "Directive Principles for the Institutions of the Future", *Commonweal*, 415–21, 419.
144. See: Andreas Musolff, *Metaphor, Nation and the Holocaust. The Concept of the Body Politics* (New York: Routledge, 2010).
145. "Preachers Will Have to Work When 'God's Chosen (?) People' Take Over U.S.A. Christianity to be abolished. Jews to rule the world. Thus says Morris Levy of World League of Liberal (?) Jews", The Pierce Printery (Oregon, US), file Néo-Canadian Activities. Articles on Jewry & Judaism 1944–1964, vol. 5, MG30 C72, LAC.
146. "Communists' Decree Regarding Women", The Pierce Printery in Oregon, file Néo-Canadian Activities. Articles on Jewry & Judaism 1944–1964, vol. 5, MG30 C72, LAC.
147. File Néo-Canadian Activities. Articles on Jewry & Judaism 1944–1964, vol. 5, MG30 C72, LAC.
148. "William Pierce", *Southern Poverty Law Centre*. Retrieved on March 30, 2020.
149. Gerald L. K. Smith, *My Fight for the Right! (A Life Story)* (St. Louis: Christian Nationalist Crusade, ca. 1950), 5, 23.

150. On Jewish stereotypes, see: Matthew Baigell, *The Implacable Urge to Defame: Cartoon Jews in the American Press, 1877–1935* (New York: Syracuse University, 2017), esp. 80; or Sara Lipton, *Dark Mirror: The Medieval Origins of Anti-Jewish Iconography* (New York: Metropolitan, 2014), esp. 171–98.
151. Gerald L. K. Smith, *Is Communism Jewish?* (St. Louis: Christian Nationalist Crusade, ca. 1950).
152. "Out of the Mouth of the Jew" (St. Louis: the Patriotic Tract Society), file Néo-Canadian Activities. Articles on Jewry & Judaism 1944–1964, vol. 5, MG30 C72, LAC. The Christian Nationalists were founded by Gerald L. K. Smith in 1942 with the aim to preserve the United States as a Christian nation and to 'oppose Communism, world government and ... all attempts to force the intermixture of the black and white races'. On the Patriotic Tract Society, see: "The Patriotic Tract Society", Philadelphia Jewish Archive Photographs, Temple Digital Collections, Temple University Libraries. Retrieved on March 30, 2020.
153. "Out of the Mouth of the Jew" (St. Louis: the Patriotic Tract Society), file Néo-Canadian Activities. Articles on Jewry & Judaism 1944–1964, vol. 5, MG30 C72, LAC.
154. G. A. Field, October 27, 1950, file Néo-Canadian Activities. Articles on Jewry & Judaism 1944–1964, vol. 5, MG30 C72, LAC.
155. On Paul-Émile Lalanne, see: Jean-François Nadeau, *The Canadian Führer: The Life of Adrien Arcand* (Toronto: James Lorimer & Company Ltd., 2011), 165. On Paul-Émile Lalanne and his association with the Canadian Gentile Congress, see: "Canada", *The American Jewish Year Book*, vol. 53 (1952): 263, American Jewish Committee Archives. See also: *Jewish Telegraphic Agency*, "Canadian Group Protests Against Anti-Jewish Propaganda", April 2, 1952.
156. File Néo-Canadian Activities. Articles on Jewry & Judaism 1944–1964, vol. 5, MG30 C72, LAC. The pamphlet had been issued by Ray (Raymond) K. Rudman, the South African leader of Die Boerenasia, a national-socialist movement founded in 1940 that promoted Anglo-Nordic supremacy. See: Steven Uran, *Afrikaners and National Socialism in South Africa: 1933–1945*, vol. 2 (US: University of Wisconsin-Madison, 1975).
157. *The Cross and the Flag*, 1946, vols. 20–1, p. 8; *The Institute Annual*, Institute of Jewish Affairs, 1957, 263; Jeffrey Kaplan and Leonard Weinberg, *The Emergence of a Euro-American Radical Right* (NJ: Rutgers University Press, 1998), 111.
158. "Archconfraternity of Prayer for the Conversion of Israel", file Néo-Canadian Activities. Articles on Jewry & Judaism 1944–1964, vol. 5, MG30 C72, LAC.
159. Charlotte Klein, "From Conversion to Dialogue. The Sisters of Sion and the Jews: a Paradigm of Catholic-Jewish Relations?", *Journal of Ecumenical Studies* (1981): 388–400.
160. Max Eisen, "Christian Missions to the Jews in North America and Great Britain", *Jewish Social Studies*, vol. 10, no. 1 (January 1948): 55.
161. Dan Mikhman, *Belgium and the Holocaust: Jews, Belgians, Germans* (New York: Berghahn Books, 1998), 132–6.
162. *L'Action Catholique*, December 1, 1956, p. 12. See also: *La Presse*, July 20, 1963, p. 23; *Le Soleil*, May 29, 1968, p. 33.
163. *La Presse*, July 20, 1963, p. 23. The Centre organized conferences on ecumenism too, of what we know because Bossy kept pamphlets advertising them. See, for instance: "Judaïsme et Oecuménisme. Conférences organisées par le Centre Ratisbonne ... 1959–1960", under the auspices of Notre Dame de Sion, vol. 5, MG30 C72, LAC.
164. Mikhman, *Belgium and the Holocaust*, 135–6.

Networks   123

165. January 30, 1956, file Néo-Canadian Activities. Articles on Jewry & Judaism 1944–1964, vol. 5, MG30 C72, LAC.
166. File Religious Activities Blue Army of Fatima Correspondence, 1958–1960, vol. 9, MG30 C72, LAC. See photo of Bossy with members of the Blue Army celebrating the inauguration of the English-speaking section of the Blue Army here: *Le Sourire, Les Buissonnets de Montréal*, January 1960, page (?), vol. 18, MG30 C72, LAC. On Bossy becoming the leader of Montreal's English-speaking section of the Blue Army of Fatima, see: Blue Army of Fatima Montreal Centre Bulletin, November 24, 1959, file Religious Activities Blue Army of Fatima Correspondence, 1958–1960, vol. 9, MG30 C72, LAC; Colgan to Bossy, August 26, 1959, file Religious Activities Blue Army of Fatima Correspondence, 1958–1960, vol. 9, MG30 C72, LAC.
167. Jeffrey S. Bennett, "The Blue Army and the Red Scare: Politics, Religion, and Cold War Paranoia", *Politics, Religion & Ideology*, vol. 16, nos. 2–3 (2015): 263–81; *L'Action Populaire*, September 22, 1955, p. 10.
168. *Le Sourire, Les Buissonnets de Montréal*, February 1960, p. 10. Edward LaPierre and John J. Fitzgerald joined Bossy's section as English-speaking members of the Blue Army of Fatima. See: List of members, June 11, 1959, file Religious Activities Blue Army of Fatima Correspondence, 1958–1960, vol. 9, MG30 C72, LAC.
169. Archbishop Lemieux to Bossy, July 23, 1959, file Religious Activities Blue Army of Fatima Correspondence, 1958–1960, vol. 9, MG30 C72, LAC.
170. In file New Canadians Service Bureau Correspondence Received on Bureau 1948–1949, vol. 5, MG30 C72, LAC.
171. Arthur B. Klyber, "Crucify the Jew?", reprinted from Catholic monthly publication *The Liguorian*, undated, in file Néo-Canadian Activities. Articles on Jewry & Judaism 1944–1964, vol. 5, MG30 C72, LAC.
172. Arthur B. Klyber, "The Jew Next Door", pp. 1–2, reprinted from Catholic monthly publication *The Liguorian*, undated, in file Néo-Canadian Activities Articles on Jewry & Judaism 1944–1964, vol. 5, MG30 C72, LAC.
173. Jacques Maritain, *Ransoming the Time* (New York: Charles Scribner's Sons, 1941), 126.
174. Maritain, *Ransoming the Time*, 150.
175. Ibid., 153–4.
176. Ibid., 155.
177. Ibid., 157.
178. Ibid., 164.
179. It is worth mentioning that, in *A Christian Looks at the Jewish Question* (New York: Longmans, Green, 1939), Jacques Maritain explicitly states that 'Christianity then is the overflowing fullness and the supernatural realization of Judaism' (pages 22–3).
180. John J. Fitzgerald, *Help! A shrill call from the Atlantic Charter* (Sault Ste. Marie: Cliffe Printing Company, 1944). On Fitzgerald becoming leader of the Social Credit of Ontario, see: *The Sudbury Daily Star*, January 20, 1946, page (?), file Correspondence Fitzgerald, J. J. 1946, vol. 3, MG30 C72, LAC.
181. Jaques to Fitzgerald, May 7, 1944, file Correspondence Fitzgerald J. J. 1944, vol. 3, MG30 C72, LAC.
182. The Social Credit Theory reached Canada just months after its institution in Britain, and was first spread by Albertan evangelist William Aberhart, who created the Social Credit Party of Canada and used his Christian radio program to promote it. In 1935, Aberhart became premier of Alberta. The Social Credit Party would remain in power in the province of Alberta until 1971. See: Alvin Finkel, *The Social Credit Phenomenon in Alberta* (Toronto: University of Toronto Press, 1989).

183. J. T. Morley, "Social Credit", *The Canadian Encyclopedia*, Last edited October 7, 2015. Retrieved on September 3, 2020.
184. Janine Stingel, *Social Discredit: Anti-Semitism, Social Credit, and the Jewish Response* (Montreal: McGill-Queen's University Press, 2000), 18.
185. Stingel, *Social Discredit*, 100; Alan Davies, ed., *Antisemitism in Canada: History and Interpretation* (Waterloo: Wilfrid Laurier University Press, 1992), 172.
186. *Edmonton Bulletin*, October 11, 1944, page (?), cited in: Stingel, *Social Discredit*, 66.
187. Davies, *Antisemitism in Canada*, 179.
188. Stingel, *Social Discredit*, 135; Martin Robin, *Shades of Right. Nativist and Fascist Politics in Canada, 1920–1940* (Toronto: University of Toronto Press, 1992), 266; Gerald L. K. Smith, *The Cross and the Flag*, vols. 4–5 (1946): 785.
189. *Today and Tomorrow*, December 9, 1943, March 2, 1944, and September 14, 1944, pages (?), cited in: Stingel, *Social Discredit*, 24, 60–1.
190. Jaques to Fitzgerald, May 7, 1944, file Correspondence Fitzgerald J. J. 1944, vol. 3, MG30 C72, LAC. For Bossy's own references to and thoughts about an alleged relationship between Judaism, communism, and liberal democracy, see Chapter 2, and especially: Walter J. Bossy, *A Call to All Socially Minded Christian Canadians* (Montreal: Classocracy League of Canada, 1934), 11, 34; Bossy to the Comité D'Aide Aux Étrangers Catholiques, "Memorandum", file Neo-Canadian Activities – New Canadian Friendship House, 1937, 6, vol. 4, MG30 C72, LAC.
191. Clerk of the House of Commons Arthur Beauchesne, February 25, 1944, 1944/45 R33 A1, 3355–11; 10 May 1944, 1944/45 R33 A1, 307–9. Accessed in May 2020.
192. Mac Reynolds, "How Social Credit Took B.C.", *Maclean's*, September 1, 1952, p. 56.
193. *The Sudbury Daily Star*, January 20, 1946, page (?), file Correspondence Fitzgerald, J. J. 1946, vol. 3, MG30 C72, LAC.
194. Bossy to Fitzgerald, December 20, 1946, file Correspondence Fitzgerald, J. J. 1946, vol. 3, MG30 C72, LAC.
195. Bossy to Lockhart, March 6, 1947, file Correspondence Fitzgerald, J. J. 1947, vol. 3, MG30 C72, LAC; Fitzgerald, "Secular Spirit Called Blight On Modern Life", *The Catholic Record*, May 11, 1946, page (?), vol. 3, MG30 C72, LAC.
196. Fitzgerald to Réal Caouette, September 18, 1946, file Correspondence Fitzgerald, J. J. 1946, vol. 3, MG30 C72, LAC.
197. Bossy to Fitzgerald, February 13, 1947, file Correspondence Fitzgerald, J. J. 1947, vol. 3, MG30 C72, LAC.
198. *The Montreal Star*, May 9, 1947, page (?), cited in: Singel, *Social Discredit*, 134.
199. *Le Canada*, May 10, 1947, p. 1; *Le Soleil*, May 10, 1947, p. 2.
200. Bossy to Fitzgerald, February 13, 1947, file Correspondence Fitzgerald, J. J. 1947, vol. 3, MG30 C72, LAC.
201. Bossy to Fitzgerald, "Thoughts Towards Christian State", March 9, 1947, file Correspondence Fitzgerald, J. J. 1947, vol. 3, MG30 C72, LAC.
202. Bossy to Fitzgerald, February 13, 1947, file Correspondence Fitzgerald, J. J. 1947, vol. 3, MG30 C72, LAC. It is worth mentioning that, even though Stingel states that the Social Credit plans for a purge can be tracked back to 'as early as April 1947' (*Social Discredit*, 131, 143), this letter shows that the leadership of the Social Credit was considering doing so since at least February 1947
203. "Canadiens Français et Néo-Canadiens. Mémoire et Projet de W. J. Bossy, ancien Directeur des classes étrangères de la Commission des Écoles Catholiques de Montréal présentés Au Gouvernement, à l'Église et à la population canadienne-française de la Province de Québec", April 1948, file "New Canadians Service Bureau Miscellaneous 1948–1962", vol. 5, MG30 C72, LAC.

204. "Canadiens Français et Néo-Canadiens. Mémoire et Projet de W. J. Bossy, ancien Directeur des classes étrangères de la Commission des Écoles Catholiques de Montréal présentés Au Gouvernement, à l'Église et à la population canadienne-française de la Province de Québec", p. 7, April 1948, file New Canadians Service Bureau Miscellaneous 1948–1962, vol. 5, MG30 C72, LAC; "Le Bureau du Service des Néo-Canadiens. General Plan of Envisaged Action", p. 1, file New Canadians Service Bureau Plans of Action 1948–1949, vol. 5, MG30 C72, LAC.
205. "Minutes of Meeting of the Quebec Regional Advisory Board, Labour Department", July 14, 1948, p. 3, file New Canadians Service Bureau Dept. of Labour Advisory Board Meetings, vol. 5, MG30 C72, LAC.
206. *Un Mouvement, Une Oeuvre*, 31, file New Canadians Service Bureau 'Un Mouvement, Une Oeuvre, Walter J. Bossy', 1948–1971, vol. 5, MG30 C72, LAC, 43, 7, 14.
207. *Un Mouvement, Une Oeuvre*, 31, file New Canadians Service Bureau 'Un Mouvement, Une Oeuvre, Walter J. Bossy', 1948–1971, vol. 5, MG30 C72, LAC, 14.
208. "Minutes of Meeting of the Quebec Regional Advisory Board, Labour Department", July 14, 1948, page 3 point 9, file New Canadians Service Bureau Dept. of Labour Advisory Board Meetings, esp. pages 2–3, vol. 5, MG30 C72, LAC. Bossy was invited to participate in the meeting as a non-board member. My emphasis. *Relations* celebrated this meeting, reporting that Bossy was able to share his ideas about immigration and the New Canadians before "the main members of a council of advisors from the Ottawa Department of Labour ... under the chairmanship of Mr. Hector Dupuis, attached to the Canadian Citizenship Service". See: *Relations*, no. 92, August 1948, p. 241.
209. See the relationship between European and Christian supremacy, as well as white privilege and racism, in: Jeannine Fletcher Hill, *The Sin of White Supremacy: Christianity, Racism, & Religious Diversity in America* (New York: Orbis Books, 2017); Andrew Sung Park, *Racial Conflict and Healing: An Asian-American Theological Perspective* (New York: Orbis Books, 1996), 21; Vincent W. Lloyd, Andrew Prevot, *Anti-Blackness and Christian Ethics* (New York: Orbis Books, 2017); Stanley R. Barrett, *Is God a Racist? The Right Wing in Canada* (Toronto: University of Toronto, 1987), 327. These works argue that Christian supremacy is a form of white supremacy.
210. *Archives Canadiennes* (Ottawa: C. H. Parmelee, 1911), 548.
211. *Le Devoir*, January 15, 1912, p. 4.
212. *Mirror Journal*, December 18, 1919, p. 2.
213. *Lomond Press*, April 20, 1923, p. 2; *Lomond Press*, November 17, 1922, p. 1; *Mirror Journal*, June 22, 1922, p. 4; *Bulletin de la Société de géographie de Québec*, vol. 4 (Quebec: Geographical Society of Quebec, 1910) 293.
214. *Le Soleil*, October 25, 1933, p. 4; *L'Ordre*, September 13, 1934, p. 4.
215. See, for instance: *Redcliff Review*, July 4, 1929, p. 3; *Stony Plain Sun*, January 8, 1925, p. 3; *Le Nouvelliste*, May 27, 1924, p. 1.
216. Henri Bourassa, *Les Canadiens-Français et l'Empire Britannique* (Quebec: S.A. Demers, 1903), 20, 29; Henri Bourassa in 1915, cited in Yves Roby, *Les Franco-Américains de la Nouvelle-Anglaterre: reves et réalités* (Quebec: Septentrion, 2000), 160.
217. *Notre Avenir Politique* (Montreal: Bibliothèque de l'Action française, 1923), 50.
218. Alfred Fitzpatrick, *Handbook for New Canadians* (Toronto: Ryerson Press, 1919), 1–2.
219. Fitzpatrick, *Handbook for New Canadians*, 221 (Chinese), 219 (Japanese), 207–8 (Jews).
220. Ibid., 13.

126   *Networks*

221. For example, in terms of clothing. The book includes the story of the 'little Japanese girl in our room', who would wear 'clothes like ours at school, but she has a Japanese dress at home'. See: D. J. Dickie, *The Book of New Canadians* (Toronto: J. M. Dent, 1930), 110–11.
222. Dickie, *The Book of New Canadians*, 9, 5.
223. Ibid., 34, 90, 93, 102–3, 110–11.
224. Victoria Hayward, *Romantic Canada* (London: Macmillan & Company, 1922), cited in John Murray Gibbon, *Canadian Mosaic. The Making of a Northern Nation* (London: J. M. Dent & Sons Ltd., 1939 [1938]), ix (Preface).
225. Gibbon, *Canadian Mosaic*, vii.
226. Watson Kirkconnell was friends with John J. Fitzgerald and was also acquainted with Bossy, whom he met at Fitzgerald's insistence. Even though Kirkconnell acknowledged that Bossy and him shared similar socio-political views on Canada, there were no significant consequences to their meeting. See: Fitzgerald to Kirkconnell, June 5, 1946, file Correspondence Fitzgerald, J. J. 1946, vol. 3, MG30 C72, LAC; Kirkconnell to Fitzgerald, June 7, 1946, file Correspondence Fitzgerald, J. J. 1946, vol. 3, MG30 C72, LAC; Bossy to Fitzgerald, June 13, 1946, file Correspondence Fitzgerald, J. J. 1946, vol. 3, MG30 C72, LAC. The reason for Kirkconnell's friendship with Fitzgerald, which seems to have started at some point during the Second World War, was essentially based on their mutual fear of communism and their (new to some) pro-democratic stance.
227. Watson Kirkconnell, *Canadians All* (Ottawa: Director of Public Information, 1941), 6, 25, 38.
228. Ruth Wodak, *Politics of Fear: What Right-Wing Populist Discourses Mean* (New York: SAGE Publications, 2015), 2, 22.
229. *Un Mouvement, Une Oeuvre*, 31, file New Canadians Service Bureau 'Un Mouvement, Une Oeuvre, Walter J. Bossy', 1948–1971, vol. 5, MG30 C72, LAC. My emphasis.
230. The book is *Un Mouvement, Une Oeuvre* (1950). See: Bossy to Richard K. Henschel, June 7, 1962, file New Canadians Service Bureau Correspondence About Bureau 1953–1962, vol. 6; *Un Mouvement, Une Oeuvre*, 31, 60, file New Canadians Service Bureau 'Un Mouvement, Une Oeuvre, Walter J. Bossy', 1948–1971, vol. 5, MG30 C72, LAC.
231. Richard S. Levy, *Antisemitism: A Historical Encyclopedia of Prejudice and Persecution*, vol. 1 (Santa Barbara, CA: ABC-Clio, 2005), 568.
232. Cited in Robert Blobaum, *Antisemitism and Its Opponents in Modern Poland* (New York: Cornell University Press, 2005), 50. See also: Josephine Z. Kopf, "Meyer Wolfsheim and Robert Cohn: A Study of Jewish Type and Stereotype", *Tradition: A Journal of Orthodox Jewish Thought*, vol. 10, no. 3 (spring 1969): 96: the Jews 'sat spider-like, in the center of an impressive commercial network'.
233. *Un Mouvement, Une Oeuvre*, 31, file New Canadians Service Bureau 'Un Mouvement, Une Oeuvre, Walter J. Bossy', 1948–1971, vol. 5, MG30 C72, LAC.
234. Ibid.
235. *La Patrie*, July 25, 1948, page (?), reporting on Joseph Saine's declarations on behalf of Bossy's New Canadians Bureau (my emphasis) in vol. 17, MG30 C72, LAC. It is worth mentioning that Bossy had been collecting notes and clippings on ecumenism and the value of "uniting people in an immense family of brothers while respecting the characters of each one", a union defined as "Christians in one Church". In such references, Syrians and Armenians as well as Greeks, Romanians, or Russians, were considered a cultural contribution. See, for example: "Nos Frères Orthodoxes et l'Unité de l'Église", file New Canadians Service Bureau Plans of Action 1948–1949, vol. 5, MG30 C72,

LAC; "Rapport Préliminaire et Privé", Père Gustave Bellemarre, March 27, 1946, file New Canadians Service Bureau Plans of Action 1948–1949, vol. 5, MG30 C72, LAC.
236. *Un Mouvement, Une Oeuvre*, 31, file New Canadians Service Bureau 'Un Mouvement, Une Oeuvre, Walter J. Bossy', 1948–1971, vol. 5, MG30 C72, LAC.
237. Bossy to J.I. Paré, April 28, 1948, file New Canadians Service Bureau Correspondence Sent 1948–1949, vol. 5, MG30 C72, LAC. See Bossy reflecting on the idea of 'modus vivendi' in: Bossy to Fitzgerald, February 13, 1947, file Correspondence Fitzgerald, J. J. 1947, vol. 3, MG30 C72, LAC.
238. Davies, *Antisemitism in Canada*, 280–1.
239. Ibid., 284.
240. Bossy to Fitzgerald, 13 February 1947, vol. 3, File Correspondence Fitzgerald, J. J. 1947, MG30 C72, LAC.

5 The 'Third Force'

> Biculturalism has its warriors, as everyone now knows. Defenders of triculturalism are less familiar. One of them is Walter J. Bossy.
> *Canada Month,* February 1964[1]

The Ethnic Canadian Mosaic Institute

After Bossy accepted funding from the Liberal Party of Canada in exchange for public support in spring of 1949, the Montreal Catholic School Commission (MCSC) showed disapproval. At that point, the MCSC had reinstated Bossy as a teacher despite disturbing allegations regarding his behaviour, namely not respecting the hours of work, and allegedly bringing women into his office. Moreover, it had allowed him to develop an independent New Canadians Bureau, which had originally been established through and financed by the MCSC. Given the close association between Bossy's activities and the MCSC, he was (it was their view) in no position to politicize his 'spiritual mission' and jeopardize the integrity of the MCSC. Even though Bossy insisted that his activities were guided by 'purely idealistic motives' and brought him 'no personal advantage or emolument', he was forced to resign from his teaching position that year.[2]

Having lost his job, Bossy had to rely on the cheques that John J. Fitzgerald began sending him.[3] Specifically, between 1950 and 1951 Fitzgerald lent Bossy a 'total [of] 3,000$ or more' to maintain the New Canadian Service Bureau, a support '[for] which he had counted on the Liberals.'[4] On the other hand, Edward LaPierre had also been making the 'most kind sacrifices' for Bossy since he returned to Montreal in 1948.[5] Since the outbreak of the Second World War, LaPierre had been in Kingston (Ontario), in the 'Eastern Ontario Headquarters doing personnel work: interviewing recruits, candidates for special training, officer candidates, COCT [COTC] candidates at Queen's University etc.'[6] Upon his return to Montreal, he helped Bossy launch the New Canadians' Service Bureau in April 1948.[7] Throughout the 1950s, LaPierre further assisted Bossy with the Bureau (especially with writing advertising material in French) and planning a new and more multifaceted centre for the 'New Canadians', which in 1963 would

DOI: 10.4324/9781003283348-5

become the Ethnic Canadian Mosaic Institute: 'Providence ... honours me in keeping me within the shadow of a great man, at the dawn of a great achievement', said LaPierre about Bossy.[8]

After repeatedly asking the MCSC to reinstate him, in 1958 Bossy came back to the MCSC through 'purely verbal arrangements' and as an employee of 'special status'.[9] His new duties were not as a teacher, however, but as a typist and a mimeographer or copyist. According to the MCSC, Bossy had been reinstated 'on a purely humanitarian basis.'[10] But, after two years of working as a mimeographer, 'the constant use and handling of wood alcohol' and 'the use of viscous black ink' caused Bossy to fall ill. He was experiencing throat 'inflammation and infection'; 'acute, repeated headaches with dizziness; muscular deterioration in ... hands and fingers'; and, due to the toxicity to which he had been exposed, his left eye had gone sightless.[11] Bossy's doctor, Marcel Wilson, suggested that Bossy be assigned to other duties.[12] But Wilson's letter was 'ignored and rebuffed' by the MCSC.[13] Bossy could not believe that a Christian institution like the MCSC, he said, would 'knowingly aggravate these ills by refusing equitable reparation.' Yet 'weeks, then months, passed', followed by silence.[14] To make matters worse, because Bossy had been reinstated 'with no recognition of years of past service' either, if he chose to retire, he would be denied access to 'the (Provincial) Pension Fund' and any 'other benefits accorded [to] teachers'.[15] Despite the fact that Bossy was not a certified teacher and that, as a consequence, having no compensation for his services at the MSCS was not entirely unexpected, he claimed that he had been 'discriminated against' by the Commission '... and not treated as a Canadian Citizen'; that he had been 'abused, as an educator, by being kept in an inferior financial status'; and 'deceived, as an employee by practices that contradicted rights and promises.'[16] Desperate, Bossy wrote to Fitzgerald for advice, but no response followed. It turned out that Fitzgerald was suffering from a serious illness. He died in October 1960.[17]

Bossy worked for the MCSC for almost three more years (his complaints and demands ceasing due to the need for income), and then retired with the little money he had left to establish the Ethnic Canadian Mosaic Institute (ECMI), which was inaugurated in October 1963. The Institute would gather data on, and look after, the wellness of the 'ethnic' Canadians – specifically the '5,000,000 of Canada's 19,000,000 people' of 'other than English or French extraction', as Bossy put it.[18] The goal of the ECMI was to coherently mobilize the 'third group [towards] a new and real [Canadian] culture'. It aimed to constitute a 'rallying center of representatives of all Canadian ethnic groups.' According to Bossy, the ECMI 'will be the answer [to] the great majority of Canadian citizens ... who are searching for means to forestall the disintegration of Canada as one nation, and who feel today more Canadian than their hyphens.'[19] This disintegration, he explained, would result from 'outmoded separatism and isolationism', said Bossy. He used the allegory of a garden to explain the variety of ethnic groups that had been 'transplanted' to 'fertile Canadian soil'. 'Insane,' he said, 'would be any attempt to uproot any one now characteristic plant, for all now definitely belong to the great undivided whole.'[20]

According to *Le Devoir* (the only major newspaper which considered the inauguration of the ECMI news), the ECMI was inaugurated 'in the presence of representatives of 13 ethnic groups'. What groups exactly participated in the inauguration of the ECMI was not specified, but what they had in common was the acceptance of official bilingualism, and their rejection of biculturalism. They argued that 'we must recognize their right to keep their identity, their culture, their customs.'[21] As Bossy explained it, the 'thesis of our Institute is, then, that the Canada of today is composed not of two, but of three, recognizable, viable and valuable demographic elements: French, English and ... the ethnic groups, which three components make up our ... inclusive Canadian mosaic.'[22] It is interesting to note that, for the first time, Bossy was replacing the term 'New Canadians' with that of 'Ethnic Canadians' or 'ethnic groups' to describe minorities of descent other than British or French. Also relevant is the fact that he incorporated the word 'Mosaic' to describe his endeavour for unity in diversity. On the one hand, 'ethnic' had become a key concept in the debates around Canadian multiculturalism spurred by the establishment of the Royal Commission on Bilingualism and Biculturalism in July 1963, whose goal was to recommend steps 'to develop the Canadian Confederation on the basis of an equal partnership between the two founding races, taking into account the contribution made by the other ethnic groups to the cultural enrichment of Canada'.[23] Thus, incorporating that term was probably a timely decision that could have allowed Bossy's endeavours to be noticed as part of the contemporary wider efforts for the recognition of the cultural contribution of ethnic minorities. On the other hand, the use of 'mosaic' helped Bossy present a more inclusive view of Canada (as we will see, he would use the words 'mosaic' and 'inclusive' beside one another), or a more egalitarian form of pluralism that was different from what Bossy had promoted up to that point. According to him, this term reflected more accurately the idea of 'fitting together' different 'pieces' of all colours, materials, and shapes under one framework.[24] Unlike his previous efforts, the ECMI seemed designed to represent, and attract, as many groups as possible.

Bossy's new and seemingly more inclusive approach to ethnic diversity started a couple of years before the establishment of the Royal Commission on Bilingualism and Biculturalism in July 1963. Specifically, it began with Bossy's participating in events organised by the Moral Re-Armament movement (MRA) in the United States between 1960 and 1961, when he learned about 'universalism'. Led by American Protestant evangelist Frank Buchman, the MRA was an international moral and spiritual movement that promoted a Christian ecumenical vision of reality.[25] Like Bossy, Buchanan believed that all groups should aspire to Christianity in order for ethnic cooperation and national unity to occur.[26] Both Buchman and

Bossy believed in Christian nationalism or, to put it differently, in the idea that faith and divine sanction should define peoples' political and social duties and aspirations as communities.[27] Yet, after the Second World War, Buchman shifted from speaking of a *Christian* common good to a *universal* common good. In doing so, he expected to appeal to as wide an audience as possible.[28] By adopting a discourse on universalism, the MRA attempted to unite 'men on a basis above party, class, race, confession, point of view ... [making] possible a true family of nations' – at least that is what they promoted.[29] Interested in the MRA's work, Bossy decided to attend its Christmas and New Year's Assembly in 1960–1961 at Mackinac Island (US). He contributed to the event by talking about his plans to establish an institute dedicated to promoting cultural diversity. Apparently, Buchman was quite impressed by Bossy's vision of Canada and told him that he had 'a great part to play in [the] universal action' against 'atheistic Communism'.[30] Bossy returned home with the promise that employing a universalist or more inclusive discourse would allow him to reach a broader audience while effectively fighting atheism.

The first step Bossy took for the promotion of his newly inaugurated Ethnic Canadian Mosaic Institute (ECMI) was accepting an invitation from the Montreal multilingual radio station CFMB, whose founder and manager was Polish Canadian Casimir Stanczykowski. In October 1963, Stanczykowski asked Bossy to share his views on 'a "tri-national nation" and the role of the Ethnic groups in our Canadian society.'[31] Bossy's radio speeches were organized in five sessions and aired between November and December of 1963. In each one of them, he mostly addressed the problem of incorporating ethnic groups into a binational and bilingual confederation. Ethnic groups, he explained, did not consider themselves English or French, 'but simply Canadian'. He argued that even though the ethnic minorities' mother tongues were often melted into an English-speaking 'pot', their traditions remained. In doing so, the result was neither an English, nor a French, or an American nation, but a 'distinctly Canadian' one which is 'ethnically heterogeneous'.[32] Against binationalism, Bossy proposed 'multiculturalism' and claimed that it was 'essential to recognize that Canada was no longer composed of two, but of three, demographic elements.'[33] He wanted ethnic groups to be able to retain 'a consciousness of their own identity' and remain 'proud of their traditions and origins', while being 'simply "Canadian"'.[34] Canada, he concluded, must be a 'multi-cultural ... mosaic', although not necessarily a 'multilingual' one.[35]

Biculturalism and bilingualism

Effectively taking 'into account the changed and charged climate of Quebec', the Royal Commission on Biculturalism and Bilingualism (henceforth B&B Commission) was the result of Prime Minister Lester B. Pearson's adopting French Canadian André Laurendeau's suggestion to inaugurate a commission to mainly 'investigate [the] cultural and linguistic disparities between the Anglophones and the Francophones.'[36] Thus, the B&B Commission was established on the assumption that Canada was composed of two linguistic and cultural groups whose fundamental relationship needed clarifying.[37] While the inauguration of the B&B Commission convinced Quebec's premier Jean Lesage that negotiations with Ottawa regarding Quebec's special status were possible, many of Canada's ethnic groups viewed Pearson's concessions with suspicion.[38] The Commission's 'terms of references', or the idea that Canada was officially composed of two languages *and* two cultures (the 'two founding races'), were especially criticized.[39] In addition, in the 1950s and early 1960s, Canadian ethnic minorities began occupying positions of power (they were now in the Senate, the Parliament, City Halls, universities, etc.), platforms from which the government could not ignore them.[40] As a result, the B&B Commission decided to welcome individuals and associations from all cultural and ethnic groups to share their understanding of and wishes for a reassessment of Canada as a nation, becoming an unprecedented space for intercultural exchanges on Canadian nationhood and power negotiation.[41] Ethnic groups and associations delivered briefs and research reports to the B&B Commission aiming to reflect or demonstrate their crucial role in Canadian political, cultural, social, and economic life.[42] The Commission received a total of 400 reports.[43]

Among such reports, there was a letter from Bossy. In it, he explained that the Ethnic Canadian Mosaic Institute (ECMI) had been established after a thorough study of the needs and expectations of ethnic groups residing in Canada. This study, he explained, was developed in 1962 through an 'extensive 18-month survey'. Specifically, he had sent a 'questionnaire letter' on the issue of binationalism to '169 Canadian ethnic group newspapers and ... to over one thousand of their associations'.[44] Even though this seems highly exaggerated, and that I have found no record of the survey or the answers to it, Bossy affirmed that the ECMI had collected the returned surveys, thereby obtaining a unique understanding of the situation. In his report, Bossy introduced himself as speaking 'on behalf of this greatest third body, the ethnic group as they are known today in Canada'. For the first time in Bossy's life as a multi-cultural activist, this body included Canadians 'of diversified ethnic origins, in Canada, whether form *Europe, Asia or Africa*'. In addition, Bossy referred to the 'Indians [as] the historically real owners of this Land'.[45] He defined all these different groups as belonging to 'the rest of heterogeneous inhabitants of Canada', consisting 'of many minorities' and forming a 'multi-cultural nation'.[46] Given that Bossy never referred to a *fourth* group, it is safe to assume that Canadians of African and Asian descent would have now fallen under his idea of the 'third force'. In regard to Indigenous groups, Bossy probably brought them into his discourse to further challenge British- and French-Canadian claims to 'historical rights', which he described as resulting from an outdated and colonial understanding of Canada.[47]

Bossy made his letter to the B&B Commission public by sending it to the press. Irish Canadian Marcus Long (*The Montreal Gazette*), professor of philosophy at the University of Toronto, appreciated Bossy's understanding of Canada, describing the concept of 'two nations' in Canada as 'absurd'. Long opposed 'the idea of "hyphenated" Canadians because this could only lead to further divisions in Canada at a time when the entire world is moving towards greater unity.'[48] More support came from Russian Canadian A. Solodovnikov (*La Nouvelle Parole Russe* or The New Russian Word), who described Bossy's letter as 'a historic document'.[49] French Canadian Jesuit Thomas Mignault (*Le Petit Journal* or The Small Newspaper)[50] also praised it, referring to Bossy as 'one of the fathers of the new Canadian federal state that MUST be born' from the elimination of 'the segregation suffered by many New Canadians.'[51] Less marginal newspapers, like *The Montreal Star*, introduced Bossy's letter to the B&B Commission as 'one of the more sensible attempts to outline this position', that is that national unity would be achieved only if Canadians 'bear in mind that Canada is composed, not of two, but of three recognizable, viable and valuable demographic elements: French, English and (collectively) the ethnic groups.'[52] On the other hand, the newspaper described Bossy as the 'most extreme of the representatives of the other ethnic groups', and pointed at the fact that his 'theory of a "tri-national" nation was flawed based on the lack of clarity concerning who exactly belonged to this third group: Where does the English-speaking 'English' group end and the English-speaking ethnic group begin? When does a New Canadian drop the adjective?'.[53] Reflecting upon similar questions surrounding Bossy's letter, *La Presse* (The Press) argued that 'the "New" is in reality a member of one of the two great "nations" of Canada', there being no 'mosaic State', as the name of Bossy's Institute suggested there was.[54] Challenging Bossy's declaration that ethnic Canadians had the right to '[equally] contribute to our present and future greatness', the newspaper explained that ethnic intervention in a constitutional revision in particular 'can only complicate the matter by introducing a point of view that is legitimate in itself but which distorts the substance of the problem to the satisfaction of one of the two parties involved in the debate, who has an interest in mixing everything up.'[55]

In his letter, Bossy associated the aspirations of the ethnic groups with French Canada. He talked about a French-Canadian 'cultural renaissance' that 'all Canadian patriots' should follow. Yet, again, Bossy was not talking about a linguistic or a political renaissance, but a religious one. He explained that French-Canadian expansion would effectively fight 'this Anglo-Saxon spiritual vacuum', spreading the 'moral and spiritual values' that would keep Canada together.[56] Bossy was once more missing the point: to many French Canadians, Catholicism was a contributing factor to their identity as a group and survival, and therefore one could not lightly disengage French-Canadian cultural renaissance from a sense of French-Canadian nationhood. But that's precisely what Bossy did. In fact, he rejected the idea that a territorial and religious expansion led by French Canadians might further justify the need for official bilingualism at the federal level. For even though the ECMI declared itself in favour of institutional bilingualism upon its inauguration, in his letter to the B&B Commission Bossy made it clear that bilingualism beyond the province of Quebec would be unjust.[57]

In the context of the *Révolution Tranquille* or Quiet Revolution, Quebec was looking at ethnic minorities as groups that must find their place within a society in the process of identity development – not the other way around.[58] Oblivious of the historical context he lived in, Bossy insisted that French-Canadian expansion must be strictly related to a 'missionary' or religious effort towards the 'unity in diversity of Canadian nationhood', rather than to the demographical and economic development of French Canada as a society.[59] And by 'missionary' venture Bossy meant a civilizing mission: his letter explained that French-Canadian 'cultural renaissance' would lead to 'transforming civilized *animals* into spiritually *elevated humans*, united by honesty, love and unselfishness'.[60] However, said Bossy, if that French-Canadian 'renaissance' turned into a threat to the integrity of the country because it was built upon ethnic rather than spiritual objectives, then it shouldn't be supported. Having experienced the hazards of nationalism in Europe, he argued, the ethnic Canadians knew that unity should prevail to 'provide justice for all'.[61] When invited to participate in a panel organized by Willingdon Elementary School of Montreal on bilingualism and biculturalism as director of the ECMI in February 1964, he insisted that French Canada must 'sacrifice for the existence of a single Canada and forget its patriotism.'[62]

That French-Canadian Catholicism could be so intimately associated with nationalism, or what he referred to as French-Canadian 'patriotism' and the idea of the 'two nation compact' was, he thought, betraying the rest of ethnic groups – who, clearly, he still perceived as mostly Catholic. They, or rather he, had been working since 1934 (when the Classocracy League of Canada was launched), claimed Bossy, to unite the 'New Canadians' with the French Canadians on a common offensive against the 'rationalist, if not atheist' English Canada towards a Christian 'multicultural nation'.[63] That was why only Christian nationalism could 'be the answer [to] the great majority of Canadian citizens, including thousands of those of French and Anglo-Saxon origin, who are searching for means to forestall the disintegration of Canada as one nation'.[64] In short, the process of rebuilding Canada was, in effect, a civilizing mission in which Catholicism (the French Canadians) must lead the way – as he had already urged back in 1936 after the 'New Canadian' demonstration at Notre-Dame Basilica of Montreal.

This religious approach to Canadian nationalism questions Bossy's more inclusive understanding of ethnic integration. It demonstrates that, in almost 30 years, Bossy's ideas on nation-building hadn't evolved, suggesting that Bossy's attempts to show more inclusiveness were not genuine, but part of a strategy to increase support.

Partial stories

Between November 7 and 8, 1963, the B&B Commission held Preliminary Hearings in Ottawa, during which those who had previously submitted their research reports on the contribution of minority groups to Canada were given an opportunity to elaborate upon their arguments.[65] On November 8, 1963, Bossy presented his own claims in front of the B&B Commission. At the hearings, he stressed the absurdity of 'these linguistic acrobatics for the benefit of French and English only.' Commissioner Royce Frith responded to Bossy's allegations by noting the inconsistencies in insisting that *'new'* Canadians wished to be both 'without the hyphen' and 'fully Canadians'.[66] Jean Charpentier (*La Presse*) wrote on Bossy's hearing, highlighting that while he represented the ECMI 'which counts on 200 members' (a number which I haven't been able to verify) and thus the Commission had the responsibility to hear his plight, it is quite 'banal that an unsuitable/unassimilated[67] immigrant tries to take advantage of this commission of inquiry to secure a legal place in the sun'.[68] Willie Chevalier (*Le Droit* or The Right) welcomed the existence of Bossy's ECMI and his defending the rights of ethnic groups to protect their culture, religion, and language at the hearings as this was, he said, their right to do so. In spite of this, the newspaper insisted that, after 1867, immigrants to Canada chose to accept and join a country that was constitutionally bicultural and bilingual. Refusing to protect that pact would inevitably mean threatening the French language specifically.[69] Bossy's view was that the Canada of 1867 had ceased to exist, and he illustrated during the hearing by referring to his family, which was gradually becoming more and more multi-ethnic – just like Canada itself:

> My oldest son, born in Canada, married a ... English... a second son, married an Irish ... the third son, married a Jewess [sic] ... another married a French Canadian ... another married a Belgian ... and another married a Scotsman from Scotland ... another married an American ... and so on ... Who are we now? ... We are Canadians![70]

It was precisely that merging, he implied, that made it possible for Canadians to exist as one people. It is worth noting that, together with his unprecedented statements on the Canadian nation, which included First Nations, and Canadians of Asian and African descent, Bossy's speech at the B&B's Preliminary Hearings mentioned for the first time the Jewish community. Based on his intervention, it would seem like Bossy accepted that his approach to multiculturalism would involve not only interethnic marriage, but also inter*faith* marriage. However, this was not the case. In order to further clarify whether his celebrating an interfaith marriage in his family in front of the B&B Commission was a product of redemption, enlightenment, or a mere strategy, a family photo is illuminating. In the 1960s, Bossy distributed a family photo whose description at the bottom omitted the specific marriage of his Christian son to a woman of Jewish descent.[71] Why this was the case can be explained by Bossy's enduring antisemitism, which he never stopped nurturing. During this period, not only did he continue consuming literature promoting the idea that Jews were inferior to Christians, but he also joined missionary groups whose main goal was to convert Jews to Christianity.

Among the literature with which he engaged in the late 1950s and early 1960s, there were the works of Catholic British conspiracy theorist Nesta H. Webster, who claimed that Jewish conversion was the path to their integration and to ethnic reconciliation.[72] Based on narratives like this, Bossy believed that the Jews must emulate Christians in order for them to effectively fight 'the corroding effects of democracy and naturalism'.[73] Encouraging emulation was an idea central to the Confraternity of the Notre Dame de Sion in Montreal, of which Bossy was a member at least until 1964. The confraternity's understanding was that Christians stood at a more elevated religious and spiritual stage than non-Christian communities, including Jews. As a matter of fact, to the Confraternity, ecumenism was directly associated with conversion.[74] Just like Webster, who believed that Britain was financially and politically dominated by Jews, throughout the 1960s Bossy sustained that 'All media – press (especially) tv, radio are if not controlled then penetrated by these persons'.[75] In his private notes, Bossy wrote about 'Our Capitulation to Jewish Offensive'.[76] From these notes, two main observations can be drawn. Firstly, that according to Bossy, Jews had seemingly achieved greater power to influence society than Christians. And secondly, that this was the case because Christians had accepted (liberal) democracy.

The truth is that, to Bossy, there never was an interfaith marriage in his family. In fact, in the early 1970s, he explained that despite the fact that his daughter-in-law 'normally feels Jewess [sic]', she ought to be considered a Catholic.[77] Clearly, Bossy's persistent antisemitic views contradicted his seemingly new inclusive views, and his religious supremacism led him to provide, in every sense of the word, a partial picture of Canadian diversity.

Another image elucidates the type of groups that Bossy really aimed to represent or speak for in the 1960s. And that is the only picture that – as far as I know – has remained from the meetings organized by the ECMI. Entitled 'Representatives of Seventeen Canadian Ethnic Groups', the image shows 14 women and 14 men, including at least three religious figures, sitting around Bossy as he speaks. All attendants are, in appearance, of European origin, and the religious figures are dressed in clothes representing Christian denominations only, specifically the Orthodox and the Catholic Church. Never mind that in the 1960s Bossy was promoting himself as 'a unique Christian who studied the Jewish problem and who is defending the Jewish Cause (since half of our century) by written and spoken words.'[78] There was no proof at all that this was true, and Bossy mentioning the existence of a Canadian Jewish community one time only (at the Preliminary Hearings) probably did not help.

The absence in the photo of a representative of the Jewish community is especially relevant given that the photo was taken in the early 1960s, that is in the midst of a new immigration wave of Jews, where a considerable number of Sephardic Jews from Africa contributed to the growth of the Jewish community of Montreal, and therefore to their importance as an ethnic minority group.[79] There is also the possibility that Bossy invited a Jewish representative but he received no answer. This would not be an exception given that none of the letters that Bossy (or his subsequent organizations) sent to Jewish associations, journals and magazines, and individuals between 1947 and 1969 were ever answered (except for the Jewish Public Library of Montreal, which sent a note of thanks to the ECMI for having sent a copy of Bossy's letter to the B&B Commission)[80]. This is not surprising, as during this period Bossy was writing about being 'on very good terms' with the Jews of Montreal (of which, again, there is no proof),[81] while at the same time actively distributing *Un Mouvement, Une Oeuvre. Walter J. Bossy* which, as we saw in earlier chapters, depicted the Jewish communities of Montreal as undesirable parasites.

Just as his accepting the Jewish community as Canadians was an isolated case, Bossy would never again refer to Canadians of Asian, African, or Indigenous origin as belonging to his idea of the 'third force' or as having the right to claim recognition as Canadian minorities or nations. In fact, in the late 1960s he ceased specifying who did or did not represent the 'third force' altogether. In the early 1970s, he explained that he made this decision on purpose, as he wanted the ECMI to strive for the unity of Canada rather than the unity of a third group specifically – as he had attempted before.[82] However, this makes no sense, given that also in the 1970s he recalled the ECMI as wanting to represent 'the Ethnic Groups from Europe' alone.[83] These declarations prove that Bossy's idea of the 'third force' and Canadian diversity did not change between 1934 and 1970. Furthermore, it shows that his tweaking his discourse on occasion was purely strategic, which is a sign that Bossy was aware that his ideas on nation-building were inadequate for the times Canadian leaders were striving to live up to.

Ambiguous goals, a confusing target, an inconsistent discourse, and the incapacity for Bossy to build a meaningful network, led the ECMI to run out of money. Between 1963 and 1966, not a single donation was made from an organized ethnic group, or an individual for that matter (that is, besides Edward LaPierre).[84] Bossy finally closed the Ethnic Canadian Mosaic Institute in 1970 unsuccessful, unrecognised, and in debt.[85]

The 'third force'

The B&B Commission saw the term 'founding races' as a reference to the undisputed role played by Canadians of French and British origin in the establishment of the first settlements in what is today Canada.[86] During the 1960s, the ethnic group that most fiercely challenged that allusion was the

138   *The 'Third Force'*

Ukrainian Canadian. This community argued that Ukrainians had shaped the land in the prairies as much as the British or the French Canadians. Indeed, in the late nineteenth century, conditions at home 'pulled' many Ukrainians abroad as Canada was in need 'for agriculturalists to settle the vast and underpopulated prairies'.[87] As a result, between 1890 and 1914, 'the Canadian prairies ... were transformed from a sparsely populated outpost of the fur trade into one of the world's major grain-producing regions.'[88] Many among the Ukrainian Canadians believed that 'the pioneering qualities and the hard work of the early settlers put Ukrainians on the same footing as the British or French Canadians.'[89] Thus, during the debate on multiculturalism, this historical event was used by Ukrainian Canadians to support their claims for recognition, participation, and equality.[90] Julia Lalande explains that this narrative was intimately connected with fears of the demise of Ukrainian culture, which they believed was occurring within Soviet-occupied Ukraine. With the proper protective measures abroad, Ukrainian culture would be able to survive – if only in the diaspora.[91]

An important supporter of the 'pioneering argument' during the 1960s was Jaroslav Rudnyckyj. Born in Przemyśl (today's Poland), he was among the 40,000 Ukrainians who moved to Canada in the early postwar period. During the interwar period, he flirted with Nazism (as did Bossy, although Bossy had more reasons to support Hitler than Rudnycky did), because Germany appeared to be the most credible threat to the survival of the Soviet Union and thus a hope for the independence of Ukraine.[92] In Canada, Rudnyckyj spoke against the marginalization of immigrants of European descent, though more specifically of Ukrainians.[93] Roberto Perin argues that his experience in Eastern Europe as a minority (Przemyśl was formed by a Polish majority and Jewish and Ukrainian minorities) shaped Rudnyckyj's understanding of Canadian pluralism. Specifically, to him it was essential that spaces be created in the diaspora, where both language *and* culture could be expressed and reproduced.[94] As opposed to Bossy, Rudnyckyj possessed the platform and the contacts to effectively voice his concerns. Appointed as a commissioner at the B&B in July 1963, Rudnyckyj fought against the thesis of the 'two founding nations' and bilingualism from above, proposing the elevation of Ukrainian as an official language and suggesting that Ukrainians were a Canadian nation just as the French Canadians or the First Nations were, overall implying that Canada could be considered a multi*national* country.[95] It was as a member of the B&B Commission that he claimed that some Ukrainians saw themselves as the 'founding races' of the prairies.[96]

Another relevant supporter of the pioneering argument was Paul Yuzyk. A Ukrainian-Canadian born in Saskatchewan, Yuzyk was a history professor at the University of Manitoba and a professor of Russian and Soviet history at the University of Ottawa. On February 4, 1963, he was appointed to the Canadian Senate, and sat as a member of the Progressive Conservative Party. Although Bossy was first in imagining a 'third group' in 1937, and was speaking of 'multiculturalism' already in October 1963 while Yuzyk didn't use that term until 1964 (during his maiden speech to the Senate),[97] it is Yuzyk who in the 1960s was in a position to become the spokesperson for the 'third force'. And so, in March 1964, Yuzyk claimed that 'we have in Canada what I call three elements: the British, the French and the Third element'.[98] Also in 1964, Yuzyk adopted the motto of 'unity in diversity',[99] which was subsequently embraced by the B&B Commission in *Book IV*,[100] despite the fact that this had been the slogan of Bossy's New Canadians movement since 1948. In 1967, Yuzyk wrote *Ukrainian Canadians: Their Place and Role in Canadian Life* to demonstrate the 'leading dynamic' of Ukrainian Canadians among Canada's ethnic group.[101] In this book, Yuzyk relied on 'pioneer history when he credited Ukrainian and other immigrant groups with setting "the vast empty lands" of the Prairies'.[102]

Joining the leading speakers of the Ukrainian-Canadian community, in early 1964 Bossy claimed that 'ethnic groups were among the founders of western Canada [i.e., the prairies], not the French Canadians.'[103] The stress upon French Canadians clearly reflects his insistence that bilingualism at the federal level was 'unjust'. In terms of what communities exactly represented the 'ethnic groups' Bossy was referring to here, it is unclear. While it is apparent that, to both Rudnyckyj and Yuzyk, the Ukrainian Canadians were the leading force of the Canadian ethnic groups (the 'third force'), to Bossy, as we have seen, the 1960s were a period of uncertainty in terms of defining what the 'third force' meant to him (or what he wanted people to think it meant). That is why his reference to the pioneering argument is revealing. At the very least, it means that Bossy saw advantages in using the pioneer narrative, either to advance his vision for Canada or himself. But it also shows that he was being influenced by the leading representatives of the Ukrainian-Canadian community on the issue of multiculturalism. And Rudnyckyj and Yuzyk were not the only Ukrainians that Bossy would closely observe throughout the 1960s in an attempt to be recognized as a leading representative of the 'third force'. The intellectual figures that influenced Bossy's thought the most during that period were André Kishka and Peter Presunka.

André Kishka was a Catholic Ukrainian who had left the USSR to establish a subsequent number of institutions in Europe dedicated to the physical and moral assistance of Eastern European Catholics. His goal was to use exiled intellectuals to establish healthy relationships between the West and the East.[104] As president of Pro-Europa, a movement established in 1949 aiming 'to the establishment of European unity to ... strengthen the ties which unite these intellectuals to Western and overseas civilization', Kishka had defended the formation of a united Europe of nations under the common framework of Christianity.[105] In spring 1956 (shortly before permanently establishing himself in Francoist Spain), Kishka visited the US and Canada promoting a similar message. In Quebec in particular, Kishka spoke of linguistic integration (specifically, that immigrants learn French) as crucial to properly understand the new cultural context in which ethnic minorities found themselves. This, in turn, was essential for ethnic minorities (he was referring here to the case of Ukrainian Canadians) to 'best assert and respect their right to preserve' their own language and cultural rights.[106] It appeared, then, that Kishka was suggesting the use of bilingualism simply as a means to the eventual establishment of structures allowing for the protection of multiculturalism as well as multilingualism – which was Rudnycky's position. To Kishka, the beauty of Canada resided in the plurality of its people and values.[107] How that plurality could be unified for the efficiency of the state, however, he didn't explain. In spite of that, it is safe to argue that he wanted for Canada what he wanted for Europe, namely the union of nations under a Christian framework.

Another influential figure who shaped Bossy's understanding of the issue of biculturalism and bilingualism during the 1960s was Peter Presunka. A Canadian of Ukrainian origin working in Ottawa as an engineer and public servant,[108] Presunka wrote in abundance in the 1960s in favour of a multicultural Canada, especially through his small magazine *My Canada*, issued in Ottawa between 1968 and 1969.[109] Presunka had often used First Nations to discredit claims for the national duality of Canada (in particular Quebec's claims to a special status)[110], which could have influenced Bossy's early incorporation of Indigenous peoples into his discourse when trying to make the case against biculturalism in front of the B&B Commission in 1963. Presunka believed that 'every minority culture' should count equally in Canada, and that the future of Canada should be built by 'a new breed of Canadians' resulting from the mixing of the multiplicity of ethnic groups.[111] As he saw it, biculturalism was 'short-sighted', and 'cultural suicide', and so he proposed 'a multi-cultural society where all the languages and all the many cultures of Canadians are brought into play, in school and in the community at large'. He said that 'the tyranny of two languages and two cultures, is not much different from the tyranny of one.'[112]

Further, Presunka thought that bilingualism made no sense beyond the province of Quebec, as beyond that territory French Canadians were a minority. He suggested that Canada should overcome historical understandings of confederation to embrace the 'mosaic' or the equal contribution of ethnic groups. How these groups would coexist was answered by 'universalism', which he thought represented the ultimate integration of all groups under a common religious framework: Christianity.[113] Even though Presunka argued that the future of Canada depended upon 'The Third Element' he, like Bossy, was very unspecific about who exactly composed this third group. All he ever said was that this element was represented by the 'ethnic groups'.[114] On the other hand, in 1968 he referred to western Canada as the big loser of Canadian biculturalism and bilingualism, and insisted that bilingualism in particular was in fact a French-Canadian strategy to finally conquer western Canada – he defined it as French Canada's 'historic dream of cultural conquest'.[115]

Both Kishka and Presunka rejected bilingualism and biculturalism but were vague about how Canadian unity would be achieved within a multicultural and multilingual state, as well as about the validity of Ukrainian Canadians to an equal partnership of three. Thus, many questions arise. For example, how should the ethnic minorities other than French and British Canadian be recognized? Would Ukrainian Canadians have the right to claim special status based on their own historical experience? Would First Nations be recognized upon different terms? And given that both Kishka and Presunka stressed the role of religion in unity, what about those groups who are not Christian: how would they fit into a multicultural nation defined by a Christian framework? The imprecision of these approaches was, to my mind, a problem in assisting Bossy when forming his own opinion on the B&B Commission and, probably, in effectively defining the nature and purposes of the ECMI. Above all, while he still wanted to lead and speak for the 'third force', he wasn't clear about who exactly formed it; as a consequence, the need for an organization like the ECMI could also be put into question. Moreover, whereas he defended multiculturalism, the Christian nationalism that framed it left unclear whether certain groups would be excluded on the basis of religion, forced to conversion, or simply ignored.

That Ukrainians and Ukrainian Canadians represented the group that most influenced Bossy's understanding of the issue of biculturalism and bilingualism in the 1960s is significant. His reliance upon the discourse of the Ukrainian community makes it seem as though he certainly believed them to be a leading force in the debate about multiculturalism, and even in the Canadian 'third group'. From a strategic point of view, as a Ukrainian, it would have also been safer for Bossy to embrace the wider Ukrainian-Canadian position on multiculturalism, as this community was the best organized, best positioned, and most active ethnic group, and could potentially lead a discussion which Bossy had strived to steer since the 1930s.[116] If this assumption is accurate, this is relevant because it makes Bossy a figure whose historical importance gradually declined as he moved from *offering* a new perspective on Canadian diversity in the interwar period, namely a trichotomic one, to *reproducing* (albeit ineffectively) a widely common narrative in the postwar era. That is, that Ukrainians were not only components of Canada, but co-founders, and as such deserved a special place in the reassessment of Canadian nationhood.

Self-preservation

In the late 1960s and early 1970s, Bossy began speaking of 'the new orientation' or the 'reorientation' of ethnic groups 'in view of our changing world conditions'. His position was now not as Canadian (or as Ukrainian, for that matter), but as *North American*, and his suggestion was not at the federal level, but at the transnational level.[117] His belief was that, because of the establishment of the B&B Commission and the terms of reference which stressed the union of two nations against the 'multicultural' ideal Bossy envisaged, the ethnic groups of Canada were 'coming closer and closer in relations with their Ethnic Brothers in U.S.A. ... and consequently feeling stronger.' An 'awakened third force of Canadians' was becoming aware of their place as 'North-Americans first', he said, thus turning towards the United States, and away from Ottawa in 'their hopes of self-preservation, security and country devotion'. Transnational cooperation and union would be the new strategy for what Bossy called 'passive resistance towards [a] new artificial "two nation" integration'.[118] He even began looking for a job in the United States as anti-communist spy.[119] So, it would seem that he didn't care too much about whether he remained in Canada or not. This implies that his concerns about Canada's fate and socio-political reconstruction were not his main concern any longer. Rather, his main concern was, as indicated above, the 'self-preservation' of ethnic groups. The fact that it didn't matter whether this self-preservation occurred in Canada, in the US, or within a new union of North American nations, suggests that Bossy was preoccupied with the survival of ethnic groups abroad rather than with the integration of ethnic groups into the Canadian nation.

Closely followed by Bossy, André Kishka's work in Europe is illuminating to further clarify whether by the late 1960s and early 1970s Bossy was thinking about the future of Canada, or the survival of the Ukrainian community abroad. In Europe, Kishka was promoting the protection (and potential leadership roles in foreign relations and peace) of Ukrainian and other eastern European communities who had fled the Soviet Union.[120] Ultimately, as suggested above, Kishka's goal was to strengthen the relationships between Christian eastern European refugees and 'western civilization' against the threat of communism and the sovietization of these communities.[121] In other words, Christian unions of nations represented a mechanism against the communist threat and, as such, a means to preserve the culture and tradition of the nations who had suffered under the expansion of the Soviet Union. Bossy was so interested in this idea that he even planned for a meeting with Kishka during his visit to Montreal to talk about the establishment of 'Societies of all races and national origins' united for a 'universalist spiritual renaissance' with a special role for eastern European communities. The meeting never took place (Kishka never responded to Bossy's invitation), but Bossy kept following Kishka's struggle for the 're-Christianization of Eastern Europe'[122] and the protection and promotion of eastern Europeans, and Ukrainians specifically, under Christian unions of nations until the 1970s.

Another event sheds light upon Bossy's intentions at the time. In 1972, Bossy brought his papers to the Library and Archives of Canada, whose importance he associated with the fact that he had been (is what he believed) the representative of the 'third force' in Montreal since 1931.[123] And yet, a ten-page long interview only makes mention of the 'third group' twice, and very vaguely. The first time Bossy is asked about it he responds by referring to 'Western Canada', explaining that this part of the country was 'not as sentimental and patriotic [towards Canada] as it used to be' due to official bilingualism, which had created an 'artificial nation' which wouldn't benefit the whole Canadian population.[124] The second time that Bossy mentioned the 'third group' was to explain that the ECMI (an institution which in the 1960s presented itself as gathering Canadian ethnic groups of descent other than British and French) was not embodying the 'third force', but 'the unity in diversity in Canada'. In other words, to him, Canadian ethnic groups of descent other than British and French were *not* the equivalent of the 'third force'. When the Library and Archives of Canada finally asked him to specify what the 'third group' was, then, and what its goals were, Bossy didn't answer directly, but instead referred to the Ukrainian struggles in Canada and the lack of help from 'rationalists Anglo-Saxons' and nationalist French Canadians.[125]

That in the 1960s Bossy adopted the pioneering narrative and that, in the 1970s, he suggested that the 'third force' was analogous to the Ukrainian-Canadian community, leads to a crucial question. That is whether Bossy used the multicultural position as a means to protect and uplift the Ukrainian-Canadian community specifically, rather than a wider sector of the Canadian population as he claimed, and since when. This question, however, cannot be fully addressed by only looking at Bossy's efforts to mobilize the 'third force' within the French- and English-speaking milieu. Rather, it requires the exploration of Bossy's discourses among the Ukrainian-Canadian community between 1924 and the postwar period. Hopefully, future research will focus on that aspect of his life to bring new light upon his overall contribution to the debate on multiculturalism.

That said, based on my research, it is my opinion that before the 1960s Bossy did not believe that the 'third group' was represented by the Ukrainian-Canadian community. I believe that he chose to see it this way once it became apparent that the Ukrainian-Canadian community was the dominant ethnic group in shaping the debate around multiculturalism, or the challenge to the terms of reference. Still, I do not think he accepted that because he believed Ukrainian Canadians were the only ones powerful enough to bring about change, but because accepting their leading role would mean increasing his own chances of finally being considered (as a Canadian of Ukrainian origin) a leading spokesman of the 'third force'. To put it simply, I think that Bossy's activism on behalf of a 'third group' from the mid-1930s until the 1960s was, after all, a pursuit for power. Thankfully, he didn't achieve the power he so desired. Indeed, his permanent inability to overcome his religious and racial prejudices, specifically towards visible minorities and the Jewish community, made him a dangerous individual whose access to power would have led to a major reversal from the politics of liberal multiculturalism and ethnic cooperation that Canadian ethnic communities were fighting for. He was, and would remain, a reactionary figure.

Conclusion

In the context of Quebec's *Révolution Tranquille,* Bossy demonstrated to have little to no knowledge regarding the French Canadians and their historical claims to a special status. After establishing the short-lived Ethnic Canadian Mosaic Institute with the help of Edward LaPierre, he used it to attack biculturalism and bilingualism – and believed that in doing so he was speaking on behalf of the 'third force'. Having previously praised the French Canadian as the leading voice of a nationwide Christian revolution, his criticism was harshly received. It cost him the little support that he had left from among the local French-Canadian press. His attempts to redirect his attention to the ethnic 'others' and present a more inclusive discourse were also a failure, which is unsurprising given that his integrating minorities that he had for years openly excluded was only sporadic, and thus clearly strategic. Bossy's late attempts to join the Ukrainian 'pioneering argument' also resulted in silence. By then, Canadians were looking at other Ukrainian representatives of the 'third force', like Jaroslav Rudnyckyj or Paul Yuzyk, who were much better positioned to create change than Bossy ever was. In the end, Bossy was alone.

This chapter demonstrates that, while the idea of a trichotomic Canada was adopted by ethnic groups in the postwar era as a means to voice their claims for cultural or national equality, Bossy's use of the 'third force' remained a means to advance himself. For 30 years, Bossy's allies changed frequently, as did his rhetoric and the projects or institutions he associated himself with. The lack of stability, including a loyal support system or friends and a source of income, seem a sign that his behaviour and interests changed with the times. Evidently, while some of his beliefs were consistently at the core of his plans for Canada (Christian supremacism, corporatism, ethnic uplifting of European nations, antisemitism …), he was willing to modify some of those principles as long as that brought him power. This suggests that Bossy's status as an individual concerned him much more than the future of the 'third force', of French Canadians, of Ukrainian Canadians, or of Canada as a whole.

Notes

1. *Canada Month*, February 1964, page (?), vol. 4, MG30 C72, LAC.
2. Bossy to MCSC, March 11, 1959, file MCSC Correspondence 1956–1969, vol. 9, MG30 C72, LAC. In this letter, Bossy reminds the MCSC of the events that occurred in 1949.
3. Fitzgerald to Bossy, March 3, 1950, file Correspondence Fitzgerald, J. J. 1949–1950, vol. 3, MG30 C72, LAC.
4. Fitzgerald to Pearson, June 11, 1951, file Correspondence Fitzgerald, J. J. 1951, vol. 3, MG30 C72, LAC. This letter also reveals that Bossy's touring western Canada with Saint-Laurent had been facilitated by Fitzgerald's connections with the Liberal Party.

The 'Third Force' 145

5. April 1948, November 1948, file Correspondence La Pierre, Edward 1935–1971, vol. 2, MG30 C72, LAC.
6. April 1948, November 1948, file Correspondence La Pierre, Edward 1935–1971, vol. 2, MG30 C72, LAC.
7. April 1948, November 1948, file Correspondence La Pierre, Edward 1935–1971, vol. 2, MG30 C72, LAC. LaPierre would continue helping Bossy throughout the 1960s, see: file Inst. of the Canadian Ethnic Mosaic Conf. Notes on Social Centre on Ile Bizard, 1963–1970, vol. 7, MG30 C72, LAC.
8. File Inst. of The Canadian Ethnic Mosaic Conf. Notes on Social Center on Ile Bizard, vol. 7, MG30 C72, LAC; Visitor's Register, Inauguration of the Institute, file Inst. of The Canadian Ethnic Mosaic Conf. Notes on Social Center on Ile Bizard 1963–1970, vol. 7, MG30 C72, LAC.
9. Bossy to MCSC, April 13, 1961, file MCSC Correspondence 1956–1969, vol. 9, MG30 C72, LAC; Secretary of New Canadians Service Bureau Jeanne Filion, July 26, 1960, file MCSC Correspondence 1956–1969, vol. 9, MG30 C72, LAC; Enclosure – List of Studies and Teaching Experience of Walter J. Bossy, file MCSC Correspondence 1956–1969, vol. 9, MG30 C72, LAC.
10. Bossy's "Answer to MCSCommission's False Information Given to Quebec Government – re: his Pension Rights", file MCSC Correspondence 1956–1969, vol. 9, MG30 C72, LAC.
11. Bossy's "Answer to MCSCommission's False Information Given to Quebec Government – re: his Pension Rights", file MCSC Correspondence 1956–1969, vol. 9, MG30 C72, LAC; Wilson to Bossy, November 11, 1960, file MCSC Correspondence, 1956–1969, vol. 9, MG30 C72, LAC.
12. Bossy to Plante, April 13, 1961, file MCSC Correspondence, 1956–1969, vol. 9, MG30 C72, LAC.
13. Bossy's "Answer to MCSCommission's False Information Given to Quebec Government – re: his Pension Rights", file MCSC Correspondence 1956–1969, vol. 9, MG30 C72, LAC; Bossy to MCSC, April 13, 1961, file MCSC Correspondence 1956–1969, vol. 9, MG30 C72, LAC.
14. Bossy's "Answer to MCSCommission's False Information Given to Quebec Government – re: his Pension Rights", file MCSC Correspondence 1956–1969, vol. 9, MG30 C72, LAC; Bossy to MCSC, April 13, 1961, file MCSC Correspondence 1956–1969, vol. 9, MG30 C72, LAC.
15. *Le Petit Journal*, August 24, 1969, p. 26; Bossy to MCSC, April 13, 1961, file MCSC Correspondence 1956–1969, vol. 9, MG30 C72, LAC; Wilson to Bossy, November 11, 1960, file MCSC CORRESPONDENCE, 1956–1969, vol. 9, MG30 C72, LAC. The salary Bossy is referring to was $4,850 yearly (see: MCSC Secretary Paul-Emile Alin to Bossy, July 26, 1960, file MCSC Correspondence 1956–1969, vol. 9, MG30 C72, LAC). In fact, Bossy's salary defers little from what a male teacher at the MCSC (or any Catholic school in Quebec) would have expected to receive after 16 years of service in the late 1950s. See: Robert Gagnon, *Histoire de la Commission des écoles catholiques de Montréal* (Montreal: Boréal, 1996), 224.
16. Bossy's "Answer to MCSCommission's False Information Given to Quebec Government – re: his Pension Rights", file MCSC Correspondence 1956–1969, vol. 9, MG30 C72, LAC; Bossy to Conseiller Juridique Jean Marcoux, October 10, 1966, file MCSC 1956–1969 Correspondence, vol. 9, MG30 C72, LAC.
17. *Sherbrooke Daily Record,* October 21, 1960, p. 3.
18. *Canada Month*, vol. 2, no. 5 (May 1962): 32–4.; *Sherbrooke Daily Record*, October 5, 1963, p. 1.
19. An Open Letter, Bossy to André Laurendeau, July 30, 1963, file Inst. of The Canadian Ethnic Mosaic Conf. Notes on 'Open Letter' 1963, vol. 7, MG30 C72, LAC.

20. Bossy to André Laurendeau, August 28, 1963, file Bossy, W. J. on Multiculturalism, vol. 8, MG31 D58, LAC. See also: file Inst. of The Canadian Ethnic Mosaic Conf. Notes on 'Open Letter' 1963, vol. 7, MG30 C72, LAC.
21. *Le Devoir*, October 21, 1963, pp. 3, 10.
22. *Le Droit*, February 7, 1964, p. 6.
23. Privy Council Minute 1106 of 19 July 1963, as reproduced in *Report of the Royal Commission on Bilingualism and Biculturalism, Book I: General Introduction: The Official Languages* (Ottawa: Queen's Printer, 1967), appendix 1, 173–4.
24. File Inst. of the Canadian Ethnic Mosaic Conf. Notes on Social Centre on Ile Bizard, 1963–1970, vol. 7, MG30 C70, LAC.
25. Philip Boobbyer, *The Spiritual Vision of Frank Buchman* (Pennsylvania: The Pennsylvania State University Press, 2013), 90, 93.
26. Boobbyer, *The Spiritual Vision of Frank Buchman*, 93.
27. Andrew L. Whitehead, Samuel L. Perry, *Taking America Back to God: Christian Nationalism in the United States* (Oxford: Oxford University Press), 10; Lori L. Bogle, *The Pentagon's Battle for the American Mind: The Early Cold War* (US: Texas A&M University Press, 2004), 65.
28. Daniel Sack, *Moral Re-Armament: The Reinventions of an American Religious Movement* (London: Palgrave Macmillan, 2009), 139.
29. Sack, *Moral Re-Armament*, 245.
30. Buchman to Bossy, March 24, 1961, file Religious Activities Moral Re-Armament Correspondence 1958–1972, vol. 9, MG30 C72, LAC; Bossy to Buchman, January 13, 1961, file Religious Activities, Ecumenism, Correspondence 1961–1969, vol. 9, MG30 C72, LAC.
31. Susan Belcourt to Bossy, October 16, 1963, Inst. Of The Canadian Ethnic Mosaic Conf. Radio Program On CFMB 1963, vol. 7, MG30 C72, LAC. On Casimir Stanczykowski and CFMB, see: *Télé-radiomonde*, February 22, 1964, page (?), vol. 18, MG30 C72, LAC; *Le Devoir*, June 27, 1966, p. 8; *La Presse*, August 1, 1966, p. 13.
32. November 4, 1963, first talk, file Inst. Of The Canadian Ethnic Mosaic Conf. Radio Program On CFMB 1963, vol. 7, MG30 C72, LAC; November 25, 1963, fourth talk, file Inst. Of The Canadian Ethnic Mosaic Conf. Radio Program on CFMB 1963, vol. 7, MG30 C72, LAC.
33. *Sherbrooke Daily Record*, October 5, 1963, p. 1.
34. *The Gazette*, March 23, 1962, page (?), vol. 18, MG30 C72, LAC.
35. *The Montreal Star*, October 2, 1963, page (?) vol. 18, MG30 C72, LAC; *Le Devoir*, October 7, 1963, p. 2; *Sherbrooke Daily Record*, October 5, 1963, p. 1.
36. Peter C. Newman, *Renegade in Power: The Diefenbaker Years* (Toronto: McClelland and Stewart, 1963), 193, 283; Shinder Purewal, "The Politics of Multiculturalism in Canada, 1963–1971", Master's thesis (Simon Fraser University, August 1992), 47.
37. Lester B. Pearson, *Memoirs*, vol. III (Toronto: University of Toronto Press, 1975), 236.
38. Bruce Thordarson, *Lester Pearson: Diplomat and Politician* (Toronto: Oxford University Press, 1974), 153.
39. *Report of the Royal Commission on Bilingualism and Biculturalism, Book IV: The Cultural Contribution of Other Ethnic Groups* (Ottawa: Queens Printer, 1969), 5–10. *Book IV* insists that 'Integration … does not imply the loss of an individual's identity and original characteristics or of his original language and culture. […] Integration is not synonymous with assimilation'. At the same time, however, it demanded that the 'other ethnic groups … choose' one of the 'two societies' (page 5).
40. Jean R. Burnet, Howard Palmer, *Coming Canadians: A History of Canada's Peoples* (Ottawa: Suppy and Services, 1988), 224.

The 'Third Force' 147

41. See: Valérie Lapointe-Gagnon, "Penser et 'Panser' les Plaies du Canada: Le Moment Laurendeau-Dunton, 1963–1971", dissertation (Université Laval, 2013).
42. Appendix V of the *Report of the Royal Commission on Bilingualism and Biculturalism, Book I* (Ottawa: Queen's Printer, 1967).
43. Lapointe-Gagnon, "Penser et 'Panser' les Plaies du Canada", 160.
44. *The Montreal Star*, October 2, 1963, page (?), vol. 18, MG30 C72, LAC; *Le Devoir*, October 7, 1963, p. 2; *The Montreal Star*, October 16, 1963, p. 11.
45. An Open Letter, Bossy to André Laurendeau, July 30, 1963, file Inst. of The Canadian Ethnic Mosaic Conf. Notes on 'Open Letter' 1963, vol. 7, MG30 C72, LAC. My emphasis.
46. "Terms of Reference", file Notes & Memoranda c. 1938–c. 1965, vol. 11, MG30 C72, LAC.
47. "An Open Letter", Bossy to André Laurendeau, July 30, 1963, file Inst. of The Canadian Ethnic Mosaic Conf. Notes on 'Open Letter' 1963, vol. 7, MG30 C72, LAC. Pioneer of liberal multiculturalism Paul Yuzyk (more on him below) included Indigenous peoples in his idea of the 'Third Element', but this is considered problematic as the colonial experience of the First Nations have little in common with the immigrant experience. See: Jonathan McQuarrie, "Another Vision for the Canadian Senate", *Active History*, October 31, 2013. Accessed in January 2021.
48. *The Montreal Gazette*, September 25, 1963, page (?), vol. 18, MG30 C72, LAC.
49. Solodovnikov to Bossy, September 11, 1963, file Inst. Of The Canadian Ethnic Mosaic Conf. Correspondence Received On 'An Open Letter' 1963–1965, vol. 7, MG30 C72, LAC.
50. According to Jean-François Nadeau, *Le Petit Journal* was the first mass-circulation weekly in Quebec. See: Nadeau, *The Canadian Führer: The Life of Adrien Arcand* (Toronto: James Lorimer Limited, 2011), 137.
51. *Le Petit Journal*, October 27, 1963, page (?), vol. 18, MG30 C72, LAC.
52. *The Montreal Star*, September 28, 1963, p. 11.
53. *The Montreal Star*, October 16, 1963, p. 11; *The Montreal Star*, November 12, 1963, page (?), vol. 18, MG30 C72, LAC. This opinion was later echoed by the B&B Commission, which insisted on the 'lack of cohesion and consistency' of the so-called 'third force'. See: Canada, *Preliminary Report*, 1965b, 67, 126, 127–8.
54. *La Presse*, October 9, 1963, p. 25.
55. Ibid.
56. November 25, 1963, fourth talk, file Inst. Of The Canadian Ethnic Mosaic Conf. Radio Program On CFMB 1963, vol. 7, MG30 C72, LAC; August 28, 1963, Bossy to André Laurendeau, file Bossy, W. J. on Multiculturalism, vol. 8, MG31 D58, LAC. See also: file Inst. of The Canadian Ethnic Mosaic Conf. Notes on 'Open Letter' 1963, vol. 7, MG30 C72, LAC.
57. "An Open Letter", Bossy to André Laurendeau, July 30, 1963, file Inst. of The Canadian Ethnic Mosaic Conf. Notes on 'Open Letter' 1963, vol. 7, MG30 C72, LAC; November 25, 1963, fourth talk, file Inst. of The Canadian Ethnic Mosaic Conf. Radio Program On CFMB 1963, vol. 7, MG30 C72, LAC; December 4, 1963, fifth talk, file Inst. Of The Canadian Ethnic Mosaic Conf. Radio Program On CFMB 1963, vol. 7, MG30 C72, LAC.
58. Martin Pâquet, *Tracer les marges de la cité. Étranger, immigrant et État au Québec 1627–1981* (Montreal: Boréal, 2005), 215.
59. "An Open Letter", Bossy to André Laurendeau, July 30, 1963, file Inst. of The Canadian Ethnic Mosaic Conf. Notes on 'Open Letter' 1963, vol. 7, MG30 C72, LAC; "Thoughts. French-Canadian Revolution vis-à-vis Canada [and the] fight for Equality", file Notes & Memoranda c. 1938–c. 1965, vol. 11, MG30 C72, LAC; *Canada Month*, vol. 2, no. 5 (May 1962): 32–4.

60. "An Open Letter", Bossy to André Laurendeau, July 30, 1963, file Inst. of The Canadian Ethnic Mosaic Conf. Notes on 'Open Letter' 1963, vol. 7, MG30 C72, LAC.
61. *The Gazette*, March 23, 1962, page (?), vol 18, MG30 C72, LAC.
62. *La Presse*, February 13, 1964, p. 28.
63. "Interview", April 1972, pp. 9–10, vol. 1, MG30 C72, LAC; Bossy to Steve Otto, January 17, 1967, file Inst. of the Canadian Ethnic Mosaic Conf. Notes on Social Center on Ile Bizard, 1963–1970, vol. 7, MG30 C72, LAC.
64. *The Gazette,* March 23, 1962, page (?), vol 18, MG30 C72, LAC.
65. Lapointe-Gagnon, "Penser et 'panser'", 161; Shinder Purewal, "The Politics of Multiculturalism in Canada, 1963-1971", Master's thesis (Simon Fraser University, August 1992), 39; Eve Haque, *Multiculturalism Within a Bilingual Framework: Language, Race, and Belonging in Canada* (Toronto: University of Toronto, 2012), 56–9.
66. *Le Soleil,* November 9, 1963, p. 2.
67. The original French word used by the source here is 'inadapté', which can mean 'unsuitable' but also 'unassimilated' or 'maladjusted'. The polysemic nature of the word could have been convenient in this context, and so used intentionally, as the source is clearly trying to undermine both Bossy and his multi-cultural project, which effectively challenges biculturalism.
68. *La Presse*, November 9, 1963, p. 29.
69. *Le Droit*, February 7, 1964, p. 6.
70. CBC Digital Archives, "Canada is actually 'tricultural'", Sunday Morning Magazine Radio Program, 10 November 1963, 2:21', 1:07'-2:21'. Accessed in May 2020.
71. See family photo in vol. 8, MG31 D58, LAC. Bossy's family ethnic groups (including Jewish) were also listed in: *The Montreal Star,* October 16, 1963, p. 11.
72. January 30, 1956, file Néo-Canadian Activities. Articles on Jewry & Judaism 1944–1964, vol. 5, MG30 C72, LAC; Nesta H. Webster, "Jewish Influence on Freemasonry. Jewish Cabala" (1964), pp. 18–9, file Néo-Canadian Activities Articles on Jewry & Judaism 1944–1964, vol. 5, MG30 C72, LAC. On Nesta H. Webster, see: Richard M. Gilman, *Behind 'World Revolution': The Strange Career of Nesta H. Webster* (London: Insight Books, 1982); Marta F. Lee, "Nesta Webster: The Voice of Conspiracy", *Journal of Women's History*, vol. 17, No. 3 (Fall, 2005): 81; Lara Trubowitz, *Civil Antisemitism, Modernism, and British Culture, 1902–1939* (New York: Palgrave Macmillan, 2012); Thomas Linehan, *British Fascism, 1918–39: Parties, Ideology and Culture* (New York: Manchester University Press, 2000), 178.
73. "Editorials, And Now – Jewish [blank]", notes on unidentified clipping, January 1965, file Religious Activities, Ecumenism, Correspondence 1961–1969, vol. 9, MG30 C72, LAC.
74. "Editorials, And Now – Jewish [blank]", notes on unidentified clipping, January 1965, file Religious Activities, Ecumenism, Correspondence 1961–1969, vol. 9, MG30 C72, LAC.
75. Notes, file Inst. Of The Canadian Ethnic Mosaic Conf. Notes & Memoranda 1963–1968, vol. 7, MG30 C72, LAC; "Editorials, And Now – Jewish [blank]", notes on unidentified clipping, January 1965, file Religious Activities, Ecumenism, Correspondence 1961–1969, vol. 9, MG30 C72, LAC.
76. Notes, file Inst. Of The Canadian Ethnic Mosaic Conf. Notes & Memoranda 1963–1968, vol. 7, MG30 C72, LAC.
77. "Interview", April 1972, p. 8, vol. 1, MG30 C72, LAC.
78. File Neo-Canadian Activities Correspondence with the Canadian Jewish Congress, 1947–1969, vol. 5, MG30 C72, LAC.

The 'Third Force' 149

79. Robert J. Brym, William Shaffir, Morton Weinfeld, *The Jews in Canada* (Oxford: Oxford University Press, 1993), 360.
80. File Inst. of the Canadian Ethnic Mosaic Conf. Correspondence Receive on 'An Open Letter', 1963–1965, vol. 7, MG30 C72, LAC.
81. Bossy to J. I. Paré, 28 April 1948, file New Canadian Service Bureau Correspondence Sent 1948–1949, vol. 5, MG30 C72, LAC. In 1972, Bossy said that this supposed shift in his ideology made Adrien Arcand very upset and, as a consequence, 'he wanted to kill me', claimed Bossy. There is no proof of these allegations, which can be found in: "Interview", April 1972, p. 8, vol. 1, MG30 C72, LAC.
82. "Interview", April 1972, p. 9, vol. 1, MG30 C72, LAC.
83. Ibid.
84. *Le Petit Journal,* August 7, 1966, p. 17; Bossy to Press Editors, June 1970, file Inst. of The Canadian Ethnic Mosaic Conf. Notes on Social Center on Ile Bizard 1963–1970, vol. 7, MG30 C72, LAC.
85. Bossy to Press Editors, June 1970, file Inst. of The Canadian Ethnic Mosaic Conf. Notes on Social Center on Ile Bizard 1963–1970, vol. 7, MG30 C72, LAC; Bossy to Steve Otto, January 17, 1967, file Inst. of The Canadian Ethnic Mosaic Conf. Notes on Social Center on Ile Bizard 1963–1970, vol. 7, MG30 C72, LAC.
86. Julia Lalande, "The Roots of Multiculturalism – Ukrainian-Canadian Involvement in the Multiculturalism Discussion of the 1960s as an Example of the Position of the 'Third Force'", *Canadian Ethnic Studies/Études ethniques au Canada XXXVIII*, no. 1, (2006): 51.
87. Orest T. Martynowych, *Ukrainians in Canada: The Formative Period, 1891–1924* (Edmonton: Canadian Institute of Ukrainian Studies Press, 1991), 59.
88. Martynowych, *Ukrainians in Canada*, 109.
89. Lalande, "The Roots of Multiculturalism", 51.
90. Ibid., 51.
91. Lalande, "The Roots of Multiculturalism", 53; Rhonda L. Hinther, Jim Mochoruk, et al., *Re-imagining Ukrainian Canadians. History, Politics, and Identities* (Toronto: University of Toronto Press, 2011), 465. See also: Paul Yuzyk, *Ukrainian Canadians: Their Place and Role in Canadian Life* (Toronto: Ukrainian Canadian Business and Professional Federation, 1967).
92. Roberto Perin, "Un adversaire du bilinguisme officiel à la commission Laurendeau-Dunton", *Le projet du bilinguisme canadien: histoire, utopie et réalisation*, vol. 26, no. 2 (Winter 2018): 122.
93. Rhonda K. Hinther, *Perogies and Politics: Canada's Ukrainian Left, 1891–1991* (Toronto: University of Toronto Press, 2018), 148.
94. Perin, "Un adversaire du bilinguisme officiel", 121; Lapointe-Gagnon, "Penser et 'Panser'", pp. 276–9; Frances Swyripa, *Ukrainian Canadians: A Survey of their Portrayal in English-language works* (Edmonton: The University of Alberta Press, 1978), 89.
95. Perin, "Un adversaire du bilinguisme officiel", 121; Lalande, "The Roots of Multiculturalism", 50.
96. Cited in: Lalande, "The Roots of Multiculturalism", 52.
97. Paul Yuzyk's Maiden Speech (Winnipeg: Ukrainian Voice, 1964).
98. Paul Yuzyk, *Voice of Freedom*, nos. 11–2, November, December 1964, vol. 8, MG30 C72, LAC. On Bossy's demands for and uses of the term 'multiculturalism', see: *Sherbrooke Daily Record*, October 5, 1963, p. 1; *The Montreal Star*, October 2, 1963, page (?), vol. 18, MG30 C72, LAC; *Le Devoir*, October 7, 1963, p. 2. On Yuzyk's first referring to Canada as a multicultural nation, see: Elspeth Cameron, ed., *Multiculturalism and Immigration in Canada: An Introductory Reader* (Toronto: Canadian Scholars' Press, 2004), 85; Haque, *Multiculturalism Within a Bilingual Framework*, 214; Paul Yuzyk, *Voice of Freedom*, nos. 11–2, November, December 1964, vol. 8, MG30 C72, LAC.

99. Paul Yuzyk's Maiden Speech, *Ukrainian Voice* (English series), no. 5, 1964, p. 21.
100. *Book IV*, 7.
101. Paul Yuzyk, *Ukrainian Canadians: Their Place and Role in Canadian Life* (Toronto: Ukrainian Canadian Business and Professional Federation, 1967), preface.
102. Jonathan McQuarrie, "Another Vision for the Canadian Senate", *Active History*, October 31, 2013. Accessed in January 2021.
103. *The Montreal Star,* February 14, 1964, p. 6.
104. *The Ukrainian Quarterly*, New York 1956, vol. XII, no. 2, file Correspondence Kishka, A. 1950–1970, vol. 2; *Pax Romana. Mouvement International des Etudiants Catholiques*, April 1948, no. 10, file Correspondence Kishka, A. 1950–1970, vol. 2, MG30 C72, LAC.
105. *La Nouvelle Gazette de Bruxelles*, February 14, 1950, page (?), file Correspondence Kishka, A. 1950–1970, vol. 2, MG30 C72, LAC.
106. *Le Devoir*, October 30, 1968, p. 4; *La Presse,* October 31, 1968, p. 4.
107. "Face aux réalités", André Kisha, October 25, 1969, file Correspondence Kishka, A. 1950–1970, vol. 11, MG30 C72, LAC.
108. *Le Droit*, November 15, 1965, p. 17.
109. *Major Ukrainian Collections in the National Archives of Canada*: https://old.archives.gov.ua/Eng/ukrainian-collections.php. Accessed in February 2021.
110. "My Canada", file Presunka, P., 1966–1972, vol. 11, MG30 C72, LAC.
111. Ibid.
112. "Canada's Choice: Bicultural Retreat or Planning for Nationhood", file Presunka, P., 1966–1972, vol. 11.
113. "Universality and World Religion", file Presunka, P., 1966–1972, vol. 11, MG30 C72, LAC.
114. "My Canada", file Presunka, P., 1966–1972, vol. 11, MG30 C72, LAC.
115. *Sherbrooke Daily Record,* March 6, 1968, p. 4; *Sherbrooke Daily Record*, September 18, 1967, p. 4.
116. *Book IV*, 8–15.
117. Bossy to Editors, June 1970, file Inst. of the Canadian Ethnic Mosaic Conf. Notes on Social Center on Ile Bizard, 1963–1970, vol. 7, MG30 C72, LAC.
118. File Inst. of the Canadian Ethnic Mosaic Conf. Notes on Social Center on Ile Bizard, 1963–1970, vol. 7, MG30 C72, LAC.
119. File RCMP, 1937–1958, vol. 11, MG30 C72, LAC.
120. *La Nation Belge*, March 31, 1950, page (?), file Correspondence Kishka, A. 1950–1970, vol. 2, MG30 C72, LAC; *Pax Romana. Mouvement International des Étudiants Catholiques*, April 1948, no. 10, file Correspondence Kishka, A. 1950–1970, vol. 2, MG30 C72, LAC.
121. *Phare-Dimanche*, April 16, 1950, page (?), file Correspondence Kishka, A. 1950–1970, vol. 2, MG30 C72, LAC.
122. *The Ukrainian Quarterly*, vol. XII, no. 2 (New York 1956), file Correspondence Kishka, A. 1950–1970, vol. 2, MG30 C70, LAC.
123. "Interview", April 1972, p. 1, file Bossy, Walter J. Biographical Notes, 1912–1972, vol. 1, MG30 C72, LAC.
124. "Interview", April 1972, p. 2, file Bossy, Walter J. Biographical Notes, 1912–1972, vol. 1, MG30 C72, LAC.
125. "Interview", April 1972, p. 9, file Bossy, Walter J. Biographical Notes, 1912–1972, vol. 1, MG30 C72, LAC.

6 Conclusion

When Walter J. Bossy died in Montreal on January 3, 1979, his passing went virtually unnoticed beyond his family and friends, his decades of activity in political life ignored or forgotten. Although, as I argue, Bossy's tri-national theory was an early expression of postwar debates on the 'third force' and multiculturalism, his thought as well as the events and institutions he led to promote it have been absent from the Canadian historical account. Until now, Bossy was yet another historical actor consigned to what E.P. Thompson called 'the enormous condescension of posterity.'[1] That is probably because, ultimately, all of Bossy's endeavours failed. He never obtained enough funds or support to develop and sustain any of his projects, and his efforts were never officially recognized. Given this, I acknowledge that by focusing on a series of failed attempts to bring about change I might be 'inflating its actual historical importance' – as Jean-François Nadeau warned about his own study of Adrien Arcand.[2] Nonetheless, ignoring them could be as harmful. As Lee Blanding's study of multicultural activism in Canada suggests, Bossy's view of the nation is worth exploring if only because it helps to understand the many Canadas that existed in the minds of those who felt they did not quite belong but wanted to.[3]

But why did he fail? Above all, Bossy's proposals for nation-building and the recognition of the 'third force' tended to be inconsistent and quite arbitrary. For example, in his first reform program, *A Call to All Socially Minded Christian Canadians* (1934–1935), Bossy incorporated as much as he could from as many theories as possible, selecting elements that he thought were interesting while rejecting others on the basis of personal appeal rather than feasibility. This is how, in the early 1930s, he managed to praise Fascism and Catholic anarchism at the same time. Bossy's insistence on the apolitical nature of his projects was of no help either even when there was some support. For instance, even though Bossy's corporatist approach to Canadian identity seemingly exercised 'a considerable influence' (according to him) among Ukrainian Canadians, this community showed more interest in learning about which provincial and federal party Bossy supported than in joining his own movement.[4] Equally, when introducing the Classocracy League of Canada in 1934, the editor of the Catholic daily

DOI: 10.4324/9781003283348-6

The Prairie Messenger Cosmas W. Krumpelmann stated: 'If I vote Liberal or Conservative I have a fair idea of what is going to happen, but when I advocate Classocracy God knows what might happen.'[5] But, far from being an apolitical person, Bossy actively supported parties such as the Union Nationale, the Parti National Social Chrétien, and the Social Credit. He didn't hesitate to pledge allegiance to the Liberal Party, however, when in the postwar period they promised to support his New Canadians Bureau in exchange.

Another major inconsistency in Bossy's plans for the mobilization of the 'third force' is that, when targeting ethnic groups to join his quest for multiculturalism, he dismissed the two biggest immigrant groups of Montreal, and eastern Canada more generally: the Italian and the Jewish communities. On the one hand, Italians appear to be listed as participating in each one of the demonstrations that Bossy organized since 1936. On the other, Bossy insisted that because Italians learned French so easily, and shared the same values as French Canadians, they were already able to advance ('assimilate', he said), and so they didn't need the support of the wider ethnic community. But this justification doesn't seem enough to explain the degree of disregard that Italians received from Bossy. While it is true that, before the Depression, Italian immigrant communities tended to settle 'in the midst of working-class French-Canadian Montreal' and 'their children attended French-language Catholic schools', in the 1930s many Italian families 'were forced to turn to Protestant social welfare agencies to survive'.[6] And getting access to these services required them to take their children to Anglo-Protestant schools. In the 1930s, Bossy's job at the Montreal Catholic School Commission consisted precisely in investigating why ethnic families would choose Anglo-Protestant schools and how to change that. In fact, Bossy believed that switching to Protestant education constituted the first step towards ethnic minorities losing their faith and eventually joining the ranks of the Communist Party. And yet he never got in touch with the Italian community. Why this was the case remains unclear, but the answer might be related to ethnic prejudice, of which Italian immigrant communities suffered greatly at the time.[7]

This study has shown that, to Bossy, ethnic prejudice ultimately outweighed religious identity and cultural values, and the most obvious example of this was his perception of Jews. From his early years of activism in Montreal in the 1930s until the 1970s, Bossy's antisemitism endured. In the 1920s and throughout the 1930s, Bossy's anti-communist work for the RCMP included targeting Jewish individuals simply on the basis of their religion; before 1938, he supported the Nazi persecution of Jewish minorities, and celebrated with Adrien Arcand a western civilization bereft of this group; he associated liberal democracy ('plutocracy') with a global Jewish conspiracy, and praised European fascism for having stopped their plans of world domination; he avidly read antisemitic conspiracy literature and propaganda material; and he established contact with openly antisemitic groups and individuals in Canada and abroad. Bossy considered Jewish communities to be 'foreign colonies' incapable of adapting and therefore contributing to harmonious inter-ethnic cooperation. Even if they converted to Christianity, something he was promoting after the Second World War, Bossy believed that they still represented a threat to national unity and the Christian world.

Besides, Bossy's new focus on Jewish conversion seems to have been a strategy to overcome the discredit that the right suffered after the Second World War. Proof of this is Bossy's private correspondence with Ontario provincial leader of the Social Credit John J. Fitzgerald in the late 1940s, in which Bossy explained that antisemitism was simply not popular and that any political movement that aspired to succeed needed to hide its anti-Jewish hatred. Indeed, Bossy's rhetoric often changed as the times did, or as opportunities for success arose. For example, with the new social activism of the 1960s, Bossy briefly attempted to incorporate Jewish groups, as well as people of African, Asian, and Indigenous descent in his discourse on multiculturalism. However, at that point the citizens of Montreal were already looking for new and more powerful representatives of the 'third force', his own ideas on nation-building being listened to only by a few enthusiasts and old friends. A persistent man, however, Bossy tried to reach out to the Jewish community a few times, but they ignored his letters – probably well aware of Bossy's pre-1960s activities and message.

Aside from rejecting certain European groups based on ethnic and religious prejudice, would Bossy have taken into consideration non-European Christians? And European agnostics? And Christian Canadians of European and other descent? We don't know. Bossy's main problem was that throughout his time in Montreal, where he tried to develop a New Canadians movement for 30 years, he thought he represented a movement that, in fact, didn't exist. Having organized several demonstrations that rallied thousands of 'New Canadians' between 1936 and 1949, he could surely state that he had been able to mobilize this 'third force'. Yet exactly who or what groups had participated in these demonstrations, or rather who Bossy was counting on doing so, was never clear-cut. For the most part, this study has argued that he believed Christians of European descent other than British and French to be the third component of the Canadian nation. However, due to the many inconsistencies found in his discourse, the last chapter suggested that Bossy could have believed Ukrainians to be the 'third force', or at least its leading ethnic group. It is plausible that Bossy was mostly preoccupied with the uplifting of his ethnic group, if only because that would imply his own socio-economic advancement. It is also possible that he extended this concern towards other ethnic groups simply for the purpose of increasing their numbers and legitimacy.

The concern about numbers also explains Bossy's many attempts to approach the French-Canadian community. In the 1930s, he argued that French Canadians must lead Canada's Christian revolution and inspire the rest with their Catholic spirituality. He also insisted that French Canadians, a minority themselves, should join the other ethnic minorities (which he described as mostly Catholic) to offset English Protestantism, which he believed led to secularism. At the same time, Bossy never really understood French-Canadian identity or its claims to a special status, and in the 1960s he blamed them for their defence of biculturalism – he argued that any type of nationalism should be abandoned for the sake of Canada's unity. Bossy's lack of consideration for French-Canadian history and Quebec's case for a higher degree of autonomy caused some hostile reactions among the French-speaking press in Montreal that up to that point had been quite sympathetic to his desire for inter-ethnic cooperation.

But even when the French-Canadian press was supportive of Bossy's ideas, financial assistance from French Canadians never actually took place. This was also true during the interwar period. At that time, lack of support from the French-Canadian community could be partly explained by a rejection of what was perceived as 'foreign' forms of corporatism. Indeed, French-Canadian corporatism was a 'made in Quebec' corporatism shaped by the narrative of *la survivance* (survival), which focused on protecting francophone culture from assimilation.[8] This conflict is exemplified by the attempts of Bossy's Classocracy League of Canada to cooperate with l'Action Corporative (AC) in the late 1930s and early 1940s. A Montreal organization composed entirely of French-speaking Canadians, AC wanted to use corporatism to reorganize Canada on the basis of professions, which would supposedly allow French Canadians to advance without ethnicity being an impediment for economic success. AC was not interested in helping Bossy and his entourage as *la survivance* was a pressing issue based on constitutional rights that other ethnic groups couldn't claim to have. And even though Bossy insisted that he accepted French as an official language, his being unable to fully master it either in written or spoken form resulted, he claimed, in discrimination.

Even though during the interwar period Bossy was able to exchange views with ethnic individuals from some relevant organizations, like Madeleine Sheridan from the Co-operative Commonwealth Federation, and arrange several meetings and symposiums with and for those who self-identified as ethnic minorities, Bossy never had a significant and/or constant number of followers from any specific ethnic group. This is partly because, at that time, most ethnic groups were already organized and could rely on their independent cultural and religious institutions or networks to protect their own lot – they didn't need Bossy to do that.[9] Future research might want to further explore if and how these ethnic communities interacted with Bossy's ideas as well as whether these shaped their own understandings of diversity, inter-ethnic cooperation, and Canadian identity. If a reaction indeed occurred, an important question to raise would be whether such

Conclusion 155

communities interpreted Bossy's projects for 'multiculturalism' from the right or from the left side of the political spectrum, and how that affected their construal of the B&B Commission and the 1971 recognition of the cultural contribution of ethnic groups – an acknowledgement that Bossy celebrated as a 'revolution'.[10]

Ultimately, however, I argue that Bossy represented no force at all. He knew of the existence of an 'ethnic other' and wanted to claim a place for it within a new nation-building project, but his personal preferences, prejudices, and paranoias shaped a vision that was neither desirable nor clear to most Canadians. As a consequence, Bossy belonged to an *unimagined* community, a constructed collective whose only member was himself: a detached and conflicted individual with no idea of what his role within a community and under the state should be. In spite of this, his trichotomic view of Canada allowed for an unprecedented conversation to take place, one that defined Canada in terms that we still hold true today. Without a doubt, those terms evolved, which is why Bossy is not responsible for the origins of Canadian liberal multiculturalism. For one thing, he rejected liberalism and maintained that individuals are unequal. The terms he used (like 'third group' and 'tri-nationalism') changed at the hands of others who saw in a plural view of Canada a step towards a more effective and fairer integration of ethnic divergence. It is thanks to those, not to Bossy, that multiculturalism as we know it emerged. And yet, Bossy still seems to have been the first Canadian to think of Canada in terms of three elements that must cooperate in order for the country to progress as a united, and culturally plural, nation. This is important. It makes it obvious that projecting our understanding of concepts we now deem progressive upon the past doesn't necessarily bring clarity to the historical contexts in which these concepts emerged. Likewise, it forces us to question the historical terms and ideas that we use to understand reality without questioning their meaning(s) and changing nature.

It is my belief that Bossy's contribution to our contemporary understanding of Canada was bypassed because his ideas at the *margin* of the concept 'third force' didn't change. These promoted the existence of a group that was privileged to the detriment of new 'others', while misusing liberal principles like equality, multiculturalism, and group rights. So, whereas in the postwar period Bossy's *core* idea of a trichotomic Canada survived and re-emerged from wider sections of Canadian society as a means to foster ethnic cooperation, he remained stuck in understandings of pluralism clouded by racism, religious prejudice, and a personal sense of victimhood. As a result, his idea of a multicultural Canada was superseded by a new liberal ideal of nationhood. In short, despite the fact that conceptual continuity persisted because the *core* idea remained the same, Bossy's vision of multiculturalism was ultimately dismissed because his illiberal ideas at the *margin* of 'third force' lingered. Canada rejected his attempt at defining a new form of supremacy, and for this History forgot him.

156 Conclusion

This monograph has demonstrated that the conceptual origins of the 'third force', and therefore the beginning of a multicultural understanding of Canada from among ethnic minorities, are rooted in Bossy and his ultraconservative entourage's assessment of diversity in the 1930s. However, Bossy's understanding of the 'third force' as a group or national element didn't relate to the ethnic minorities the Canadian Liberal government recognized in 1971 as cultural contributors to the nation. Rather, his 'third force' embodied an illiberal project that used liberal tenets for reactionary purposes. This is what Aurelien Mondon and Aaron Winter have called 'liberal racism'[11]: a history of the far right.

Notes

1. Edward Palmer Thompson, *The Making of the English Working Class* (Toronto: Harmondsworth: Penguin, 1980 [1963]), 958.
2. Jean-François Nadeau, *The Canadian Führer: The Life of Adrien Arcand* (Toronto: James Lorimer Limited, 2011), 19.
3. Lee Blanding, "Re-branding Canada: The Origins of Canadian Multiculturalism Policy, 1945–1974", dissertation (University of Victoria, 2013), 335. Although Blanding only briefly refers to Bossy's postwar New Canadian Service Bureau, the conclusion reads: 'If we want to understand what multiculturalism "is", we should begin by reexamining the assumptions that guided ... activists like Scott Symons, Walter Lindal, Walter Bossy, and others. Their understanding of Canadian society, perhaps ironically, mirrors that of many modern critics of multiculturalism policy. All were interested in mitigating the negative (and accentuating the positive) effects of cultural and ethnic diversity, while maintaining common goals, institutions, and values to which all Canadians – new and old – could cling to as their own. The Canadian state's adoption of "multiculturalism within a bilingual framework" both recognized the power and strength of its two "founding peoples," even as it looked to a future in which ethnic and linguistic diversity would play an increasing role in the lives of Canadians' (p. 335).
4. Bossy to J. J. Penverne, Conservative Candidate, October 2, 1935, file Political Activities Correspondence 1930–1965, vol. 8, MG30 C72, LAC.
5. Cosmas W. Krumpelmann, March 16, 1935, vol. 8, MG30 C72, LAC.
6. Yves Frenette, "National minorities, immigration, and responsibility: French Canada as a case study, 1840–1960", in S. Karly Kehoe, Eva Alisic, Jan-Christoph Heilinger, eds., *Responsibility for Refugee and Migrant Integration* (Berlin: De Gruyter, 2019), 92–3.
7. See, for example: Jennifer Guglielmo, Salvatore Salerno, eds., *Are Italians White? How Race is Made in America* (New York: Routledge, 2012).
8. Filippo Salvatore, *Fascism and the Italians of Montreal: An Oral History, 1922–1945* (Toronto: Guernica, 1998), 8–9. It is interesting to note that, in a sense, Bossy's idea that social and political grievance could overcome ethnic divergence echoed the efforts from the Communist Party of Canada which, also unsuccessfully, expected class solidarity to surpass ethnic conflict. See: Paula Maurutto, "Private Policing and Surveillance of Catholics: Anti-communism in the Roman Catholic Archdiocese of Toronto, 1920–1960", *Labour/Le Travail* (fall 1997): 117; Stephen Endicott, *Raising the Workers' Flag: The Workers' Unity League of Canada, 1930–1936* (Toronto: University of Toronto Press, 2012), 28; Donald Avery, *Dangerous Foreigners: European Immigrant Workers*

and Labour Radicalism in Canada, 1896–1932 (Toronto: McClelland and Steward, 1979), 128; Penner, Norman, *Canadian communism: the Stain years and beyond* (Toronto: Methuen, 1988), 276.
9. Raymond Breton, "Institutional Completeness of Ethnic Communities and the Personal Relations of Immigrants", *American Journal of Sociology*, vol. 70, no. 2 (September 1964): 193–205.
10. Vol. 18, MG30 C72, LAC.
11. Aurelien Mondon and Aaron Winter, *Reactionary Democracy: How Racism and the Populist Far Right Became Mainstream* (London: Verso, 2020).

References

Archives

Archives of the Roman Catholic Archdiocese (ARCAT), Toronto

- MN AP02.01, Neil McNeil Papers

Bibliothèque et Archives nationales du Québec (BAnQ), Montreal

- Patrimoine québécois/Texte (Numérique)
- Patrimoine québécois/Revues et journaux (Numérique)

Canadian Broadcasting Corporation (CBC) Digital Archives
  Library and Archives Canada (LAC), Ottawa

- MG30 C72, Walter J. Bossy Fonds
- MG30 D211, Francis Reginald (Frank) Scott Fonds
- MG31 D58, Jaroslav Bohdan Rudnyckyj Fonds
- MG30 D91, Adrien Arcand Fonds

Morisset Library, University of Ottawa

- FC 2924.1, Adrien Arcand Collection

People's History Museum Archives (PHM), Manchester (Britain)

- LP/SCW/16, Friends of National Spain Collection

United Church of Canada Archives (ARCHEION), Toronto

- F3363, R.B.Y. Scott Fonds

Newspapers and Magazines

Canada Month
Clairon-Montreal
Commonweal
Jewish Telegraphic Agency
L'Étoile du Lac St. Jean
L'Action Catholique
L'Action Nationale
L'Avenir du Nord
L'École Sociale Populaire
L'Illustration Nouvelle
L'Ordre
L'Ordre Nouveau
La Liberté et le Patriote
La Patrie
La Presse
La Tribune
Le Bien Public
Le Canada
Le Devoir
Le Droit
Le Montréal-Matin
Le Nouvelliste
Le Petit Canadien
Le Petit Journal
Le Progrès du Saguenay
Le Soleil
Lomond Press
Macleans
Mirror Journal
Oeuvre des Tracts
Redcliff Review
Relations
Sherbrooke Daily Record
Social Forum
Stony Plain Sun
The Christian Century
The Cross and the Flag
The Herald
The Montreal Gazette
The Montreal Beacon
The Montreal Daily Star
The Raymond Recorder
The Standard

The Sudbury Daily Star
The Toronto Daily Star
Ukrainian Voice

Bibliography

A. Small, Charles, ed. *Global Antisemitism: A Crisis of Modernity*. Leiden: Martinus Nijhoff Publishers, 2013.

Abrams, Paula. *Cross Purposes: Pierce V. Society of Sisters and the Struggle over Compulsory Public Education*. Michigan: The University of Michigan Press, 2009.

Adamson, G., Carlbom, A., Ouis, P. "Johann Herder: Early Nineteenth-Century Counter-Enlightenment, and the Common Roots of Multiculturalism and Right-Wing Populism". *Télos*, vol. 169 (2014): 131–46.

Anderson, Benedict. *Imagined Communities: Reflections on the Origin and Spread of Nationalism*. London: Verso, 1983.

Anderson, Kay. "Thinking 'Postnationally': Dialogue across Multicultural, Indigenous, and Settler Spaces", *Annals of the Association of American Geographers*, vol. 90, no. 2 (2000): 381–91.

Anderson, Kevin P. *Not Quite Us: Anti-Catholic Thought in English Canada since 1900*. Montreal: McGill-Queen's University Press, 2019.

Angus, Ian. *A Border Within: National Identity, Cultural Plurality, and Wilderness*. Montreal: McGill-Queen's University Press, 1997.

Archambault, Joseph P. *Sous la menace rouge*. Montreal: École Sociale Populaire, 1936.

Archer, Jules. *Twentieth-Century Caesar: Benito Mussolini*. Folkestone, NZ: Bailey Bros and Swinfen, 1972.

Avery, Donald. *Dangerous Foreigners: European Immigrant Workers and Labour Radicalism in Canada, 1896–1932*. Toronto: McClelland and Steward, 1979.

Backes, Uwe, Moreau, Patrick, eds. *The Extreme Right in Europe: Current Trends and Perspectives*. Göttingen: Vandenhoeck and Ruprecht, 2012.

Baigell, Matthew. *The Implacable Urge to Defame: Cartoon Jews in the American Press, 1877–1935*. New York: Syracuse University, 2017.

Balan, Jars. *Salt and Braided Bread: Ukrainian Life in Canada*. Oxford: Oxford University Press, 1984.

Bannerji, Himani. *The Dark Side of the Nation: Essays on Multiculturalism, Nationalism and Gender*. Toronto: Canadian Scholars' Press, 2000.

Bar-On, Tamir. "Fascism to the Nouvelle Droite: The Dream of Pan-European Empire", *Journal of Contemporary European Studies*, vol. 16, no. 3 (2008): 327–45.

Bar-On, Tamir. *Where Have All the Fascists Gone?* London: Routledge, 2016.

Barrett, Stanley R. *Is God a Racist? The Right Wing in Canada*. Toronto: University of Toronto, 1987.

Bartley, Allan. *The Ku Klux Klan in Canada: A Century of Promoting Racism and Hate in the Peaceable Kingdom*. Toronto: James Lorimer & Company, 2020.

Baum, Gregory. *Catholics and Canadian Socialism: Political Thought in the Thirties and Forties*. Toronto: James Lorimer Ltd., 1980.

Beaulieu, André, Hamelin, Jean. *La Presse Québécoise des Origines à Nos Jours. 1920–1934*, third volume. Sainte-Foy: Presses de l'Université Laval, 1984.

Behiels, Michael D. "The Commission des écoles catholiques de Montréal and the Néo-Canadian Question: 1947–1963". *Canadian Ethnic Studies*, vol. 18, no. 2 (1986): 38–64.
Behiels, Michael D., Martel, Marcel, eds. *Nation, Ideas, Identities: Essays in Honour of Ramsay Cook*. Oxford: Oxford University Press, 2000.
Bélanger, André-J. *L'Apolitisme des Idéologies Québécoises 1934–1936*. Quebec: Les Presses de l'Université Laval, 1974.
Bellamy, Richard. *Modern Italian Social Theory: Ideology and Politics from Pareto to the Present*. Stanford: Stanford University Press, 1987.
Bennett, Jeffrey S. "The Blue Army and the Red Scare: Politics, Religion, and Cold War Paranoia". *Politics, Religion & Ideology*, vol. 16, no. 2–3 (2015): 263–81.
Berger, Carl. *The Sense of Power*. Toronto: University of Toronto Press, 1970.
Berry, Damon T. *Blood and Faith: Christianity in American White Nationalism*. New York: Syracuse University Press, 2017.
Betcherman, Lita-Rose. *The Swastika and the Maple Leaf: Fascist movements in Canada in the Thirties*. Toronto: Fitzhenry & Whiteside, 1978.
Bevir, Mark. *The Logic of the History of Ideas*. Cambridge: Cambridge University Press, 1999.
Blanding, Lee. *"Re-branding Canada: The Origins of Canadian Multiculturalism Policy, 1945–1974"*, unpublished PhD dissertation. University of Victoria, 2013.
Blobaum, Robert. *Antisemitism and Its Opponents in Modern Poland*. New York: Cornell University Press, 2005.
Blondel, Jean, ed. *Comparative Government: A Reader*. London, UK: Macmillan Education, 1969.
Bock, Michel. *A Nation Beyond Borders: Lionel Groulx on French-Canadian Minorities*. Ottawa: University of Ottawa Press, 2014.
Bogle, Lori L. *The Pentagon's Battle for the American Mind: The Early Cold War*. College Station, TX: Texas A&M University Press, 2004.
Bohachevsky-Chomiak, Martha. *Ukrainian Bishop, American Church: Constantine Bohachevsky and the Ukrainian Catholic Church*. Washington: Catholic University of America Press, 2018.
Boily, Frédéric. *La pensée nationaliste de Lionel Groulx*. Sillery, QC: Septentrion, 2003.
Boobbyer, Philip. *The Spiritual Vision of Frank Buchman*. Pennsylvania: The Pennsylvania State University Press, 2013.
Bourassa, Henri. *Les Canadiens-Français et l'Empire Britannique*. Quebec: S.A. Demers, 1903.
Bradbury, Bettina, Myers, Tamara, eds. *Negotiating Identities in 19th and 20th Century Montreal*. Vancouver: University of British Columbia, 2005.
Bradbury, Bettina. *Working Families*. Toronto: University of Toronto Press, 2007.
Brady, Bernard V. *Essential Catholic Social Thought*, 2nd ed. New York: Orbis Books, 2017.
Breton, Raymond. "Institutional Completeness of Ethnic Communities and the Personal Relations of Immigrants". *American Journal of Sociology*, vol. 70, no. 2 (September 1964): 193–205.
Brodkin, Karen. *How Jews Became White Folks & What That Says About Race in America*. London: Rutgers University Press, 1998.
Brym, Robert J., Shaffir, William, Weinfeld, Morton. *The Jews in Canada*. Oxford: Oxford University Press, 1993.

162 References

Buckner, Phillip, Francis, R. Douglas eds. *Canada and the British World: Culture, Migration, and Identity*. Vancouver: UBC Press, 2006.

Burnet, Jean R., Palmer, Howard. *Coming Canadians: A History of Canada's Peoples*. Ottawa: Suppy and Services, 1988.

Caccia, Ivana. *Managing the Canadian Mosaic in Wartime*. Montreal: McGill-Queen's University Press, 2010.

Cameron, Elspeth, ed. *Multiculturalism and Immigration in Canada: An Introductory Reader*. Toronto: Canadian Scholars' Press, 2004.

Canada. Privy Council Office. *Report of the Royal Commission on Bilingualism and Biculturalism, Book I: General Introduction: The Official Languages*. Ottawa: Queen's Printer, 1967.

Canada. Privy Council Office. *Report of the Royal Commission on Bilingualism and Biculturalism, Book IV: The Cultural Contribution of Other Ethnic Groups*. Ottawa: Queens Printer, 1969.

Cau, Maurizio. "An inconvenient legacy: corporatism and Catholic culture from Fascism to the Republic". *Dossie. Corporatismos: experiencias históricas e suas representaçoes ao longo do século XX*, vol. 25 no. 1 (Jan./Abr. 2019): 219–38.

Cawley, Art. "The Canadian Catholic English-Language Press and the Spanish Civil War". *CCHA Study Sessions*, vol. 49 (1982): 25–51.

Cerasi, Laura. "From corporatism to the 'foundation of labour': notes on political cultures across Fascist and Republican Italy". *Dossie. Corporatismos: experiencias históricas e suas representaçoes ao longo do século XX*, vol. 25, no. 1 (Jan./Abr., 2019): 239–55.

Chan, Kwok B. *Smoke and Fire: The Chinese in Montreal*. Hong Kong: Chinese University Press, 1991

Chappel, James. *Catholic Modern: The Challenge of Totalitarianism and the Remaking of the Catholic Church*. Cambridge: Harvard University Press, 2018.

Christie, Nancy. *Engendering the State: Family, Work, and Welfare in Canada*. Toronto: University of Toronto Press, 2000.

Clark, Anna. *The Struggle for the Breeches: Gender and the Making of the British Working Class*. Berkeley: University of California Press, 1995.

Cooper, John Irwin. "The Origins and Early History of the Montreal City and District Savings Back 1846–1871". CCHA *Report*, vol. 13, no. 460 (1945): 15–25.

Costa Pinto, Antonio. *Corporatism and Fascism: The Corporatist Wave in Europe*. London: Routledge, 2017.

Coupland, Philip M. "Western Union, 'Spiritual Union', and European Integration, 1948–1951". *Journal of British Studies*, vol. 43, no. 3 (July 2004): 366–94.

Croteau, Jean-Philippe. "Les commissions scolaires et les immigrants à Toronto et à Montréal (1900–1945): quatre modèles d'intégration en milieu urbain", *Francophonies d'Amérique*, no. 31 (Spring 2011): 49–85.

Crowe, Frederick E. *Lonergan*. Collegeville, MN: Liturgical Press, 1992.

Daly, George. *Catholic Problems in Western Canada*. Toronto: Macmillan, 1921.

Dard, Olivier, ed. *Le Corporatisme dans l'aire francophone au XXe siècle*. Bern: Peter Lang AG, 2011.

Davies, Alan, ed. *Antisemitism in Canada: History and Interpretation*. Waterloo: Wilfrid Laurier University Press, 1992.

Day, Dorothy. *All the Way to Heaven: The Selected Letters of Dorothy Day*. New York: Image Books, 2012.

Day, Richard. *Multiculturalism and the History of Canadian Diversity*. Toronto: University of Toronto, 2000.

Delâge, Denys. "Quebec and Aboriginal Peoples", in *Vive Quebec! New Thinking and New Approaches to the Quebec Nation*. Edited by M. Venne. Toronto: James Lorimer & Co., 2001.

Dickie, D. J. *The Book of New Canadians*. Toronto: J. M. Dent, 1930.

Dirks, Patricia. *Failure of l'Action Libérale Nationale*. Montreal: McGill-Queen's University Press, 1991.

Dorrien, Gary. *Social Ethics in the Making: Interpreting an American Tradition*. Chichester, UK: Wiley-Blackwell, 2011.

Dreisziger, Nador F. "The Rise of a Bureaucracy for Multiculturalism: The Origins of the Nationalities Branch, 1939–1941", in *On Guard for Thee: War, Ethnicity, and the Canadian State, 1939–1945*. Edited by Norman Hillmer, Bohdan S Kordan, Lubomyr Luciuk. Ottawa: Ministry of Supply and Services, 1988.

Dunleavy, Patrick. *Theories of the State: The Politics of Liberal Democracy*. Basingstoke: Macmillan Education, 1987.

Eisen, Max. "Christian Missions to the Jews in North America and Great Britain". *Jewish Social Studies*, vol. 10, no. 1 (January 1948): 31–66.

Elliott, Jean Leonard. *Two Nations, Many Cultures: Ethnic Groups in Canada*. Scarborough: Prentice-Hall of Canada, 1983.

Endicott, Stephen. *Raising the Workers' Flag: The Workers' Unity League of Canada, 1930–1936*. Toronto: University of Toronto Press, 2012.

Este, David, Sato, Christa, McKenna, Darcy. "The Coloured Women's Club of Montreal, 1902–1940. African-Canadian Women Confronting Anti-Black Racism". *Canadian Social Work Review*, vol. 34, no. 1 (August 29, 2017): 81–99.

Evans, David. *Mussolini's Italy*. Pennsylvania: McGraw-Hill Companies, 2005.

Fay, Terence J. *A History of Canadian Catholics*. Montreal: McGill-Queen's University Press, 2002.

Feldman, Matthew, Turda, Marius, eds. *Clerical Fascism in Interwar Europe*. London: Routledge, 2008.

Filipeko, Anton S. ed. *A Social and Solidarity Economy: The Ukrainian Choice*. Cambridge: Cambridge Scholars Publishing, 2017.

Finkel, Alvin. *The Social Credit Phenomenon in Alberta*. Toronto: University of Toronto Press, 1989.

Fitzpatrick, Alfred. *Handbook for New Canadians*. Toronto: Ryerson Press, 1919.

Fogg-Davis, Hawley. "The Racial Retreat of Contemporary Political Theory". *Perspectives on Politics*, vol. 1 (2003): 555–64.

Fortin, Nicole M., Huberman, Michael. "Occupational Gender Segregation and Women's Wages in Canada: An Historical Perspective". *Canadian Public Policy*, Scientific Series, vol. 28, no. s1 (2002): 11–39.

Foucault, Michel. *Power/Knowledge: Selected Interviews and Other Writings, 1972–1977*. New York: Pantheon Books, 1980.

Francis, R. D., Jones, Richard, Smith, Donald B. *Canadian History since Confederation: Destinies*. Scarborough: Nelson Education Limited, October 11, 2011.

Francis, R. D., Jones, Richard, Smith, Donald B. *Journeys: A History of Canada*. Toronto: Nelson Education, 2009.

Friedländer, Saul. *Nazi Germany and the Jews: The Years of Persecution*. London: Weidenfeld & Nicolson, 1997.

Frye Jacobson, Matthew. *Whiteness of a Different Color*. Cambridge: Harvard University Press, 1999.

Fudge, Judy, Tucker, Eric. *Labour Before the Law: the Regulation of Workers' Collective Action in Canada, 1900–1948*. Toronto: Oxford University Press, 2001.
Gagnon, Robert. *Histoire de la Commission des écoles catholiques de Montréal*. Montreal: Boréal, 1996.
Gélinas, Xavier. *La droite intellectuelle québécoise et la révolution tranquille (1956–1966)*. Dissertation. York University, 2001.
Gerald L. Gold, ed. *Minorities and Mother Country Imaginary*. St. John's: ISER, Memorial University of Newfoundland, 1984.
Gibbon, John Murray. *Canadian Mosaic. The Making of a Northern Nation*. London: J. M. Dent & Sons Ltd., 1939.
Gilman, Richard M. *Behind 'World Revolution': The Strange Career of Nesta H. Webster*. London: Insight Books, 1982.
Givens, Terri E. *Voting Radical Right in Western Europe*. Cambridge: Cambridge University Press, 2005.
Godden, Gertrude M. *Mussolini. The Birth of the New Democracy*. New York: PJ Kennedy, 1923.
Goeschel, Christian. "Staging Friendship: Mussolini and Hitler in Germany in 1937". *The Historical Journal*, vol. 60, no. 1 (March 2017): 149–72.
Gorski, Philip. *American Covenant: A History of Civil Religion from the Puritans to the Present*. Princeton: Princeton University Press, 2017.
Grace, Robert J. *The Irish in Quebec. An Introduction to the Historiography*. Toronto: University of Toronto, 1993.
Gualtieri, Sarah. "Becoming 'White': Race, Religion and the Foundations of Syrian/Lebanese Ethnicity in the United States". *Journal of American Ethnic History*, vol. 20, no. 4 (summer 2001): 29–58.
Guglielmo, Jennifer, Salerno, Salvatore, eds., *Are Italians White? How Race Is Made in America*. New York: Routledge, 2012.
Guo, Shibao, Wong, Lloyd, eds. *Revisiting Multiculturalism in Canada: Theories, Policies and Debates*. Rotterdam: Sense Publishers, 2015.
Hage, Ghassan. *White Nation: Fantasies of White Supremacy in a Multicultural Society*. New York: Routledge, 2000.
Haider, Carmen. "The Italian Corporate State". *Political Science Quarterly*, vol. 46, no. 2 (June 1931): 228–47.
Hall, Catherine. *Civilizing Subjects: Metropole and Colony in the English Imagination, 1830–1867*. Chicago: University of Chicago Press, 2002.
Hamelin, Jean, Gagnon, Nicole. *Histoire du catholicisme québécois*, Tome 1, 1898–1940. Montreal: Boréal Express, 1984.
Hanebrink, Paul. *A Specter Haunting Europe: The Myth of Judeo-Bolshevism*. Cambridge: Harvard University Press, 2018.
Haque, Eve. *Multiculturalism within a Bilingual Framework: Language, Race, and Belonging in Canada*. Toronto: University of Toronto, 2012.
Harmon, Katharine E. *There Were Also Many Women There: Lay Women in the Liturgical Movement in the United States: 1926–59*. Minnesota: A Pueblo Book, 2013.
Harrigan, Camille. "Storied Stones: St. Patrick's Basilica. History, Identity, and Memory in Irish Montréal, 1847–2017", Master's thesis. Concordia University, 2018.
Harvard Ukrainian Studies. "The Political and Social Ideas of Vjačeslav Lypyns'kyj," Special Issue, Guest Editor Jaroslaw Pelenski, vol. 9, no. 3–4 (1985).

Hayward, Victoria. *Romantic Canada*. London: Macmillan & Company, 1922.
Herf, Jeffrey. *The Jewish Enemy*. Harvard: Harvard University Press, 2006.
Herzstein, Robert Edwin. *Western Civilization: From the Seventeenth Century to the Present*. Boston: Houghton Mifflin, 1975.
Hill Fletcher, Jeannine. *The Sin of White Supremacism: Christianity, Racism, & Religious Diversity in America*. London: Orbis, 2017.
Hinther, Rhonda, Mochoruk, Jim, eds. *Re-Imagining Ukrainian Canadians: History, Politics, and Identity*. Toronto: University of Toronto Press, 2010.
Holdcroft, David. *Saussure: Signs, System, and Arbitrariness*. Cambridge: Cambridge University Press, 1991.
Hollinger, David A. "Amalgamation and Hypodescent: The Question of Ethnoracial Mixture in the History of the United States". *The American Historical Review*, vol. 108, no. 5 (December 2003): 1363–1390.
Holubnychy, Vsevolod. *Soviet Regional Economics: Selected Works of Vsevolod Holubnychy*. Edmonton: Canadian Institute of Ukrainian Studies, University of Alberta, 1982.
Horn, Michiel. *The League for Social Reconstruction: Intellectual Origins of the Democratic Left in Canada 1930–1942*. Toronto: University of Toronto Press, 1980.
Howard, Victor. *MacKenzie-Papineau Battalion: The Canadian Contingent in the Spanish Civil War*. Carleton: Carleton University Press, 1986.
Hugh Donald Forbes, *Multiculturalism in Canada: Constructing a Model Multiculture with Mulicultural Values*. Toronto: Palgrave Macmillan, 2019.
Iacovetta, Franca. *Gatekeepers: Reshaping Immigrant Lives in Cold War Canada*. Toronto: Between the Lines, 2006.
Igartua, José. *The Strange Demise of British Canada: The Liberals and Canadian Nationalism, 1964–1968*. Montreal: McGill-Queen's University Press, 2010.
Ignatiev, Noel. *How the Irish Became White*. London and New York: Routledge Classics, 1995.
Isaiv, Ivan [John Esaiw], ed. *Za Ukrainu: Podorozh Velmozhnoho Pana Hetmanycha Danyla Skoropadskoho do Zluchenykh Derzhav Ameryky I Kanady, osin 1937–vesna 1938*. Chicago: United Hetman Organizations, 1938.
Jardina, Ashley. *White Identity Politics*. Cambridge: Cambridge University Press, 2019.
Joshee, Reva. "An Historical Approach to Understanding Canadian Multicultural Policy", in *Multicultural Education in a Changing Glocal Economy: Canada and the Netherlands*. Edited by T. Wotherspoon and P. Jungbluth. New York: Waxmann Munster, 1995.
Kallen, Evelyn. *Ethnicity and Human Rights in Canada*. Oxford: Oxford University Press, 2010.
Kaplan, Jeffrey, Weinberg, Leonard. *The Emergence of a Euro-American Radical Right*. New Brunswick, NJ: Rutgers University Press, 1998.
Katzenstein, Peter J. *Corporatism and Change: Austria, Switzerland, and the Politics of Industry*. Ithaca: Cornell University Press, 1984.
Kehoe, S. Karly, Alisic, Eva, Heilinger, Jan-Christoph, eds., *Responsibility for Refugee and Migrant Integration*. Berlin: De Gruyter, 2019.
Kelley, Ninette, Trebikcock, M. J., eds. *The Making of the Mosaic: A History of Canadian Immigration Policy*. Toronto: University of Toronto Press, 2010.
Kertzer, David I. *The Pope and Mussolini: The Secret History of Pius XI and the Rise of Fascism in Europe*. Oxford: Oxford University Press, 2014.

Kirkconnell, Watson. *Canadians All*. Ottawa: Director of Public Information, 1941.
Klein, Charlotte. "From Conversion to Dialogue. The Sisters of Sion and the Jews: a Paradigm of Catholic-Jewish Relations?" *Journal of Ecumenical Studies*, vol. 18, no. 3 (1981): 388–400.
Kopf, Josephine Z. "Meyer Wolfsheim and Robert Cohn: A Study of Jewish Type and Stereotype". *Tradition: A Journal of Orthodox Jewish Thought*, vol. 10, no. 3 (spring 1969): 93–104.
Kordan, Bohdan S. *Canada and the Ukrainian Question, 1939–1945: a study in statecraft*. Montreal: McGill-Queen's University Press, 2001.
Kröller, Eva-Marie. "*Le Mouton de Troie*: Changes in Quebec Cultural Symbolism", *American Review of Canadian Studies*, vol. 27, no. 4 (1997): 523–44.
Kuukkanen, Jouni-Matti. "Making Sense of Conceptual Change", *History and Theory*, vol. 47, no. 3 (October 2008): 351–72.
Kymlicka, Will. *Multicultural Citizenship: A Liberal Theory of Minority Rights*. Oxford: Oxford Clarendon Press, 1995.
L. Klein, Ruth, ed. *Nazi Germany, Canadian Responses: Confronting Antisemitism in the Shadow of War*. Montreal: McGill-Queen's University Press, 2012.
Lacoursière, Jacques. *Histoire populaire du Québec: 1896–1960*. Montreal: Septentrion, 1997.
Laforest, Guy. *Trudeau and the End of a Canadian Dream*. Montreal: McGill, Queen's University Press, 1995.
Lalande, Julia. "The Roots of Multiculturalism – Ukrainian-Canadian Involvement in the Multiculturalism Discussion of the 1960s as an Example of the Position of the 'Third Force'". *Canadian Ethnic Studies/Études ethniques au Canada*, vol. XXXVIII, no. 1 (2006): 47–64.
Lanouette, Mélanie. "Pense l'Éducation, Dire Sa Culture. Les écoles Catholiques anglaises au Québec, 1928–1964". Dissertation. Université Laval, 2004.
Lapointe-Gagnon, Valérie. "Penser et 'Panser' les Plaies du Canada: Le Moment Laurendeau-Dunton, 1963–1971". Dissertation. Université Laval, 2013.
Lavoie, André, ed. *Répertoire des parlementaires québécois, 1867–1978*. Quebec: Bibliothèque de la Législature, 1980.
Lazare, Bernard. *Antisemitism: Its History and Causes*. New York: Cosimo Classics, 2006.
Lee, Marta F. "Nesta Webster: The Voice of Conspiracy", *Journal of Women's History*, vol. 17, no. 3 (Fall, 2005): 81–104.
Leo XIII. *Rerum Novarum; On the Rights and Duties of Capital and Labour*. May 15, 1891.
Lévesque, Andrée. *Virage à gauche interdit. Les Communistes, les socialistes et leurs ennemis au Québec 1929–1939*. Montreal: Boréal Express, 1984.
Levy, Richard S. *Antisemitism: A Historical Encyclopedia of Prejudice and Persecution*, vol. 1. Santa Barbara, CA: ABC-Clio, 2005.
Linehan, Thomas. *British Fascism, 1918–39: Parties, Ideology and Culture*. New York: Manchester University Press, 2000.
Linteau, Paul-André, Durocher, René, Robert, Jean-Claude, Ricard, François, eds. *Quebec Since 1930*. Toronto: James Lorimer&Company, 1991.
Linteau, Paul-André, Durocher, René, Robert, Jean-Claude. *Histoire du Québec contemporain: de la Confédération à la crise, 1867–1929*. Montreal: Boréal Express, 1979.
Lipton, Sara. *Dark Mirror: The Medieval Origins of Anti-Jewish Iconography*. New York: Metropolitan, 2014.

Lloyd, Vincent W., Prevot, Andrew. *Anti-Blackness and Christian Ethics*. New York: Orbis Books, 2017.

Lupul, Manoly R. *A Heritage in Transition: Essays in the History of Ukrainians in Canada*. Toronto: McClelland and Stewart, 1982.

Maccody, Hyam. *Antisemitism and Modernity: Innovation and Continuity*. London: Routledge, 2006.

Mackey, Eva. *The House of Difference. Cultural Politics and National Identity in Canada*. London: Routledge, 1999.

Maclure, Jocelyn. *Quebec Identity: The Challenge of Pluralism*. London: McGill-Queen's University Press, 2003.

Mann, Michael. *The Dark Side of Democracy: Explaining Ethnic Cleansing*. Cambridge: Cambridge University Press, 2005.

Mannion, Patrick. "The 'Irish Question' in St. John's, Newfoundland, and Halifax, Nova Scotia, 1919–1923". *Acadiensis*, vol. 44, no. 2 (Summer/Autumn 2015): 27–49.

Marcel, Marcel, Pâquet, Martin. *Speaking Up: A History of Language and Politics in Canada and Quebec*. Toronto: Between the Lines, 2012.

Mardiros, Anthony. *William Irvine: The Life of a Prairie Radical*. Toronto: James Lorimer Ltd., 1979.

Margalit, Yotam. "Economic Insecurity and the Causes of Populism, Reconsidered", *The Journal of Economic Perspectives*, vol. 33, no. 4 (2019): 152–70.

Maritain, Jacques. *A Christian Looks at the Jewish Question*. New York: Longmans, Green, 1939.

Maritain, Jacques. *Ransoming the Time*. New York: Charles Scribner's Sons, 1941.

Martel, Marcel. "Managing Ethnic Pluralism: The Canadian Experience, 1860–1971", in *Meeting Global and Domestic Challenges: Canadian Federalism in Perspective*. Edited by T. Greven and H. Ickstadt. Berlin: John F. Kennedy-Institut fur Nordamerikastudien/Freie Universitat, 2004.

Martel, Marcel. *Deuil d'un Pays Imaginé: Rêves, Luttes et Déroute du Canada Français*. Ottawa: University of Ottawa Press, 1997.

Martin, Robin. *Shades of Right: nativist and fascist politics in Canada, 1920–1940*. Toronto: University of Toronto Press, 1992.

Martynowych, Orest T. *Ukrainians in Canada: The Formative Period, 1891–1924*. Edmonton: Canadian Institute of Ukrainian Studies Press, 1991.

Martynowych, Orest T. *Ukrainians in Canada: The Interwar War*. Canadian Institute of Ukrainian Studies Press, 2016.

Maurutto, Paula. "Governing Charities: Church and State in Toronto's Catholic Archdiocese, 1850–1950", dissertation. York University, 1998.

Maurutto, Paula. "Private Policing and Surveillance of Catholics: Anti-communism in the Roman Catholic Archdiocese of Toronto, 1920–1960", *Labour/Le Travail*, vol. 40 (Fall 1997): 113–36.

Mayeur, Jean-Marie, Pietri, Luce, Vauchez, André. *Guerres mondiales et totalitarismes (1914–1958): Histoire du christianisme*. Paris: Desclée-Fayard, 1990.

Mazower, Mark. *Hitler's Empire: Nazi Rule in Occupied Europe*. New York: The Penguin Press, 2008.

McGowan, Mark, Clarke, Brian P. *Catholics at the Gathering Place*. Toronto: The Canadian Catholic Historical Association, 1993.

McKay, Ian. "The Liberal Framework", in *Liberalism and Hegemony. Debating the Canadian Liberal Revolution*. Edited by Jean-François Constant, Michel Ducharme, eds. Toronto: University of Toronto Press, 2009.

McRoberts, Kenneth. *Misconceiving Canada: The Struggle for National Unity.* Toronto: Oxford University Press, 1997.

Miedema, Gary Richard. *For Canada's Sake: Public Religion, Centennial Celebrations, and the Re-making of Canada in the 1960s.* Montreal: McGill-Queen's University Press, 2005.

Miedema, Gary. "For Canada's Sake: The Centennial Celebrations of 1967, State Legitimation and the Restructuring of Canadian Public Life". *Journal of Canadian Studies*, vol. 34 (spring 1999): 139–60.

Mikhman, Dan. *Belgium and the Holocaust: Jews, Belgians, Germans.* New York: Berghahn Books, 1998.

Mills, Allen George. *Fool for Christ: The Political Thought of J.S. Woodsworth.* Toronto: University of Toronto Press, 1991.

Mills, Sean. "When Democratic Socialists Discovered Democracy: The League for Social Reconstruction Confronts the Quebec Problem", *The Canadian Historical Review*, vol. 86, no. 1 (March 2005): 53–82.

Mochoruk, Jim, Hinther, Rhonda L. eds. *Re-Imagining Ukrainian Canadians: History, Politics, and Identity.* Toronto: University of Toronto Press, 2011.

Moir, John S. *Christianity in Canada: Historical Essays.* Yorkton: Redeemer's Voice Press, 2002.

Molas, Bàrbara. "Transnational Francoism: The British and the Canadian Friends of National Spain", *Contemporary British History*, vol. 35, no. 2 (2021): 165–86.

Mondon, Aurelien, Winter, Aaron. *Reactionary Democracy: How Racism and the Populist Far Right Became Mainstream.* London: Verso, 2020.

Morelock, Jeremiah, ed. *Critical Theory and Authoritarian Populism.* London: University of Westminster Press, 2018.

Morgan, Philip. *Fascism in Europe, 1919–1945.* London: Routledge, 2003.

Morgan, Philip. *The Fall of Mussolini: Italy, the Italians, and the Second World War.* Oxford: Oxford University Press, 2007.

Motyl, Alexander J. "Viacheslav Lypyns'kyi and the Ideology and Politics of Ukrainian Monarchism". *Canadian Slavonic Papers*, vol. 27, no. 1 (March 1985): 31–48.

Mudde, Cas. *Populist Radical Right Parties in Europe.* Cambridge: Cambridge University Press, 2007.

Muller, Ja-Wener. *What Is Populism?* Philadelphia: University of Pennsylvania Press, 2016.

Murphy, Terrence, Perin, Roberto, eds. *A Concise History of Christianity in Canada.* Oxford: Oxford University Press, 1996.

Murphy, Terrence, Stortz, Gerald, eds. *Creed and Culture. The Place of English-speaking Catholics in Canadian Society 1750–1930.* Montreal: McGill-Queen's University Press, 1993.

Musolff, Andreas. *Metaphor, Nation and the Holocaust. The Concept of the Body Politics.* New York: Routledge, 2010.

Nadeau, Jean-François. *The Canadian Führer: The Life of Adrien Arcand.* Toronto: James Lorimer Limited, 2011.

Nesbitt, Bruce. *Conversations with Trotsky: Earle Birney and the Radical 1930s.* Ottawa: University of Ottawa Press, 2017.

Neville, Peter. *Mussolini.* London and New York: Routledge, 2004.

Newman, Peter C. *Renegade in Power: The Diefenbaker Years.* Toronto: McClelland and Stewart, 1963.

Niremberg, David. *Anti-Judaism: The Western Tradition*. New York: W.W. Norton & Company, 2013.

Noll, John Francis. *Civilization's Builder and Protector*. Huntington: Our Sunday Visitor Press, 1940.

Noll, John Francis. *The Decline of Nations: Its Causes and Cure*. Huntington: Our Sunday Visitor Press, 1940.

O'Brien, Kathleen, Gauthier, Sylvie. "Montréal: Re-Imagining the Traces". *The Canadian Journal of Irish Studies*, vol. 26, no. 1 (Spring 2000): 25–34.

O'Neill, Daniel I. "*Symposium:* The Logic of the History of Ideas". *The Journal of the History of Ideas*, vol. 73, no. 4 (October 2012): 583–92.

Odale, Walter B. *Americanism or Communism?* Portland: Priv. Printed, 1935.

Pal, Leslie A. *Interests of State: the Policies of Language, Multiculturalism, and Feminism in Canada*. Montreal: McGill-Queen's University Press, 1993.

Palonen, Kari. "The Politics of Conceptual History", *Contributions to the History of Concepts*, vol. 1, no. 1 (March 2005): 37–50.

Pâquet, Martin. *Tracer les marges de la cité. Étranger, immigrant et État au Québec 1627–1981*. Montreal: Boréal, 2005.

Payne, Stanley G. *A History of Fascism, 1914–1945*. Madison, WI: The University of Wisconsin Press, 1996.

Peacocke, Christopher. *A Study of Concepts*. Cambridge: MIT Press, 1992.

Pearson, Lester B. *Memoirs*, vol. III. Toronto: University of Toronto Press, 1975.

Pelletier, Lucien. "Les Jésuites de Sudbury ves 1960: une mutation difficile". *Revue du Nouvel-Ontario*, no. 37 (2012): 9–178.

Penner, Norman. *Canadian Communism: the Stain Years and Beyond*. Toronto: Methuen, 1988.

Perin, Roberto. "Saint-Boniface au coeur d'un catholicisme continental et pluraliste". *SCHEC, Études d'histoire religieuse*, vol. 85, nos. 1–2 (2019): 23–38.

Perin, Roberto. "Un adversaire du bilinguisme officiel à la commission Laurendeau-Dunton". *Le projet du bilinguisme canadien: histoire, utopie et réalisation*, vol. 26, no. 2 (Winter 2018): 114–27.

Perin, Roberto. *The Immigrant's Church: The Third Force in Canadian Catholicism, 1880–1920*. Toronto: Canadian Historical Association, 1998.

Perry, Samuel L., Whitehead, Andrew. "Christian Nationalism and White Racial Boundaries: Examining White's Opposition to Interracial Marriage". *Ethnic and Racial Studies*, vol. 38, no. 10 (August 9, 2015): 1671–89.

Perry, Samuel L., Whitehead, Andrew, Baker, Joseph O. "Make America Christian Again: Christian Nationalism and Voting for Donald Trump in the 2016 Presidential Election". *Sociology of Religion*; Washington, vol. 79, no. 2 (summer 2018): 147–71.

Pitsula, James M. *Keeping Canada British: The Ku Klux Klan in 1920s Saskatchewan*. Vancouver: UBC Press, 2013.

Pons, Silvio, Service, Roberto. *A Dictionary of 20th-Century Communism*. Princeton: Princeton Reference, 2012.

Prestiss, Craig R. *Debating God's Economy: Social Justice in America on the Even of Vatican II*. Pennsylvania: Pennsylvania University Press, 2008.

Principe, Angelo. *The Darkest Side of the Fascist Years. The Italian-Canadian Press: 1920–1942*. Toronto: Guernica, 1999.

Prymak, Thomas M. *Gathering a Heritage: Ukrainian, Slavonic, and Ethnic Canada and the USA*. Toronto: University of Toronto Press, 2015.

Prymak, Thomas M. *The Maple Leaf and Trident: The Ukrainian Canadians During the Second World War.* Toronto: Multicultural History Society of Ontario, 1988.
Purewal, Shinder. "The Politics of Multiculturalism in Canada, 1963–1971". Master's thesis. Simon Fraser University, August 1992.
Resnick, Philip. "Towards a Multinational Federalism," in *Federalism and Nationalism*. Edited by Murray Forsyth. Leicester: Leicester University Press, 1989.
Rich, Norman. *Hitler's War Aims: Ideology, the Nazi State, and the Course of Expansion.* New York: Norton & Company, 1992.
Roberts, Nancy L. *Dorothy Day and the Catholic Worker.* New York: State University of New York, 1984.
Robertson, E. M. *Hitler's Pre-War Policy and Military Plans 1933–1939.* New York: Citadel Press, 1967.
Robin, Martin. *Shades of Right: Nativist and Fascist Politics in Canada, 1920–1940.* Toronto: University of Toronto Press, 1992.
Roby, Yves. *Les Franco-Américains de la Nouvelle-Anglaterre: reves et réalités.* Quebec: Septentrion, 2000.
Roediger, David R. *The Wages of Whiteness: Race and the Making of the American Working Class.* London: Verso, 1999.
Roediger, David. *Working Toward Whiteness: How America's Immigrants Became White.* New York: Basic Books, 2006.
Rossolinski-Liebe, Grzegorz. "Celebration of fascism and war crimes in Edmonton. The political myth and the cult of Stepan Bandera in multicultural Canada". *Pamięć i Sprawiedliwość*, vol. 20, no. 2 (2012): 453–78.
Rudling, Per A. "Multiculturalism, memory, and ritualization: Ukrainian nationalist monuments in Edmonton, Alberta". *The Journal of Nationalism and Ethnicity*, vol. 39, no. 5 (2011): 733–68.
Rudnytsky, Ivan L. *Essays in Modern Ukrainian History.* Edmonton: Canadian Institute of Ukrainian Studies Press, 1987.
Rudnytsky, Peter L. ed. *Essays in Modern Ukrainian History.* Edmonton: Canadian Institute of Ukrainian Studies, 1987.
Rutherdale, Myra, Miller, Jim. "'It's Our Country': First Nations' Participation in the Indian Pavilion at Expo 67". *Journal of the Canadian Historical Association/ Revue de la Société historique du Canada*, vol. 17, no. 2 (2006): 3–173.
Rydgren, Jens, ed. *The Oxford Handbook of the Radical Right.* Oxford: Oxford University Press, 2018.
Sack, Daniel. *Moral Re-Armament: The Reinventions of an American Religious Movement.* London: Palgrave Macmillan, 2009.
Salvatore, Filippo. *Fascism and the Italians of Montreal: An Oral History, 1922–1945.* Toronto: Guernica, 1998.
Salvemini, Gaetano. *Under the Axe of Fascism: The definitive study of the creation of the Italian Fascist State.* New York: Citadel Press, 1971 (originally published in 1936).
Sanctuary, Eugene. *Are These Things So?* New York: E.N., 1934.
Scott, Joan. *Gender and the Politics of History.* Columbia: Columbia University Press, 2018.
Seldes, George. *The Catholic Crisis.* New York: Julian Messner, 1945.
Seljak, David. "Protecting religious freedom in multicultural Canada", *Diversity Magazine*, vol. 9, no. 3 (2012): 40–43.

Seymour Wilson, Vince. "The Tapestry Vision of Canadian Multiculturalism", *Canadian Journal of Political Science*, vol. 26, no. 4 (1993): 645–69.

Shore, Marlene. *The Science of Social Redemption: McGill, the Chicago School, and the Origins of Social Research in Canada*. Toronto: University of Toronto Press, 1987.

Siegel, Arthur. *Politics and the Media in Canada*. Toronto: McGraw-Hill Ryerson, 1983.

Smith, Gerald L. K. *Is Communism Jewish?* St. Louis: Christian Nationalist Crusade, ca. 1950.

Smith, Gerald L. K. *My Fight for the Right! (A Life Story)*. St. Louis: Christian Nationalist Crusade, ca. 1950.

Smith, Miriam, ed. *Group Politics and Social Movements in Canada*. Toronto: University of Toronto Press, 2014.

Spektorowski, Alberto. "The French New Right: multiculturalism of the right and the recognition/exclusionism syndrome", *Journal of Global Ethics*, vol. 8, no. 1 (2012): 41–61.

St-Amant, Jean-Claude. "L'École Sociale Populaire et Le Syndicalisme Catholique 1911–1949". Master's thesis. L'École des Gradues de l'Université Laval, Décembre 1976.

St-Amant, Jean-Claude. "La propagande de l'École sociale populaire en faveur du syndicalisme catholique 1911–1949". *Revue d'histoire de l'Amérique française*, vol. 32, no. 2 (September 1978): 203–28.

Stanley, Timothy J. "White Supremacy, Chinese Schooling, and School Segregation in Victoria: The Case of the Chinese Students' Strike, 1922–23". *Historical Studies in Education*, vol. 2, no. 2 (Fall 1990): 287–305.

Sternhell, Zeev. *The Birth of Fascist Ideology*. Princeton: Princeton University Press, 1995.

Stingel, Janine. *Social Discredit: Anti-Semitism, Social Credit, and the Jewish Response*. Montreal: McGill-Queen's University Press, 2000.

Stoler, Ann. *Race and the Education of Desire: Foucault's History of Sexuality and the Colonial Order of Things*. Durham: Duke University Press, 1995.

Struk, Danylo H., ed. *Encyclopedia of Ukraine*, vol. III. Toronto: University of Toronto Press, 1993.

Sung Park, Andrew. *Racial Conflict and Healing: An Asian-American Theological Perspective*. New York: Orbis Books, 1996.

Swyripa, Frances. *Ukrainian Canadians: A Survey of their Portrayal in English-language Works*. Edmonton: The University of Alberta Press, 1978.

Taylor, Barbara. *Eve and the New Jerusalem: Socialism and Feminism in the Nineteenth Century*. Harvard: Harvard University Press, 1993.

Taylor, Charles. *Multiculturalism and the Politics of Recognition*. Princeton, NJ: Princeton University Press, 1992.

Théoret, Hughes. *The Blue Shirts: Adrien Arcand and Fascist Anti-Semitism in Canada*. Ottawa: University of Ottawa Press, 2017.

Thompson, Edward Palmer. *The Making of the English Working Class*. Harmondsworth: Penguin, 1980 [1963].

Thordarson, Bruce. *Lester Pearson: Diplomat and Politician*. Toronto: Oxford University Press, 1974.

Torrelli, Maurice. "Le nationalisme intégral, c'est selon Maurras, la monarchie". *L'Action nationale*, vol. 65, no. 1 (September 1975): 16–27.

Trépanier, Pierre. "Le maurrassisme au Canada français". *Les Cahiers des dix*, vol. 53 (1999): 167–233.
Trubowitz, Lara. *Civil Antisemitism, Modernism, and British Culture, 1902–1939*. New York: Palgrave Macmillan, 2012.
Tulchinsky, Gerald J. J. *Taking Root: The Origins of the Canadian Jewish Community*. Toronto: Lester Publishing, 1992.
Uran, Steven. *Afrikaners and National Socialism in South Africa: 1933–1945*, vol. 2. Madison, WI: University of Wisconsin-Madison, 1975.
Valerie Knowles, *Strangers at Our Gates: Canadian Immigration and Immigration Policy, 1540–2006*. Toronto: Dundurn Press, 2007.
Valverde, Mariana. *The Age of Light, Soap, and Water: Moral Reform in English Canada 1885–1925*. Toronto: University of Toronto Press, 2008.
Veryha, Wasyl. "The Ukrainian Canadian Committee: Its Origins and War Activity". Master's thesis. University of Ottawa, 1967.
Walker, James. *"Race", Rights and the Law in the Supreme Court of Canada*. Toronto: Osgoode Society for Canadian Legal History, 2006.
Walkowitz, Judith. *City of Dreadful Delight: Narratives of Sexual Danger in Late-Victorian London*. Chicago: The University of Chicago Press, 1992.
Wallot, Jean-Pierre, Lanthier, Pierre, Watelet, Hubert. *Constructions identitaires et pratiques sociales*. Ottawa: Presses de l'Université d'Ottawa, 2002.
Warren, Jean-Philippe. "Le corporatisme canadien-français comme 'système total'. Quatre concepts pour comprendre la popularité d'une doctrine". *Recherches sociographiques*, vol. 45, no. 2 (May–August 2004): 219–38.
Whitehead, Andrew L., Perry, Samuel L. *Taking America Back for God*. Oxford: Oxford University Press, 2020.
Whitehead, Andrew, Perry, Samuel L., Baker, Joseph O. "Make America Christian Again: Christian Nationalism and Voting for Donald Trump in the 2016 Presidential Election". *Sociology of Religion*; Washington, vol. 79, no. 2 (summer 2018): 147–71.
Winter, Elke. "Bridging Unequal Relations, Ethnic Diversity, and the Dream of Unified Nationhood: Multiculturalism in Canada". *Zeitschrift für Kanada-Studien*, vol. 1 (2007): 38–57.
Wodak, Ruth. *Politics of Fear: What Right-Wing Populist Discourses Mean*. New York: SAGE Publications, 2015.
Woodsworth, J. S. *Strangers within Our Gates*. Toronto: F.C. Stephenson, 1909.
Yuzyk, Paul. *The Ukrainians in Manitoba: a Social History*. Toronto: University of Toronto Press, 1954.
Yuzyk, Paul. *Ukrainian Canadians: Their Place and Role in Canadian Life*. Toronto: Ukrainian Canadian Business and Professional Federation, 1967.
Zhu, Lianbi. "National Holidays and Minority Festivals in Canadian Nation-building". Dissertation. University of Sheffield, January 2012.

Index

Note: Page numbers followed by "n" refer to notes

Aberg, Einar 104
Aberhart, William 21, 123n182
absolutism 6, 92
Adamson, G. 16n46
Allegiance Day 62–66
American Federation of Labour (AFL) 59, 60
Anderson, Kay 14n28, 119n103
Angers, François-Albert 97, 118n85
Anglophones 3, 34, 35, 96, 109, 132
Angus, Ian 13n6
antisemitism 2, 25, 43n86, 65, 69, 75n15, 93, 102, 106–108, 136, 144, 152, 153
Arcand, Adrien 2, 25, 26, 57, 69, 75n17, 93, 104, 106, 151, 152
Archambault, Joseph-Alfred 56
Archambault, Joseph P. 21, 32, 33, 47n153, 47n154, 47n158, 52, 55, 61, 64, 74n9, 76n28, 84n118, 90, 91
Archconfraternity 104, 122n158
Arès, Richard 93, 115n39
Aster, Howard 42n81

Backes, Uwe 16n42
Baigell, Matthew 122n150
Baker, Joseph O. 16n51
Balan, Jars 86n153
Bannerji, Himani 3, 13n15
Bar-On, Tamir 15n38, 16n42, 16n49
Bastien, Hermas 90, 114n25
Baum, Gregory 39n36, 44n117
Beaudin, Dominique 97, 98, 118n86
Beaulieu, Michel S. 120n107
Bégin, L. N. 56
Bélanger, André J. 113n2
Belcourt, Susan 146n31
Bellamy, Richard 38n18

Bennett, Jeffrey S. 123n167
Bennett, Richard Bedford 1
Berger, Carl 6, 15n35
Berry, Damon T. 15n38
Bevir, Mark 9, 10, 16n55
biculturalism and bilingualism (B&B commission) 131–135, 137–141, 147n53, 155; British- and French-Canadian claims 132; French-Canadian Catholicism 134; *The Montreal Star* 133; Preliminary Hearings 135; Royal Commission on 130
Blanding, Lee 15n29, 156n3
Blobaum, Robert 126n232
Blondel, Jean 42n74
Blue Army 105, 123n166, 123n167, 123n169
Bobinas, Jean 48n176, 98
Bock, Michel 114n12, 115n38
Bohachevsky-Chomiak, Martha 38n23
Boily, Frédéric 86n148
Bonin, René 97
Boobbyer, Philip 146n25, 146n26
Bossy, Walter J. 1, 2, 5, 6, 7, 9, 10, 11, 18–26, 18–36, 23, 36n2, 36n4, 37n6, 37n7, 37n13, 37n14, 38n24, 38n27, 39n37–n40, 40n43, 40n44, 40n50, 40n51, 40n57, 41n58, 41n60, 41n63, 41n64, 41n66, 41n68, 41n72, 42n76, 42n81, 42n84, 42n86, 43n94, 43n97, 43n99, 43n102, 43n103, 43n106, 44n110, 45n123, 45n131, 45n134, 45n135, 45n136, 46n137, 46n141, 46n142–n147, 47n148–n151, 47n150, 47n154, 47n155, 47n157, 47n159, 47n161, 47n162, 47n163, 48n164–n167,

Index

48n175, 48n176, 49n178, 49n180, 49n181, 49n186, 50n189, 50n190, 50n191, 51–58, 61–73, 74n1–n8, 75n11–n15, 75n17, 76n23, 76n27–n33, 77n34, 77n40, 77n41, 77n44, 77n45, 77n46, 78n50, 78n51, 78n59, 78n60, 78n61, 79n63, 79n64, 80n85, 81n88–n91, 81n93, 82n94, 82n96, 82n97, 83n108, 83n111–n114, 83n116, 84n117, 84n118, 84n119, 85n131, 86n144, 86n151, 86n153, 87n159, 87n161, 87n164, 87n165, 88n169–n172, 88n174, 88n176, 88n179, 88n182, 88n183, 89n184, 89n185, 89n186, 89n188–n191, 89n196, 90, 91, 93–105, 107, 108, 109, 111, 112, 113n1, 114n8, 115n34, 115n37, 115n41, 115n43, 115n45, 116n46–n52, 116n54, 116n55, 117n60, 117n62, 117n63, 117n65–n68, 117n70, 118n76, 118n85, 118n86, 119n94, 119n100, 119n102, 120n115, 121n132, 121n133, 121n136, 121n141, 122n163, 123n166, 123n169, 124n190, 124n194, 124n195, 124n197, 124n200–n203, 125n204, 125n206, 125n207, 125n208, 126n226, 126n229, 126n230, 126n233, 126n235, 127n236, 127n237, 127n240, 128–144, 144n2, 144n3, 145n7, 145n9, 145n11–n16, 145n19, 146n20, 146n30, 146n31, 147n45, 147n47, 147n49, 147n56, 147n57, 147n59, 148n60, 148n63, 148n67, 149n81, 149n84, 149n85, 150n117, 150n123, 150n124, 150n125, 151–156, 156n3, 156n4, 118n75
Bosyi, Volodymyr 42n82
Bouchard, Daniel 119n95
Boulanger, Trefflé 116n49
Bourassa, Henri 8, 109, 125n216
Breton, Raymond 157n9
Brodkin, Karen 15n39
Brotherhood of Ukrainian Classocrats-Monarchist Hetmanites (BUKMH) 19
Bryan, William X. 22, 30, 34, 45n130, 50n190, 51, 54, 61, 74n2, 74n5, 78n61
Brym, Robert J. 149n79
Buchman, Frank 130, 131, 146n30
Buckner, Phillip 15n32
Burnet, Jean R. 146n40

Canadian Mosaic 66, 82n105, 85n132, 110, 126n224, 126n225
Canadian multiculturalism: French-Canadian claims 3–4; history of 2–4; liberal framework 3; postwar debates 5
Canadian Officers Training Corps (COTS) 68, 72, 88n171, 89n186, 128
Caouette, Réal 124n196
Carlbom, A. 16n46
Caron, Maximilen 90, 91, 114n15, 114n18, 114n20, 114n21, 114n22, 114n23
Carpatho-Ukraine 69, 70
Catholic anarchism 28, 151
Catholic Church Extension Society (CCES) 56, 57
Catholic spirit 51, 154
Catholic Worker 25, 28, 31, 44n111
Cawley, Art 40n48
Cerasi, Laura 38n29
Chappel, James 87n163
Charbonneau, Joseph 101
Charpentier, Jean 135
Chevalier, Willie 135
The Christian Century 53, 54, 76n24, 76n25
Christian corporatism 20, 21
Christian framework 2, 9, 22, 57, 67, 140, 141
Christian left 26–27
Christian nationalism 7, 9, 16n51, 16n52, 56, 131, 134, 146n27, 141
Clark, Anna 44n109
Clarke, Brian P. 46n141
classocracy 19, 22, 23, 27, 28, 30, 31, 51, 62, 69, 74, 93, 94, 116n48
Classocracy League of Canada (CLC) 8, 29–31, 33, 45n130, 54, 61, 62, 90–94
Colgan, Harold V. 105
Communistic elements 59
Coonan, T. J. 33, 47n149, 47n157, 47n159, 47n160, 47n162, 48n164, 61
Cooperative Commonwealth Federation (CCF) 26, 27, 28, 43n106, 48n168, 108
corporatism 2, 5, 6, 8, 20, 21, 28, 31, 38n29, 59, 91–94, 115n42, 144, 154
cosmopolitanism 24, 25
Costa Pinto, António 15n30
Courteau, Guy 68, 99
Crowe, Frederick E. 40n52
cultural integration 12, 55, 56, 74, 105

Dagneau, Georges-Henri 97
Daly, George 77n47
Dann, T. 39n41
Datzkiw, Teodor 71, 88n179

Davies, Alan 124n187, 127n238
Day, Dorothy 3, 13n15, 28, 29, 31, 43n105, 44n112, 44n113, 44n116, 44n118
Day, Ralph C. 66
Debelt, Adalbert 48n176
de Hueck, Catherine 29, 46n141, 51
Delâge, Denys 13n10
Dickie, D. J. 49n186, 110, 126n221, 126n222
Dirks, Patricia 39n34
Doré, Victor 35, 46n144, 46n145, 46n146, 47n148, 77n44
Dorrien, Gary 44n111
Douglas, C. H. 21, 106
Dreisziger, Nador F. 14n29
Duhamel, Roger 97
Dunleavy, Patrick 38n19
Duplessis, Maurice 32, 33, 54, 58
Dupuis, Armand 84n117, 86n144
Durand, Louis 67, 86n146
Durocher, René 12n1

Eisen, Max 122n160
elitist theory 19
English-speaking group 1, 2, 5, 14n28, 22, 53, 55, 57, 65, 74, 91, 94, 109, 120n115, 123n168, 131, 133, 143
Ethnic Canadian Mosaic Institute (ECMI) 128–132, 134–137, 141, 143
Eurocentric approach 5
Evans, David 79n67

far right 1, 6, 7, 26, 156
Fay, Terence J. 43n98, 79n65
Feldman, Matthew 38n26
Felicko, Félix C. 50n188
Field, G. A. 122n154
Filipeko, Anton S. 38n22
Fitzgerald, John J. 22, 29, 30, 31, 33, 40n44, 40n45, 40n47, 40n49, 43n94, 43n102, 43n103, 44n121, 44n122, 45n131, 45n134, 45n136, 46n143, 47n161, 48n164, 49n180, 58, 59, 60, 61, 62, 73, 73n1, 74n1, 74n7, 76n29, 76n30, 76n32, 77n34, 77n35, 77n40, 78n60, 79n63, 80n85, 81n90, 81n91, 82n97, 83n109, 89n191, 89n196, 91, 93, 94, 96, 106, 107, 114n8, 115n35, 115n36, 115n37, 115n40, 115n41, 115n43, 116n46, 116n47, 116n48, 116n51, 117n63, 117n66, 123n168, 123n180, 123n181, 124n190, 124n194, 124n196, 124n197, 124n200, 124n201, 124n202, 127n240, 128, 129, 144n3, 144n4, 153
Fitzpatrick, Alfred 109, 110, 125n218, 125n219
Forbes, Hugh D. 14n26
foreign problem 29–36
Forsey, Eugene 43n106, 113n2
Fortin, Nicole M. 44n108
Foucault, Michel 11, 17n59
Francis, R. D. 14n28, 15n32, 66, 85n137
Fréchette, L. A. 90
French-Canadian Catholics 32–34, 52, 56, 58, 95, 134
French-speaking group 1, 2, 5, 14n28, 47n151, 53, 55, 65, 74, 96, 98, 105, 115n38, 118n90, 154
Frenette, Yves 156n6
Friedländer, Saul 121n142
Frye Jacobson, Matthew 15n39
Fudge, Judy 48n170
fundraising 56, 91

Gagnon, A. R. 88n171, 117n59
Gagnon, Nicole 12n1, 13n5
Gagnon, Robert 37n6, 95, 116n53, 116n54, 117n62
Gardiner, Albert A. 32, 35, 47n151, 47n153, 47n158
Gauthier, Georges 33, 34, 35, 48n168, 48n176, 49n180, 50n191, 54, 64, 77n41, 78n50, 78n59
Gibbon, John M. 66, 82n105, 85n132, 110, 126n225
Girard, Philippe 34
Givens, Terri E. 15n38
Godden, Gertrude M. 115n30
Goeschel, Christian 113n3
Gold, Ben 80n82, 80n84
Gorski, Philip 16n52
Gouin, L. M. 94, 113n4, 115n35, 115n36, 115n40, 115n45
Gouin, Paul 21
Greven, T. 14n27
Groulx, Lionel 8, 67
Gualtieri, Sarah 65, 84n125
Guénette, René 118n74
Guglielmo, Jennifer 156n7
guild system 2, 6, 7, 20, 73, 90, 91, 93, 115n40, 116n48
Guo, Shibao 15n29

Haider, Carmen 38n27
Hall, Catherine 82n102
Hambly, Rose A. 110

Index

Hamelin, Jean 12n1, 13n5
Handbook for New Canadians 109, 125n218, 125n219
Hanebrink, Paul 87n162
Hanley, Frank 102
Hansell, George 107
Haque, Eve 3, 13n15
Harmon, Katharine E. 44n115
Harris,Walter 121n141
Hayward, Victoria 126n224
Heidt, Daniel 13n12, 13n13
Henschel, Richard K. 126n230
Herder, Johann G. 8
Herf, Jeffrey 42n73
Herzstein, Robert E. 79n67
Hethman, Michael 68
Hill Fletcher, Jeannine 57, 78n57, 125n209
Hillmer, Norman 14n29
Hinther, Rhonda K. 37n9, 37n12, 37n14, 43n97, 80n77, 86n155, 86n157, 149n93
historic novelty 35, 49n188
Hitler, Adolf 26, 69, 86n154, 93, 100
Hladun, John 60, 80n76
Holdcroft, David 16n57
Hollinger, David A. 77n39
Holubnychy, Vsevolod 38n21
Horn, Michiel 39n33
Houde, Camillien 119n100
Howard, Victor 88n174
Huberman, Michael 44n108
Hughes, Katherine 22

Iacovetta, Franca 14n29
Ickstadt, H. 14n27
Igartua, José 14n29
Ignatiev, Noel 15n39
immigrant communities: and communism 79n72; and ethnic prejudice 152; guidance of 57; integration of 67; Italian 152; 'physical and economic' amelioration of 51–52; Ukrainian 14n28
immigrants: bolshevization of 38n24; British 109; Canadian 35, 51; Catholic 28, 29, 32, 95; English-born 109; European 109; marginalization of 138; Syrians as 65; Ukrainian 19, 139
Italian immigrant communities 152

Jaques, Norman 107, 123n181, 124n190
Jardina, Ashley 15n40, 16n44
Jenkins, J. H. 88n172

Jewish community 25, 65, 87n164, 111, 112, 135, 136, 137, 143, 153
Jones, Richard 14n28, 85n137
Joseph Boulanger, Franco-Albertan 97
Judeo-Communism 104, 111
Julien, Maurice 49n178
Jungbluth, P. 14n29

Karmis, Dimitrios 13n21
Katzenstein, Peter J. 115n42
Kelley, Ninette 13n4
King George VI 65, 83n107
King, Mackenzie 100
Kirkconnell, Watson 110, 116n51, 126n226, 126n227
Kishka, André 139, 140, 141, 142
Klein, Charlotte 122n159
Klyber, Arthur B. 105, 123n171, 123n172
Kopf, Josephine Z. 126n232
Korchinsky, J. N. 67
Kordan, Bohdan S. 14n29, 88n175, 88n178
Krumpelmann, Cosmas W. 23, 152, 156n5
Kuukkanen, Jouni-Matti 11, 17n62
Kymlicka, Will 4, 13n6, 13n21

Labarre, J.P. 119n94
l'Action Corporative (AC) 90–94, 97, 101, 113n2, 114n7, 114n17, 115n40, 154
Laforest, Guy 3, 4
Lalande, Julia 14n26, 15n31, 149n86, 149n89, 149n91
Lalanne, Paul-Émile 104
Langevin, Adélard 57
Lanouette, Mélanie 96, 117n56, 118n72, 118n76, 118n87
LaPierre, Edward 30, 31, 33, 36n4, 45n135, 46n139, 46n140, 46n142, 54, 55, 61, 62, 63, 66, 74n6, 76n31, 78n62, 78n63, 79n63, 81n88, 81n90, 81n91, 81n93, 82n94, 82n96, 82n104, 83n107, 83n111, 84n130, 85n138, 91, 94, 114n8, 115n41, 115n43, 123n168, 128, 129, 145n5, 145n6, 145n7
Lapointe-Gagnon, Valerie 147n41, 147n43, 147n45, 147n47, 148n65
Laprès, Joseph-Arthur 59, 60, 61, 74n3, 78n60, 78n63, 79n63, 79n64, 79n66, 79n68, 79n69, 81n89, 81n92, 119n99
La Presse 34, 38n24, 38n27, 39n37, 44n114, 45n130, 46n137, 46n138, 47n156, 48n169, 48n173, 52, 53, 76n18, 87n159, 102, 114n11, 114n18, 118n74,

120n109, 120n124, 120n125, 120n126, 121n136, 122n162, 122n163, 133, 135, 146n31, 147n54, 148n62, 148n68, 150n106
Larose, Alfred F. 116n50
Laurendeau, Andre 145n19, 146n20, 147n45, 147n56, 147n57, 147n59, 148n60
Lazare, Bernard 42n80, 48n176
League for Social Reconstruction (LSR) 6, 27
Lebon, Gustave 19
L'École Sociale Populaire (ESP) 21, 27, 30, 32, 38n27, 45n124, 45n128, 45n130, 55, 91, 98, 114n23, 115n39
Le Monde Ouvrier 92, 114n26
Leo XIII 38n25
Lesage, Jean 132
Levy, Richard S. 126n231
Liberal Party 66, 95, 99, 100, 102, 128, 152
Linteau, Paul-André 12n1
Logan, Jack 60
Long, Marcus 133
Luciuk, Lubomyr 14n29
Lypynsky, Viacheslav 18, 19, 20, 22, 25

Mackey, Eva 13n9
Maclure, Jocelyn 4, 13n23, 13n24
Manning, J. M. 39n37, 83n108, 83n113, 83n114
Mannion, Patrick 40n46
Marcel, Marcel 13n16
Margalit, Yotam 15n41
Maria, Benedetto 49n176
Maritain, Jacques 105, 123n173, 123n174, 123n179
Marples, David R. 37n14
Martel, Marcel 3, 5, 13n18, 14n27
Martynowych, Orest T. 42n86, 87n160, 149n87, 149n88
Massé, Paul 98
Maurault, Olivier 98, 101
Maurras, Charles 8
Maurutto, Paula 44n119, 44n120, 75n10
Mayeur, Jean-Marie 114n7
McGowan, Mark 46n141
McKay, Ian 3, 11, 13n7, 14n28, 17n60
McKenna, Léo 34, 54
McNeil, Neil 21
McQuarrie, Jonathan 150n102
McRoberts, Kenneth 3, 4, 13n11, 13n16, 13n17

Mead, Frederick John 21, 22, 33, 40n43, 72, 73, 79n63, 86n151, 87n159, 87n161, 87n164, 87n165, 88n169, 88n170, 88n176, 88n182, 88n183, 89n184, 89n185, 89n188, 89n189, 89n190
Mead, Jack 33, 69, 70
Mercier-Gouin, Léon 90, 92, 93, 101, 102
Miedema, Gary 15n32
Mignault, Thomas 98, 99, 133
Mikhman, Dan 122n161, 122n164
Miller, Jim 62, 82n101
Mills, Allen G. 41n63
Mills, Sean 15n34
Minville, Esdras 8, 90, 92, 114n13, 114n24
Mochoruk, Jim 37n12, 37n14, 43n97, 80n77, 86n155, 86n157
Molas, Bàrbara 115n44
Mondon, Aurelien 157n11
Monette, Gustave 116n52
Montpetit, André 94
The Montreal Beacon 22, 23, 29, 30, 33, 36n1, 40n43, 40n44, 40n56, 40n57, 45n130, 45n135, 47n160
Montreal Catholic School Commission (MCSC) 21, 31–35, 39n37, 41n66, 46n144–n147, 46n147, 47n148, 47n149, 47n153, 47n154, 47n155, 47n157, 47n158, 47n159, 47n161, 47n162, 47n163, 48n164–167, 48n175, 49n180, 56, 63, 77n44, 77n45, 77n46, 78n51, 78n59, 83n108, 83n113, 83n114, 84n117, 86n144, 86n151, 95, 96, 98, 116n49, 116n50, 116n55, 117n56, 117n58, 117n62, 128, 129, 144n2, 144n3, 145n9–n16; Comité des Néo-Canadiens 95; Ethnic Canadian Mosaic Institute (ECMI) 128, 129; during interwar period 95; New Canadians 32, 33, 35, 56, 63, 96
The Montreal Daily Star 53, 76n22, 102, 121n137
Moral Re-Armament movement (MRA) 130–131
Moreau, Patrick 16n42
Morgan, Philip 42n75
Morley, J. T. 124n183
Mosca, Gaetano 19
Motyl, Alexander J. 38n17
multiculturalism of the right 8, 16n45
Murphy, Stortz 77n48
Musielak, Stephen 48n176

Musolff, Andreas 121n144
Mussolini, Benito 6, 31, 59, 92

Nadeau, Jean-François 42n85, 49n188, 78n53, 78n54, 122n155, 147n50, 151, 156n2
Narodna Hazeta 70
Narodnia Gazeta 70–72
Neville, Peter 114n20, 115n29
New Canadian Citizens Federation (NCF) 54, 61, 66
New Canadians 10, 11, 16n54, 32–36, 49n186, 51, 54, 55, 56, 61–68, 83n110, 84n120, 84n127, 85n138, 85n140, 86n149, 91, 95–102, 108–112, 125n208, 128, 130, 133, 134, 135, 153
New Canadians Friendship House (NCFH) 51–55; foreign groups 52; French and English lessons 53; problem of foreigners 53; Slav and Germanic Catholic communities 52
Newman, Peter C. 146n36
Noll, John F. 73, 89n192
Norman, Wayne 13n21
Notre Dame Basilica 34, 101, 134
Notre Dame de Sion 104, 122n163, 136

Odale, Walter B. 52, 59, 75n16, 79n71, 79n72, 80n73, 80n74, 80n75
Oeuvre, Une 118n75
O'Neill, Daniel I. 17n58
Osewsky, Thaddeus 48n176
Otto, Steve 148n63
Ouis, P. 16n46

Pal, Leslie A. 14n29
Pâquet, Martin 3, 13n16, 13n18, 147n58
Paré, J. I. 127n237, 149n81
Pareto, Vilfredo 19
Peacocke, Christopher 17n61
Pearson, Lester B. 131, 144n4, 146n37
Pelenski, J. 38n16
Penverne, Jean-Joseph 63, 66, 83n112, 85n138, 156n4
Perin, Roberto 13n26, 15n33, 78n52, 118n90, 149n92, 149n94, 149n95
Perry, Samuel L. 16n51, 16n53, 56, 77n42, 146n27
Peverne, Jean-Joseph 83n109
Pierce, William Luther 103
Pietri, Luce 114n7
Pitsula, James M. 15n32
Pius XI 5, 20, 21, 39n30, 39n31
plutocracy 24, 25, 152

plutocratic democracy 24, 92
Pope Leo XIII 20
Potichnyj, Peter J. 42n81
Power, C. G. 116n48
The Prairie Messenger 23, 40n52, 152
Prentice, Howard 121n141
Prestiss, Craig R. 38n28
Presunka, Peter 140, 141
Protocols of the Elders of Zion 106, 108, 111

Quadragesimo Anno 2, 5, 20, 22, 31, 39n30, 39n31
Quinn, Herbert F. 53, 54, 76n22, 76n23, 76n26, 76n27

radical right 6–8, 12, 57
Rawlyk, G. A. 120n122
Raynault, Adhémar 65, 84n130, 85n131
Rensmann, Lars 115n28, 115n32
Representatives of Seventeen Canadian Ethnic Groups 136
Rerum Novarum 20–23, 38n25
Reynolds, Mac 124n192
Ricard, François 12n1
Rich, Norman 87n166
Robert, Jean-Claude 12n1
Robertson, E. M. 88n168
Robin, Martin 12n2
Roediger, David R. 15n39, 17n59, 41n63
Rossolinski-Liebe, Grzegorz 14n28
Routhier, Henri 98
Royal Canadian Mounted Police (RCMP) 18, 21, 33, 39n42, 40n43, 42n84, 69, 70, 152
Rudling, Per A. 14n28
Rudman, Ray K. 122n156
Rudnyckyj, Jaroslav 138, 139, 140
Rudnytsky, Ivan L. 37n10, 37n15
Rutherdale, Myra 62, 82n101
Rydgren, Jens 6, 15n36

Sack, Daniel 146n28, 146n29
Saine, Joseph 99, 101, 120n116, 126n235
Saint Laurent 99, 100, 119n102, 121n141
Salazar, Oliveira 92
Salerno, Salvatore 156n7
Salvatore, Filippo 156n8
Sanctuary, Eugene 26
Scott, Francis R. 21, 27
Scott, Joan 44n109
Scott, R. B. Y. 27, 43n104
Seljak, David 15n29
Seymour Wilson, Vince 13n19

Shaffir, William 149n79
Sheridan, Madeleine 27, 28
Sinclair, Stuart 121n141
Skoropadsky, Danylo 68, 69, 87n159, 87n160
Skoropadsky, Pavlo H. 18, 19, 37, 68, 86n152
Smith, Donald B. 14n28, 85n137
Smith, Gerald L. K. 103, 107, 121n149, 122n151
Smith, Miriam 14n26
Smyth, Thomas T. 61
Snyder, Timothy 37n14
Social Credit Party 2, 21, 106–108, 123n182
social Darwinism 8, 41n63, 57
The Social Forum 31, 46n141, 113n4
Sorel, Georges 19
Spektorowski, Alberto 8, 16n45
St-Amant, Jean-Claude 45n125, 119n92
Stanley, Timothy J. 76n17
Sternhell, Zeev 16n48
Stingel, Janine 13n4, 39n35, 124n184, 124n185, 124n188
Stoler, Ann 17n59
Subtelny, Orest 37n11

Tarnovych, J. 36n5
Taschereau, Louis-Alexandre 56
Taylor, Barbara 44n109
Taylor, Charles 14n28
The Canadian Social Crediter 106
Théoret, Hughes 13n3, 13n4, 115n33
Thibeault, Mercier G. 34
third force, the 1, 2, 5, 6, 9–12, 91, 100, 102, 128–150; biculturalism and bilingualism (B&B commission) 131–134, 137; conceptual origins 9–12, 156; Ethnic Canadian Mosaic Institute (ECMI) 128–132; ethnic groups 140; idea of 12; partial stories 135–137; pioneering argument 138, 139; self-preservation 141–143
third group 2, 6, 54, 101, 129, 133, 137, 138, 140–143, 155
Thompson, Edward P. 151, 156n1
Thordarson, Bruce 146n38
Torrelli, Maurice 16n50

Trebikcock, M. J. 13n4
Trépanier, Pierre 16n50
Trudeau, Pierre E. 3, 4
Trudeau's multiculturalism 4
Tucker, Eric 48n170
Turda, Marius 38n26
Tymochko, J. 48n176

Ukrainian-Canadian community 18, 25, 26, 139, 143
Ukrainian Labour-Farmer Temple Association (ULFTA) 60, 70, 80n77
Ukrainian question 68–73
Ukrainskyi Robitnyk 25, 42n84, 68
Underhill, Frank 21
The Union Nationale 32, 35, 53, 153
United Hetman Organization (UHO) 68, 71, 86n153
unity in diversity 101, 130, 134, 139, 143

Vauchez, André 114n7
Villeneuve, Jean-Marie-Rodrigue 54, 69
Vinet, Jean-Baptiste 101

Walker, James 41n59, 76n17
Warren, Jean-Philippe 92, 114n19
Webster, Nesta H. 136, 148n72
Weinfeld, Morton 149n79
Wesselenje, Nicolaus 48n176
Whitehead, Andrew L. 16n51, 16n53, 56, 77n42, 146n27
white 'third force' 108–113
Wilson, Marcel 129
Winnipeg Free Press 23, 40n55, 60
Winter, Aaron 13n20, 157n11
Winter, Elke 13n8
Wodak, Ruth 126n228
Wong, Lloyd 15n29
Woodsworth, J. S. 79n70
World Alliance Against Jewish Aggressiveness (WAAJA) 26
Wotherspoon, T. 14n29

Yuzyk, Paul 88n177, 138, 139, 149n97, 149n98, 150n99, 150n101

Zhu, Lianbi 85n136
Zieger, Robert H. 80n86

Printed and bound by CPI Group (UK) Ltd, Croydon, CR0 4YY
01/12/2024
01797774-0019